THE MANY LIVES OF
KHRUSHCHEV'S THAW

The Many Lives of Khrushchev's Thaw

EXPERIENCE AND MEMORY IN

MOSCOW'S ARBAT

Stephen V. Bittner

CORNELL UNIVERSITY PRESS

ITHACA AND LONDON

First published 2008 by Cornell University Press

Printed in the United States of America

Library of Congress Cataloging-in-Publication Data

Bittner, Stephen V.
    The many lives of Khrushchev's thaw : experience and memory in Moscow's Arbat/
Stephen V. Bittner.
        p. cm.
    Includes bibliographical references and index.
    ISBN 978-0-8014-4606-1 (cloth : alk. paper)
    1. Arbat (Moscow, Russia)—Intellectual life.   2. Moscow (Russia)—Intellectual
life.   3. Soviet Union—Intellectual life—1917–1970.   4. Soviet Union—History—
1953–1985.   I. Title.

DK604.3.A73.B58   2008
947'. 31—dc22

2007048077

Cornell University Press strives to use environmentally responsible suppliers and
materials to the fullest extent possible in the publishing of its books. Such materials
include vegetable-based, low-VOC inks and acid-free papers that are recycled,
totally chlorine-free, or partly composed of nonwood fibers. For further information,
visit our website at www.cornellpress.cornell.edu.

Cloth printing   10   9   8   7   6   5   4   3   2   1

For Christel

Contents

Acknowledgments

The title page indicates that I am the sole author of this book, but it has been a collaborative effort throughout. I have benefited in countless ways, both personal and professional, from the input of Sheila Fitzpatrick, Ron Suny, and Richard Hellie, my former mentors at the University of Chicago. Their high scholarly standards are tempered only by their infectious confidence in the abilities of their students. I am also indebted to the extraordinary cohort of aspiring scholars who were part of Russian history at Chicago during my time there: Golfo Alexopoulos, Jon Bone, Chris Burton, Michael David, Mark Edele, Julie Gilmour, Elise Giuliano, Charles Hachten, James Harris, Steve Harris, Yoi Herrera, Julie Hessler, Terry Martin, John McCannon, Matt Lenoe, Elena Pavlova, Matt Payne, Steve Richmond, Josh Sanborn, Alison Smith, Kiril Tomoff, and the late Jenifer Stenfors. Although we have all gone our separate ways—to universities around the globe—I feel fortunate that our paths once crossed. I hope this book reflects the high standards of scholarship I came to know in our old workshop.

I would have been unable to complete this book had it not been for the generous assistance of several different organizations. Fellowships from the International Research & Exchanges Board (IREX) and the Social Science Research Council (SSRC) funded the initial research and writing. In 2000–2001, I was a fellow at the Kennan Institute for Advanced Russian Studies at the Woodrow Wilson International Center for Scholars in

Washington, D.C. Special thanks go to my Wilson Center friends—Kent Hughes, Martha Merritt, Maggie Paxson, Chris Chulos, Blair Ruble, and Willard Sunderland—for challenging me to think about the broad implications of my work, and to my research assistant, Corynn Cushman. In 2003, a RSCAP Summer Fellowship from Sonoma State University funded research in Moscow. Finally, postdoctoral fellowships from SSRC and the National Council for Eurasian and East European Research (NCEEER) allowed me to take two sabbaticals from teaching to complete work on the book.

Since I began this project, I have called a number of different institutions home. I wrote an early draft in Columbus, Ohio, while my wife completed an M.B.A. at Ohio State University. I am grateful to Eve Levin, Nick Breyfogle, and David Hoffmann for making an outsider feel welcome at OSU. In 2001–2, I was a visiting professor in the Department of History at Lafayette College, where I was blessed by the hospitality of Josh Sanborn, my old graduate school friend, as well as Paul Barclay, Andy Fix, and Arnie Offner. And since 2002, I have been in the Department of History at Sonoma State University. Out of the admirable conviction that a productive scholarly life makes for good pedagogy, my colleagues at Sonoma have graciously accommodated the many demands of my research and writing. Special thanks go to Steve Estes, who unwittingly contributed to this project when he asked why historians of Russia use a flawed metaphor like "thaw."

My time in Moscow was enriched by the help of Sigurd Shmidt, the foremost Arbat *kraeved* (local historian), who kindly invited me to his apartment on Krivoarbatskii Lane for tea and conversation. I am also grateful to Boris Bushmelev, Maia Levidova, Vadim Konchalovskii, and Lev Roshal', Arbat residents who happily shared memories of the neighborhood with a curious American, and to Liudmila Kiseleva and Yuri Slezkine for putting me in touch with several of them. On numerous occasions, Elena Drozdova and Galina Kuznetsova pointed me toward relevant archival sources and helped me navigate the Russian visa bureaucracy with nary a snafu. Finally, Heidy Berthoud and Andrey Shlyakhter tied up a few loose ends for me in Moscow when I was too busy to make the trip.

An earlier version of chapter 4 appeared in the journal *Kritika* ("Remembering the Avant-garde: Moscow Architects and the 'Rehabilitation' of Constructivism, 1961–1964," *Kritika* 2, no. 3 (Summer 2001): 553–76). Michael David-Fox's published response to the article informed many of the revisions I later undertook. I presented other material from this book to helpful audiences at Ohio State University, Indiana University, Georgetown University, Lehigh University, the University of California, Berkeley, and at several AAASS conferences.

No one is more relieved that this book is done than my friend (and quasi-family member) Ethan Pollock, who has read more drafts than either of us cares to remember, and who always offered the right advice to keep me working. I am also grateful to Doug Weiner, who occasionally checked in on my progress with a phone call. John Farrell, Susan Constanzo, Eleonory Gilburd, David Engerman, Karl Loewenstein, Andy Day, Louise McReynolds, Kelly Smith, Anna Krylova, Denis Kozlov, and Paul Hagenloh also shared their expertise with me on numerous occasions. At Cornell University Press, John Ackerman expressed an early interest in this project, which was just enough to keep me committed to its completion. And two anonymous readers struck the perfect balance between encouragement and honesty in their appraisal of my manuscript. I could not have asked for more.

Through it all, my parents, Rodger and Barbara Bittner, have supported my career in ways I hope I can one day replicate for my own children. And my wife, Christel Querijero, has postponed many of her own dreams so I can achieve mine. This book would never have made it into print had I not met Christel in my sophomore Russian class many years ago.

As I was finishing these acknowledgments—sequestered, as usual, in my office at home—I overheard my four-year-old daughter, Mia, tell her two-year-old brother, Ethan, that "we have to leave Daddy alone so he can make money." With this book out of the way, I look forward to having more time to spend with my children, if only so I can teach them how lucrative scholarly publishing really is!

STEPHEN V. BITTNER

Santa Rosa, California

THE MANY LIVES OF
KHRUSHCHEV'S THAW

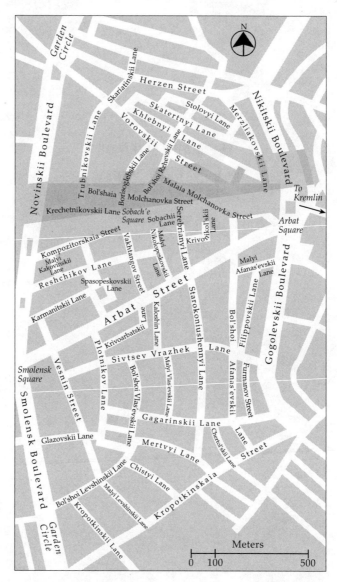

Map of the Arbat neighborhood. The darker-shaded area indicates the corridor along which Novyi Arbat was built in the 1960s.

History of a Metaphor

On March 5, 1953, the day Joseph Stalin died of a cerebral hemorrhage at his dacha on the outskirts of Moscow, few Soviet citizens could have imagined the stunning events that would follow. Within weeks of Stalin's funeral, newspapers carried reports that prosecutors had dropped outlandish charges against a group of mostly Jewish doctors, alleged conspirators in a plot to murder Kremlin leaders. By early summer, the gaunt faces and shabby clothes of newly released gulag prisoners could be seen in queues at train stations and bakeries. In the years that followed, Nikita Khrushchev, the principal victor in the succession struggle that followed Stalin's death, implemented a host of reforms to improve living standards: a mass housing campaign that moved millions of people out of communal apartments; the cultivation of virgin lands in Siberia, the Urals, and Kazakhstan; greater investment in light industry and the retail sector; and the empowerment of local governmental institutions to respond better to popular concerns. In the spring of 1956, Soviet citizens were astonished and, in some cases, angered by rumors that Khrushchev had attacked Stalin from the podium at the Twentieth Party Congress. Gathered around kitchen tables, they whispered with friends and family members about bloody uprisings in Tbilisi and Budapest, and about other topics that had once been taboo: life in the West, past repressions, even the failures of political leaders. In time, they realized that these developments, almost unimaginable on the eve of Stalin's death, were indicative of a new era that went by a simple metaphor.

1

After the seemingly eternal freeze of Stalinism, the Soviet Union had begun to "thaw."

In this book, I ask how artists, writers, and scholars in Moscow's Arbat neighborhood experienced the thaw. Often described as a Russian version of the Faubourg Saint-Germain, the old aristocratic quarter on the Left Bank in Paris that became famous in the interwar years as a gathering spot for intellectuals, the Arbat was unusual in the social and cultural geography of Moscow because of its longstanding ties with the intelligentsia. It was also transformed in the 1950s and '60s in physical and cultural ways, and emerged from the thaw wrapped in a myth that emphasized its own special suffering by contrasting an edenic past with a dismal present. These were not unrelated developments: the thaw provoked the changes in the Arbat that underlay the myth, and the myth was in many ways reflective of the thaw. In the chapters that follow, I stroll through the neighborhood's history and backstreets to explore the interconnections between thaw and neighborhood. On occasion, I stop to open the doors of prominent cultural institutions: the Gnesin Music Academy, the Vakhtangov Theater, and the Institute of World Literature. Because of growing institutional autonomy and scholarly freedom, these institutions became relatively freewheeling forums after Stalin's death, where the intelligentsia was able to explore the dimensions of the thaw in ways that were impossible in public. I also step outside the neighborhood to follow discussions about the Arbat's architecture and streetscape, irreplaceable embodiments of its unique history and "sites of memory" that were the focus of many discussions about the past.[1] Through it all, I show that the thaw the intelligentsia experienced differed in important ways from the thaw it later remembered. That simple metaphor—deceptively simple, really—hides many contradictory meanings.

It was not always this way. As a device that structures popular and scholarly understandings of the post-Stalin years, the thaw metaphor dates to May 1954, when the journal *Znamia* (Banner) published Ilya Ehrenburg's first work of fiction since Stalin's death, a novella entitled *Thaw*. Ehrenburg, then one of the most famous writers in the Soviet Union, settled on the title after reminiscing about a group of children playing outside his

1. Jay Winter, *Sites of Memory, Sites of Mourning: The Great War in European Cultural History* (Cambridge, 1995), 5–8. Frederick C. Corney investigates something similar, "institutions of memory" that embodied and shaped collective memories of the October Revolution. See *Telling October: Memory and the Making of the Bolshevik Revolution* (Ithaca, N.Y., 2004), 97–125.

country home during a temperate spell the previous spring. He never denied that its reference was political, even in the face of criticism in the press and the Union of Writers, the organization that looked after literary orthodoxies and the material welfare of writers. Indeed, it would have been disingenuous for him to do so: his novel broached previously taboo topics like official anti-Semitism and mass arrests, and challenged the socialist-realist precept that true happiness could be found only by selflessly devoting oneself to the construction of socialism. Nonetheless, Ehrenburg did not want readers to mistake thaw for spring, since "slight frosts" lay ahead. He instead hoped that thaw would evoke images of impermanence, instability, and uncertainty about how the weather would turn. It was suggestive of short-term ambiguity amid a long-term process.[2] It was precisely this understanding of thaw that Khrushchev denounced after the publication of Ehrenburg's memoir in 1963. In Khrushchev's mind, thaw implied an overall lack of direction that belied the eschatological claims of the party and did not properly depict the "clear, bright prospects of the Communist future." It was impossible, Khrushchev claimed, "by means of a literary image of this kind, to arrive at a correct opinion on the essence of those changes . . . which have occurred since Stalin's death."[3]

Ehrenburg's metaphor captured an era that was, from its first days, uncertain. The thaw could be exhilarating, to be sure, largely because so many things seemed possible. "Yesterday the wife of [the Pushkin scholar Sergei] Bondi was here radiating rumors of the 'new regime,'" the children's writer Kornei Chukovskii wrote in his diary in April 1953.

'The Kremlin will be opened for all the public. The Stalin Prizes have been abolished. There will not be [obligatory] bonds. Kolkhozniks will be given relief,' etc., etc., etc. 'The Union of Writers will be abolished. [Aleksandr] Fadeev [the secretary of the union] has been replaced. The number of police will be reduced by five times,' etc., etc., etc. Everything that a philistine could want is being passed off as part of the government program.[4]

---

2. Ilya Ehrenburg, *Post-War Years, 1945–1954*, trans. Tatiana Shebunina (Cleveland, 1967), 322–23, 327. For a more detailed analysis of the meanings embedded in thaw and alternate framing devices, see Nancy Condee, "Cultural Codes of the Thaw," in *Nikita Khrushchev*, ed. William Taubman, Sergei Khrushchev, and Abbott Gleason (New Haven, Conn., 2000), 169–76.
3. "Khrushchev Speaks Again," in *Khrushchev and the Arts: The Politics of Soviet Culture, 1962–1964*, ed. Priscilla Johnson and Leopold Labedz (Cambridge, Mass., 1965), 180.
4. K. Chukovskii, *Dnevnik, 1930–1969*, ed. E. Ts. Chukovskaia (Moscow, 1994), 197–98.

Like Chukovskii, artists, writers, and scholars across the Soviet Union were often thrilled by the possibilities that the thaw presented. But the flipside of their enthusiasm was dashed expectations and apprehension for the future. They struggled to reconcile developments and policies that were contradictory in the extreme. Only a few months after the publication of Ehrenburg's novella, speakers at the Second Congress of Writers attacked "bourgeois nationalism" and "cosmopolitanism," rhetoric eerily akin to the xenophobia and anti-Semitism of the late-Stalin period. In February 1955, Khrushchev dismissed the consumption initiatives of Georgii Malenkov, one of his rivals for supreme power, in terms reminiscent of the intraparty opposition struggles of the late 1920s. Malenkov's plans were "right-deviationist belching, a vomiting of the anti-Leninist ideas that Rykov, Bukharin, and their sort once disseminated." Khrushchev did not need to mention that Aleksei Rykov and Nikolai Bukharin, opponents of Stalin's forced collectivization of agriculture, were executed in 1938. Nor did he apologize to Malenkov when he later advocated similar policies.[5] At the Twentieth Party Congress in February 1956, Khrushchev denounced Stalin's boundless egomania and gross violations of Marxism-Leninism. Yet Khrushchev became far more equivocal about his predecessor during the domestic and international upheavals that followed—the dangerously unrestrained discussions about Stalin in workplaces across the Soviet Union, the anti-Soviet strife in Poland and Hungary, and the pro-Stalin demonstration in Georgia. In November 1962, Khrushchev personally approved publication of Aleksandr Solzhenitsyn's landmark novella about the gulag, *One Day in the Life of Ivan Denisovich;* in December, he curbed much of the good cheer by vulgarly denouncing a group of abstract artists who had gathered to narrate their work at the Manège Exhibit Hall, just beyond the western wall of the Kremlin: "Are you pederasts or normal people? . . . What is hung here is simply anti-Soviet. It's amoral."[6] Contemporaries spoke not of one contiguous thaw, but of numerous thaws and freezes, of cloudy weather, and of uncertain forecasts. For them, as for Ehrenburg, the thaw was a fickle thing.

5. "Ob uvelichenii proizvodstva produktov zhivotnovodstva. Doklad N. S. Khrushcheva na plenume Tsentral'nogo komiteta KPSS, 25 ianvaria 1955 goda," *Pravda,* February 3, 1955, 1, quoted in Harry Schwartz, *The Soviet Economy since Stalin* (Philadelphia, 1965), 69.
6. "Khrushchev on Modern Art," in *Khrushchev and the Arts,* 103. On the Manège affair, see Susan E. Reid, "In the Name of the People: The Manège Affair Revisited," *Kritika* 6, no. 4 (Fall 2005): 673–716.

This was the first phase in the evolution of the thaw metaphor. The second phase began during the late 1960s, when the Soviet intelligentsia began to reformulate the meanings embedded in thaw. In official parlance, the intelligentsia encompassed persons with university or technical educations; it was a sociological category that could be easily quantified by demographers eager to prove the success of Soviet educational programs. Yet the traditional meaning of intelligentsia, which had roots in Russia's belated encounter with the Enlightenment in the late-eighteenth century, suggested something different: individuals whose worldviews made them estranged from the state. The intelligentsia that redefined the thaw was all the latter and more: self-identified victims of the new government of Leonid Brezhnev, defying the old adage about victors being the writers of history by recasting the meanings implicit in the rapidly fading thaw.

The pivotal events in the transformation of the thaw were the dissident trials, which seemed to signal what the journalist Anatole Shub, drawing a parallel to the reactionary policies of Tsar Alexander III in the 1880s, called a "restoration of old ways."[7] In 1968 more than one hundred signatories of a letter to Brezhnev claimed that it was "impossible to conclude otherwise": the dissident trials were "an attempt to resurrect the methods and processes of 1937," the year Stalinist terror peaked. Fifty-two signatories of another letter noted that evidence suggesting a link between dissidents and an anti-Soviet émigré organization was so sketchy that it forced Soviet citizens to fear a return of the 1930s, when millions of people were "executed, tormented, and imprisoned for decades."[8] To underscore the parallels between Stalinist terror and the fate of the two most prominent dissidents of the era, Andrei Sinyavsky and Iulii Daniel, who were imprisoned in 1966 for publishing anti-Soviet materials abroad, letter-writers made generous use of adverbs signifying repetition: "Again lawlessness reigns," "Again society has lost control of the judicial mechanism," "Our country is immersed anew in an atmosphere of judicial arbitrariness," and in a creative attempt at reverse psychology, "Again our investigators, prosecutors, and courts give hope to our opponents' arguments."[9]

7. Anatole Shub, *An Empire Loses Hope: The Return of Stalin's Ghost* (New York, 1970), 420.
8. Gosudarstvennyi arkhiv Rossiiskoi federatsii [hereafter GARF], f. 8131, o. 31, d. 89189b, l. 89 (52 signatories); and l. 100 (100 signatories).
9. GARF, f. 8131, o. 31, d. 89189a, l. 127 (lawlessness reigns); l. 166 (opponents' arguments); and l. 195 (lost control and immersed).

The perception of intensified repression generated a great deal of nostalgia for the seemingly lost world of the thaw. In a letter to Brezhnev, Mar'ia Rozanova-Kruglikova, Sinyavsky's wife, claimed that writers of fiction should never be held criminally responsible for the content of their work, and then added the caveat, "at least that's what I became accustomed to thinking after the Twentieth Party Congress." Another letter-writer eulogized a decade of socialist legality, the official euphemism for due process: it was born out of the Twentieth Party Congress, where Khrushchev denounced Stalin, and died alongside Sinyavsky and Daniel in a Moscow courtroom.[10] Letter-writers' nostalgia for the thaw is all the more ironic when contrasted with the popular enthusiasm that followed Khrushchev's dismissal from the post of party first secretary in October 1964. Khrushchev never enjoyed much esteem among Soviet citizens, despite a host of reforms that improved living standards and ended terror. Among artists and writers, Khrushchev's reputation was even worse, largely because he was a meddler *par excellence*, known for his casual threats and banal artistic tastes. After being forced to decline the Nobel Prize for Literature in 1958, the writer Boris Pasternak, voicing the feelings of many, derided Khrushchev as a "fool and a pig."[11] Consequently, many persons in the intelligentsia thought that Khrushchev's forced retirement signaled a deepening of the thaw. In February, Aleksei Rumiantsev, the editor of *Pravda*, reinforced these expectations by writing that the new "collective leadership" in the Central Committee Presidium, Brezhnev and his colleagues, had eschewed the overbearing style of Khrushchev and Stalin for good. "It was not surprising," he argued, "that an individual 'boss,' certain of his own righteousness, considered himself to be the final arbiter in all spheres of human activity, but most of all in the realm of intellectual work."[12]

In light of the dissident trials and the Soviet invasion of Czechoslovakia in August 1968, assessments of Khrushchev and the thaw changed dramatically. The leader once pegged as a "fool and a pig" became, for many, a saint and a sage. In the memoir she wrote in emigration in the 1980s, the

10. GARF, f. 8131, o. 31, d. 99561, l. 43 (Rozanova-Kruglikova); and d. 99563, l. 120 (socialist legality).
11. Iurii Aksiutin, *Khrushchevskaia "ottepel'" i obshchestvennye nastroeniia v SSSR v 1953–1964 gg.* (Moscow, 2004), 368–77; idem, "Popular Responses to Khrushchev," in *Nikita Khrushchev*, 199.
12. A. Rumiantsev, "Partiia i intelligentsia," *Pravda*, February 21, 1965, 2. On the official and public reaction to the article, see L. Kurin, "Vspominaia proshloe, dumaia o nastoiashchem. Besedy s akademikom A. M. Rumiantsevym," *Pravda*, January 1, 1990, 4.

human-rights activist Ludmilla Alexeyeva described the thaw as "our time of awakening." For her, it was fundamentally about the "pursuit of liberty" and "seeing the truth," a time when it was possible to read, write, and speak "without asking permission from the party or the government."[13] As David Nordlander has observed, it was not uncommon for supporters of Mikhail Gorbachev's reforms in the late 1980s to acknowledge their own debt to Khrushchev, the "linchpin in the resuscitation of Soviet socialism from the depths of Stalinism," and if they were old enough, to underscore the seminal impact of the thaw in their own development.[14] From the vantage point of October 1964, when Khrushchev was removed from power, the thaw seemed like a long sequence of missed opportunities and squelched reforms. From the vantage point of 1968 and later, the thaw was a "magical era [that] ended as quickly as it had begun."[15]

Scholarly accounts of the thaw parallel the evolving views of the intelligentsia. During the 1950s and early '60s, outside observers were every bit as perplexed as the intelligentsia about the changes that occurred after Stalin's death. They recognized that the political climate had warmed significantly, but few dared to guess how long it would last or what its broader repercussions would be. In an insightful essay about Soviet culture after Khrushchev's denunciation of modern art at the Manège, Priscilla Johnson wondered how far artists and writers would "go in exploiting any opening, either now or in years hence?" Inertia, after all, was a powerful force in the Soviet Union. Outside observers also questioned the magnitude and sincerity of Khrushchev's reforms. In the introduction to a collection of essays on Soviet culture after the Twentieth Party Congress that first appeared in *Soviet Survey* (the journal of the anticommunist Congress for Cultural Freedom), Walter Laqueur and George Lichtheim emphasized the "perpetuation of unadulterated Zhdanovism," a reference to the *zhdanovshchina*, the vitriolic campaign against Western culture that Andrei Zhdanov orchestrated at Stalin's behest in the late 1940s. What Laqueur and Lichtheim described was not a full-fledged warming by any means, but contra-

13. Ludmilla Alexeyeva and Paul Goldberg, *The Thaw Generation: Coming of Age in the Post-Stalin Era* (Pittsburgh, 1993), 4–5.
14. David Nordlander, "Khrushchev's Image in Light of Glasnost and Perestroika," *Russian Review* 52, no. 2 (April 1993): 249. Robert D. English traces the origins of Gorbachev's reforms to the "new thinking" of the thaw. See *Russia and the Idea of the West: Gorbachev, Intellectuals, and the End of the Cold War* (New York, 2000).
15. Masha Gessen, *Dead Again: The Russian Intelligentsia after Communism* (London, 1997), 12.

dictory impulses toward thaw and freeze, toward reform and retrenchment.[16]

Beginning in the late 1960s, however, and especially in the 1980s when it became common to speak of the Brezhnev period (1964–82) as "stagnation," scholars began to use thaw to refer to the liberal, reformist interlude between the Stalin and Brezhnev periods. In fact, liberal may be the adjective most commonly attached to the thaw. Along with its variations and synonyms, it is widespread in textbook discussions and the work of period specialists.[17] Scholars tend to imagine a thaw that pits Stalinists, reactionaries, and conservatives against Khrushchevists, reformists, and liberals.[18] For the better part of fifteen years, from 1953–68, the latter group had the upper hand. Proof of the thaw's liberal credentials lay in the flood of unconventional, even deviant works that Soviet artists and writers produced, and the newfound willingness of Soviet citizens to speak their minds.[19] Katerina Clark once observed that Western scholars use thaw to describe "ideological shake-up" in the Soviet Union only if they "like the kind of literature and values which are permitted freer access to public forums."[20] Indeed, for many scholars, the thaw was about the greatest of liberal values: free speech. For Paul Josephson, a historian of Soviet science, it was a "decade of academic freedom" and the "golden years" of Akademgorodok, the scientific community in

16. Priscilla Johnson, "The Politics of Soviet Culture, 1962–1964," in *Khrushchev and the Arts*, 88; and Walter Z. Laqueur and George Lichtheim, *The Soviet Cultural Scene, 1956–1957* (New York, 1958), 3–5.

17. See, for instance, Gregory L. Freeze, "From Stalinism to Stagnation, 1953–1985," in *Russia: A History*, ed. Gregory L. Freeze (New York, 1997), 353; Roy Medvedev, *Khrushchev: A Biography*, trans. Brian Pearce (Garden City, N.Y., 1984), 216, 220–21; Dina Spechler, *Permitted Dissent in the USSR: Novyi Mir and the Soviet Regime* (New York, 1982), xv–xxii; Ronald Grigor Suny, *The Soviet Experiment: Russia, USSR, and the Successor States* (New York, 1998), 405–6; William J. Tompson, *Khrushchev: A Political Life* (New York, 1997), 132–33; and M. R. Zezina, *Sovetskaia khudozhestvennaia intelligentsiia v 1950-e—60-e gody* (Moscow, 1999), 5.

18. Stephen Cohen was among the first to warn of the limitations of the dominant "two pole" approach to Soviet politics after Stalin. See *Rethinking the Soviet Experience: Politics and History since 1917* (New York, 1985), 109, 128–34. In recent years, other scholars have issued similar warnings in reference to the thaw. See Anna Krylova, "The Tenacious Liberal Subject in Soviet Studies," *Kritika* 1, no. 1 (Winter 2000): 131–33; and Miriam Dobson, "Contesting the Paradigms of De-Stalinization: Readers' Responses to *One Day in the Life of Ivan Denisovich*," *Slavic Review* 64, no. 3 (Fall 2005): 580–600.

19. On the latter as a characteristic of the Khrushchev years, see Erik Kulavig, *Dissent in the Years of Khrushchev: Nine Stories about Disobedient Russians* (New York, 2002).

20. Katerina Clark, "Rethinking the Past and Current Thaw," in *Glasnost' in Context: On the Recurrence of Liberalizations in Central and East European Literatures and Cultures*, ed. Marko Pavlyshyn (New York, 1990), 1.

central Siberia. For Vladimir Shlapentokh, an émigré sociologist, the latter part of the thaw was a "heroic period," when "intellectuals managed to break the state's monopoly in many fields," not least in the realm of political discourse.[21]

The tendency among scholars to cast the thaw as a liberal age, however relative it may have been, marks the beginning of the third phase in the evolution of the thaw metaphor. It is not an altogether unwarranted assessment. From the very first days of the thaw, for instance, party leaders encouraged a greater amount of public criticism in order to revitalize the political system. With its connotations of increasing tolerance, liberalization also anticipates the end of mass terror, the most important development of the 1950s and '60s. Marc Junge points out that Khrushchev reversed a strategy honed by Stalin. Stalin maintained the party line through the exclusionary practices of purge, imprisonment, and execution; Khrushchev, in contrast, relied on an inclusionary policy of selective rehabilitation, the legal process that restored, often posthumously, the civil rights and party memberships of millions of repressed persons (but not, importantly, of high-profile intraparty opposition figures like Leon Trotsky and Nikolai Bukharin).[22] Junge's observation nicely illustrates a broader predilection for characterizing the Khrushchev regime in opposition to its predecessor. Inclusion was only possible in a context where many have been excluded; liberalization was the only cure for a regime that was reactionary, xenophobic, and terroristic. Here, perhaps, lies the chief reason why the thaw is often characterized as a liberal age: it just seems different from what came before, and to a lesser extent, what came after. Even the catchword for Khrushchev's reforms, de-Stalinization, suggests that the thaw was somehow the antipode of its predecessor, in intent if not reality.[23]

Yet there are good reasons to question the extent of the thaw's uniqueness and its liberal pedigree relative to earlier and later periods.

21. Paul Josephson, *New Atlantis Revisited: Akademgorodok, the Siberian City of Science* (Princeton, N.J., 1997), 263; and Vladimir Shlapentokh, *Soviet Intellectuals and Political Power: The Post-Stalin Era* (Princeton, N.J., 1990), 148. For a similar appraisal, see Alexander Yanov, *The Soviet 1960s: A Lost Reform* (Berkeley, Calif., 1984), xi–xix.
22. Marc Junge [Mark Iunge], *Strakh pered proshlym: reabilitatsiia N. I. Bukharina ot Khrushcheva do Gorbacheva* (Moscow, 2003), 263–70.
23. Polly Jones points out that the term de-Stalinization, like the thaw metaphor, has its own history; it originated among Western Sovietologists as a way of focusing "on the systemic enquiry which *domestic* commentators were forced to avoid." See Introduction to *The Dilemmas of De-Stalinization: Negotiating Cultural and Social Change in the Khrushchev Era*, ed. Polly Jones (London, 2006), 3.

Khrushchev, of course, liked to think of himself as progressive and often dismissed opponents of his reforms as dogmatists. But he would have rejected assertions that he was in any way liberal, a deeply opprobrious word for a Marxist-Leninist. Moreover, recent work on postwar Stalinism challenges the abruptness of the 1953 caesura by locating the roots of Khrushchev's reforms in the late-Stalin period, and by belying perceptions that the late-Stalinist regime was fully calcified. In his analysis of postwar "discussions" in philosophy, biology, physics, linguistics, physiology, and political economy, Ethan Pollock depicts a Stalin who is fully engaged with the complexities and ambiguities of Marxist-Leninist theory. Not only is Pollock's depiction of Stalin a far cry from the stereotypical portrait of a paranoid dictator, but it suggests that Stalin himself struggled to keep flexible theory from becoming rigid dogma. At lower levels, Elena Zubkova shows that the cultural vibrancy and political deviance normally associated with the thaw had roots in the heightened (and ultimately dashed) expectations of the postwar years. Andrew Day has uncovered a similar provenance for the mass housing campaign of the 1950s and '60s. Julie Hessler shows how the Stalinist government flirted with free market reforms after the war to alleviate shortages, an example of what she calls "the politics of possibility."[24] Postwar Stalinism, in short, was by no means static, and many of its features anticipated the developments of the Khrushchev years.

Sharp juxtapositions of the Khrushchev and Brezhnev periods, and their corollary, assertions that the Brezhnev government was Stalinist at its core, are even more dubious.[25] The end of the thaw was ambiguous and uneven, falling somewhere between the arrest of the Leningrad poet Joseph Brodsky for "parasitism" (having no job) in 1963 and the

24. Ethan Pollock, *Stalin and the Soviet Science Wars* (Princeton, N.J., 2006), 212–22; idem, "Conversations with Stalin on Questions of Political Economy," Working Paper no. 33, Cold War International History Project (Washington, D.C., 2001); Elena Zubkova, *Russia after the War: Hopes, Illusions, and Disappointments, 1945–1957*, trans. Hugh Ragsdale (Armonk, N.Y., 1998), 74–98; idem, *Poslevoennoe sovetskoe obshchestvo: politika and povsednevnost', 1945–1953* (Moscow, 1999), 136–70; Andrew Day, "Home Is Where the Heart Is: Housing and the Architecture of the Stalinist Welfare State" (unpublished ms., 2002); and Julie Hessler, "A Postwar Perestroika? Toward a History of Private Enterprise in the USSR," *Slavic Review* 57, no. 3 (Fall 1998): 516–42. For a similar attempt to locate the roots of the thaw in postwar Stalinism, see Maria Zezina, "Crisis in the Union of Soviet Writers in the Early 1950s," *Europe-Asia Studies* 46, no. 4 (1994): 649–61.

25. Victor Zaslavsky argues that the Brezhnev regime restored and maintained essential features of Stalinism and partially rehabilitated Stalin, but sought to mobilize society through social consensus rather than mass terror. See *The Neo-Stalinist State: Class, Ethnicity, and Consensus in Soviet Society* (Armonk, N.Y., 1982), vii–xii, 3–21.

invasion of Czechoslovakia in 1968.[26] At the very moment Soviet writers were in retreat in the wake of the dissident trials, the unorthodox economist Evsei Liberman watched Aleksei Kosygin, the head of state and the second-ranking figure in Brezhnev's collective leadership, partially implement his plan to decentralize the economy and augment local initiative. Throughout the late 1960s and '70s, the Brezhnev government continued to grant wide latitude to certain segments of the intelligentsia, especially those with Russian nationalist sympathies like the village prose writers, who glorified peasant life and nature, and historical preservationists. For them, the end of Khrushchev's thaw marked the beginning of a "truly golden era," a thaw in its own right.[27] Moreover, many dissidents who bemoaned the events of the late 1960s became participants in a bona fide human-rights movement that survived the so-called soft repression—the police harassment, forced hospitalizations, arrests on non-political charges, and deportations—of the 1970s and early '80s. Their activism suggests that the impact of the thaw on Soviet society was indelible.[28] Finally, despite the widespread perception of a resurgent Stalinism in the late 1960s that was so critical to recasting the thaw as a gentler era, the dissident trials occurred against a backdrop of steeply declining convictions for anti-Soviet activities under articles 70 and 190 of the RSFSR criminal code. In 1957 there were 1,964 persons convicted of anti-Soviet activities; from 1966 and 1970, there were only 679 total.[29]

What does this mean? Mainly, scholars should treat blanket assertions about the thaw as an era of liberalization, unique from what came before and after, with care. As Iurii Aksiutin points out in a recent study of the public's response to the thaw, the period defies simple categorization.

26. On the difficulty of identifying a clear end to the thaw, see Stephen V. Bittner, "Remembering the Avant-garde: Moscow Architects and the 'Rehabilitation' of Constructivism, 1961–64," *Kritika* 2, no. 3 (Summer 2001): 575–76.
27. Andrew Jenks, "Palekh and the Forging of a Russian Nation in the Brezhnev Era," *Cahiers du Monde russe* 44, no. 4 (October–December 2003), 642. Katerina Clark similarly notes that the Brezhnev era can be considered a "thaw" for the pro-Stalin intelligentsia. See "Rethinking the Past and Current Thaw," 1–2.
28. Ludmilla Alexeyeva, *Soviet Dissent: Contemporary Movements for National, Religious, and Human Rights* (Middletown, Conn., 1985).
29. V. A. Kozlov, "Kramola: inakomyslie v SSSR pri Khrushcheve and Brezhneve, 1953–1982 gody," *Obshchestvennaia istoriia* 4 (2003): 99. Kozlov also points out that "mass uprisings"—ethnic conflicts, religious revolts, widespread hooliganism, and other forms of overt, collective defiance of Soviet law—became less common after 1964. See *Mass Uprisings in the USSR: Protest and Rebellion in the Post-Stalin Years*, trans. and ed. Elaine McClarnand MacKinnon (Armonk, N.Y., 2002), 305–10.

It was not Stalinism, to be sure. But neither was it a "robust spring" that produced democratization and an autonomous civil society. Moreover, as Aksiutin and others have shown, many core assumptions about the period, like the view that Soviet citizens quickly and willingly shed the ways of Stalinism, are erroneous.[30] The thaw is often couched as a precursor to the great popular upwelling that accompanied glasnost and perestroika, when Soviet citizens from all walks of life—striking miners, Baltic nationalists, and dissident writers—demanded further reform from Gorbachev. Yet there was also an element in the thaw that the first Russian reformer, Peter the Great, would have recognized: a deep, popular mistrust of any reform initiated at the top of the political hierarchy that bred opposition and fear at the bottom.

Scholars also need to be explicit in their writings about what they mean when they invoke the thaw metaphor to describe the period following Stalin's death. I am no exception. Václav Havel once described the Czechoslovakian variant of the thaw as a time of "accelerated metabolism."[31] The same description is apt for the Soviet context, where the common denominator of Khrushchev's contradictory, uneven, and sometimes ill-planned reforms was rapid ideological change. Stalinism offered an evolving set of "systemically structured processes and experienced social relations" that shaped individual identity and consciousness, explained the Soviet role in the world, and presented a vision of the communist future that justified present sacrifice and repression. Consequently, when Stalin died, more changed in the Soviet Union than the inhabitant of the Kremlin and the amount of repression he employed. A universe of meaning was thrown into disarray, a process that was akin to the "cosmic reorganization" that followed the collapse of communism.[32] The thaw could be dangerous, uncomfortable, and disorienting. The Soviet Union during the thaw was like a jalopy careening down the highway. Signs that were legible at

30. Aksiutin, *Khrushchevskaia "ottepel'*," 479–82; Miriam Dobson, "'Show the Bandit-Enemies No Mercy!': Amnesty, Criminality, and Public Response in 1953," and Denis Kozlov, "Naming the Social Evil: The Readers of *Novyi mir* and Vladimir Dudintsev's *Not by Bread Alone*, 1956–59 and beyond," in *The Dilemmas of De-Stalinization*, 21–40, and 80–98, respectively.
31. Václav Havel, *Open Letters: Selected Writings, 1965–1990*, ed. Paul Wilson (New York, 1992), 6.
32. Katherine Verdery, *National Ideology under Socialism: Identity and Cultural Processes in Ceauşescu's Romania* (Berkeley and Los Angeles, 1991), 9; and idem, *The Political Lives of Dead Bodies: Reburial and Postsocialist Change* (New York, 1999), 35. On the destruction of Stalinist patterns of subjectivity, see David MacFadyen, *Red Stars: Personality and the Soviet Popular Song, 1955–1991* (Montreal and Kingston, Ont., 2001), 6–32.

slower speeds were blurry at thaw speed. Potholes jarred the jalopy's engine and strained the shock absorbers. Narrow shoulders tested the driver's acumen. And all the while, one passenger tried to keep the windshield from fogging with a handkerchief, another angrily criticized the driver for not going fast enough, and a third tried to mitigate nausea by reminiscing about the slow cars and smooth roads of childhood.

This thaw resists many of the rosy hues that the Soviet intelligentsia retrospectively applied to it. Yet it is consonant with the meanings that Ilya Ehrenburg first saw in the metaphor—impermanence, uncertainty, instability—and with recent work that challenges longstanding perceptions about postwar Stalinism and the Brezhnev period. It is also the thaw that is at the center of this book.

Three big themes are woven through the chapters that follow. Most important is an emphasis on the thaw as a lived experience. Artists, writers, and scholars in the Arbat were constantly struggling to navigate the turbulent waters of de-Stalinization. In some instances, they relied on strategies honed during the Stalin period, like patronage and letters to political leaders asking for intervention or clarification. In other instances, they patiently waited for the seemingly inevitable directive from above, keeping their heads low to minimize risk. Yet increasingly, they set out on their own, boldly testing the parameters of reform and asserting their own roles as independent cultural arbiters. This was especially common in response to the innumerable conflicts and inconsistencies that were caused by the uneven pace and scope of de-Stalinization. Did Khrushchev's denunciation of Stalin in 1956 negate decrees on music and culture from the late 1940s? Did the empowerment of public "self-administration" organizations spell the end of the party and state's monopoly over cultural policy and urban planning? Did Khrushchev's criticism of Stalinist architects in 1954 amount to the rehabilitation of constructivist architecture? The party's reticence on these questions forced cultural figures to extrapolate from political signposts like the Twentieth Party Congress to determine on their own which of their cultural and political projects were consonant with the spirit of the thaw. Sometimes they correctly anticipated (and even served as a catalyst for) future reforms. Other times, they stepped beyond what political leaders had intended, and had to be reined in with threats of punishment.

The experience of thaw varied, of course, according to individual and institution, but there was a great deal of commonality by generation, a second theme in the pages that follow. The "fathers" who had come of age in the 1920s and '30s were demoralized by the *zhdanovshchina* of the late 1940s. Initially, at least, many of them reacted to the thaw in a guarded manner: they were confused, fearful, and, in some cases, painfully aware of their own complicity for past repression and obscurantism. Some responded by dragging their feet and opposing any initiatives that reflected poorly on them. Some settled scores with old nemeses who bore greater guilt than they. Others were nostalgic for the pre-Stalin period, before they had been forced to make the difficult choices that Stalinism demanded. And still others freely confessed to past mistakes and promised to atone for their sins by working to rid the present of the remnants of Stalinism. The "sons," in contrast, were teenagers and young adults at the time of Stalin's death. They were galvanized by the Twentieth Party Congress and generally supportive of de-Stalinization. They mocked elders who feared that they were unduly interested in Western music and fashion. And they flaunted conventional Soviet morality and even political strictures in ways that frightened older people, who better remembered, perhaps, what the cost of deviance had once been. Ludmilla Alexeyeva, who was born in 1927, called them the "thaw generation." Because of their age, the sons "knew no other life . . . [and] were not prepared to picture what came next." But they were also the most bold in "sharing views, knowledge, beliefs, questions" that eroded the pillars of Stalinism.[33] Finally, there is evidence in the pages that follow of a third cohort: persons for whom the trial of Sinyavsky and Daniel constituted a final breaking point in their feelings about the party and government. Even though the dissident Andrei Amalrik called them the "generation of 1966," they were, in fact, a cross-generational group, comprising people whose ages varied widely. Most considered themselves part of the intelligentsia, and many participated in the dissident movement in the 1960s and '70s.[34] In truth, none of these generational categories were entirely discrete. As Amalrik notes, they were "philosophical" rather than "chronological": many persons whose age put them in one group were galvanized by the same events that became touchstones for others. Nonetheless, these generational divides correspond to the broad

33. Alexeyeva and Goldberg, *The Thaw Generation*, 4.
34. Andrei Amalrik, *Notes of a Revolutionary*, trans. Guy Daniels (New York, 1982), 21–22. Of course, not all persons who opposed the trial considered themselves part of the "generation of 1966." See, for instance, the interview with Aleksandr Aleksandrovich Konstantinov in *Russia's Sputnik Generation: Soviet Baby Boomers Talk about Their Lives*, trans. and ed. Donald J. Raleigh (Bloomington, Ind., 2006), 33–35.

trajectory of the Arbat's experienced thaw: it went from uncertainty to enthusiasm, and then, to anger and disappointment.

A third theme is the centrality of the past in the politics and culture of the present. De-Stalinization may have engendered optimism for the future, but it was accompanied by a widespread obsession with Soviet history before 1953. This is often mentioned in studies of the thaw, particularly in efforts to remember Stalin's victims.[35] Yet the past was present in many other ways as well. For political leaders, the past was the cause of unexpected problems: ill-conceived and ad hoc reforms bred contradictions with extant decrees from the Stalin era that were difficult to reconcile and always confusing. Conversely, artists, writers, and scholars frequently looked for answers in the past. They found plenty in the 1920s, the relatively permissive decade before Stalin came to power: the art and architecture of the avant-garde, a greater degree of cultural pluralism, and an overall sense of vibrancy, especially in the Arbat. Their focus on the past posed potentially destabilizing questions about their own right to reassess past culture, and implicitly, about the party's long-standing monopoly in these matters. Much of their retrospective gaze, of course, falls under the rubric of collective memory, understandings of the past that were shared (and were thus different from individual memory) and mediated, typically through cultural tools like literature and architecture. Collective memory in the Arbat was always dynamic, shifting, and contingent on the sociopolitical context. Just as Khrushchev's denunciation of Stalin encouraged the Arbat intelligentsia to look anew at the 1920s, so too the dissident trials transformed understandings of the thaw. Consequently, collective memory had little to do with the accurate recall of events that were experienced firsthand. Instead, it was about "reorganizing, or reconstructing, bits of information into a general scheme" that was recognizable, that had emotional appeal, and, oftentimes, that had some political utility.[36]

The first chapter traces the history of the Arbat and its animating myth, which cast the neighborhood as a victim of Soviet power and explained

---

35. On the popular obsession with the past, see Denis Kozlov, "The Historical Turn in Late Soviet Culture: Retrospectivism, Factography, Doubt, 1953–1991," *Kritika* 2, no. 3 (Summer 2001): 577–600; Petr Vail' and Aleksandr Genis, *60-e: Mir sovetskogo cheloveka* (Ann Arbor, Mich., 1988), 116–17; and N. P. Milonov, Iu. F. Kononov, A. M. Razgon, M. N. Chernomorskii, A. S. Zavad'e, *Istoricheskoe kraevedenie (osnovnye istochniki izucheniia istorii rodnogo kraia)* (Moscow, 1969), 12–26. On efforts to remember Stalin's victims, see Kathleen E. Smith, *Remembering Stalin's Victims: Popular Memory and the End of the USSR* (Ithaca, N.Y., 1996), 4–11.

36. James V. Wertsch, *Voices of Collective Remembering* (Cambridge, 2002), 7, 9.

its suffering in terms of its longstanding ties with the intelligentsia. It shows how the myth originated in the works of Bulat Okudzhava and Anatolii Rybakov, writers who celebrated as an intellectual and cultural utopia the Arbat they had known as children in the 1920s and early '30s, and who mourned the changes that occurred in later decades, such as terror, large-scale demolition, and the resettlement of thousands of life-long residents. As subsequent chapters show, the myth was appealing, in part, because it encapsulated the ways the Arbat intelligentsia experienced the thaw.

The tour of prominent cultural institutions begins in the second chapter. The first stop is the Gnesin Music-Pedagogy Institute, a university-level program attached to the famous Gnesin Music Academy. In the years following Stalin's death, Gnesin teachers struggled to make sense of the incongruity between the xenophobic decrees from the Stalin period that still governed culture, on the one hand, and Stalin's growing disgrace and Khrushchev's lenient policies, on the other hand. In time, they determined that the friction between past and present was manifested in a growing wave of student disciplinary problems, including excessive interest in the music of Western composers like George Gershwin, Igor Stravinsky, and Paul Hindemith. In private, they shared fears that the "sons" who came of age in the heady climate of the thaw held the "fathers" responsible for the enduring obscurantism of Stalinism. Their fears were all the more painful because many teachers wanted students to be familiar with modern Western music, if only to appreciate more fully the achievements of Soviet composers. They imagined the Gnesin Academy as a participant in a cultural world that transcended Soviet boundaries. Until the party revised decrees from the Stalin period, however, they were obligated to restrain students, even though they were undermining their own moral and cultural authority by doing so.

The third and fourth chapters examine the search for alternate political and cultural models in the pre-Stalinist past. The second chapter follows the revival of Carlo Gozzi's 1762 play *Princess Turandot* at the Vakhtangov Theater in the early 1960s. *Turandot* was the Vakhtangov's most celebrated production from its formative years in the 1920s. It was also a symbol of the cultural dynamism of old Arbat. For many, it embodied the art for art's sake ideal that had been lost under Stalin. The decision to restage it spoke to the possibilities of the present, when theaters were allowed greater independence to determine their own repertoire. It also turned out to be an unexpected commentary on a controversy that engulfed the theater during the early 1960s. The controversy involved the anti-Stalinist play *Rainstorm,* by the obscure playwright Boris Voitekhov. The theater initially refused to perform *Rainstorm,* citing artistic deficiencies. It relented after the Minister of Culture intervened, but only under protest. The minister's meddling in affairs normally reserved for the theater struck many as a remnant of the very policies Voitekhov's play tried to criticize.

The fourth chapter uses the construction of the Novyi Arbat radial street, the largest urban renewal project in Moscow in the post-Stalin period, to explore efforts to rehabilitate the architectural avant-garde. During the early 1960s, Khrushchev spearheaded a campaign to reshape the Arbat neighborhood into his vision of communist modernity. Hundreds of buildings were razed and thousands of residents were displaced to make way for the Novyi Arbat thoroughfare and its concrete and glass skyscrapers. After the Twenty-second Party Congress, architects in Moscow began to associate these skyscrapers with the utopian social mandate of Khrushchev's "new-life" campaign, and with the related attempt to build "communist social relations" by 1980. This convergence elicited a series of lengthy debates on the similarities between contemporary Soviet architecture and the constructivist experiments of the 1920s, which had been declared "formalist" during the Stalin period. The campaign to rehabilitate constructivism serves as a reminder that the retrospective gaze of the thaw impacted the Arbat in different ways. The agenda of the architects may have been restorative, but its implications for the Arbat were transformative, a fact that was not lost on the neighborhood's defenders.

The fifth chapter examines a question that arose during efforts to rehabilitate constructivism. Who rightfully determines the value of past culture? The question came to a head in the Arbat when landmarks associated with Vladimir Lenin, Leo Tolstoy, and Alexander Herzen, one of the founding fathers of Russian socialism, were razed to accommodate Novyi Arbat. Preservationists criticized the scale of demolition and the preservation policies of Moscow's Architectural-Planning Administration. They tried to halt the demolition by calling for a greater degree of public input in the urban-planning process. They initially conceived of this public in professional terms; they had in mind the capital's architects and the collective expertise architects brought to issues concerning preservation. In the wake of Khrushchev's dismissal in 1964, however, preservationists determined that their cause was better served by a wider definition of the public, one that incorporated the opinion of all Muscovites. They cited Leninist injunctions about the public ownership of cultural treasures and Khrushchev's penchant for treating Moscow as if it were his own "estate." Their campaign on behalf of monuments reflected the thaw at its most radical. By allowing the public a greater role in evaluating the past, preservationists proposed the creation of a very different relationship between citizen and state.

The sixth chapter pushes the narrative into the early-Brezhnev years, when the fading thaw joined the 1920s as an object of nostalgia. It examines the fallout from Sinyavsky and Daniel's trial at the Institute of World Literature, an Academy of Sciences affiliate north of Arbat Street. Sinyavsky worked at the institute until his arrest in 1965; Daniel was friendly with many of its scholars. During the late 1960s, their friends and colleagues rallied to defend a host of scholarly reforms that critics identified as the root cause of dissidence. Likewise, thousands of persons outside the institute wrote letters to political leaders and publications in support of socialist legality and other reforms associated with the thaw that now appeared to be in jeopardy. Sinyavsky and Daniel's trial reinforced an old dichotomy between intelligentsia and state that resonated in the myth of the Arbat. It also created a new dichotomy between thaw (the Khrushchev period) and freeze (the Brezhnev and Stalin periods) that transformed understandings of the recent past.

Taken together, these chapters show that the thaw experienced by the Arbat intelligentsia was not always idyllic and often perilous. In its turmoil there were both risks and rewards. But most of all, there was change—sometimes sweeping—that had unknown consequences. After more than two decades of Stalinism, that was not easy to grasp.

History and Myth of the Arbat

West of the Kremlin, beyond the leafy boulevard where the white stone wall of medieval Moscow once stood, is the Arbat, part of a centuries-old road between Moscow, Smolensk, and Warsaw. The Arbat stretches a kilometer southwest from Arbat Square, where the busy Novyi Arbat radial street intersects the quiet pedestrian paths on the Boulevard Circle, to Smolensk Square on the Garden Circle, the ring artery that defines central Moscow. The oldest buildings on the Arbat date from the early nineteenth century; they were built atop the cinders of the fire that engulfed Moscow before Napoleon occupied the city in 1812. Today their stucco exteriors are painted in pastels of green, yellow, and pink, and their cornices in white. They sit aside early twentieth-century brick and stone buildings inspired by Art Nouveau. Their upper floors and balconies are decorated with concrete vines and wrought-iron branches. The few Soviet structures on the Arbat are distinguished either by the austere, constructivist lines of the 1920s, or the classical embellishments preferred by Joseph Stalin. Since the end of communism, a small number of glass and steel buildings have also appeared on the Arbat. By mayoral edict, they resemble their nineteenth-century counterparts, albeit with modern amenities like tinted windows. Muscovites call them "elite houses." Maps typically depict the Arbat as a straight line, but anyone who has walked its length knows that it curves gently so it is impossible to see either end from the middle. The uncharted curve creates a sense of distance from the rest of Moscow, which is what the writer Ivan Bunin had in mind in 1906 when he wrote of the "special city" that existed in the backstreets of the Arbat.[1]

The Arbat first appeared in the historical record in 1493, during the reign of Ivan III Vasil'evich, when a candle in a nearby church ignited a fire that destroyed most of Moscow. The Church of Boris and Gleb "on Orbat" was among the recorded casualties. What the poet Bulat Okudzhava called the "strange name" in his popular "Little Song about the Arbat" probably derives from the Arabic word *rabad*, meaning a place set apart from the city, or the old Slavic word *gorbat*, meaning a place with rough terrain. Little is known about the Arbat during this early period. It was located in a part of Moscow known as Zaneglimen', the land beyond the Neglinnaia River, which now flows underground along the western wall of the Kremlin before emptying into the Moscow River. According to some accounts, Zaneglimen' was a meeting place for merchants from Central Asia, the lower Volga, and Persia. The Arbat's historical obscurity persisted until 1565, when Ivan the Terrible moved much of the administration for the *oprichnina*, which refers to those parts of Russia that were under his direct control, into the fields west of the city walls. The *oprichnina* palace, where Ivan's loyalists oversaw the military campaign against hostile boyar families, was built somewhere between Arbat and Bol'shaia Nikitskaia Streets (Herzen Street during the Soviet period), near present-day Arbat Square. Until the early 1700s, the Arbat remained a district of palace servitors. Zubovskii Boulevard (south of the Arbat on the Garden Circle), Bol'shoi Levshinskii Lane (Shchukin Street), and Malyi Kakovinskii Lane bear the surnames of commanders of the *strel'tsy*, musketeers who guarded the tsar. Several communities of artisans and laborers in the service of the tsar also lent their professional titles to the Arbat's toponymy: Malyi Kislovskii Lane (east of Arbat Square) derives from *kisloshniki*, the persons who pickled cabbage and prepared hard cider and kvass; Starokoniushennyi Lane derives from the stable tenders; Khlebnyi Lane from the bakers; and Skatertnyi Lane from the weavers. When Peter the Great relocated the capital to the swamps along the Neva River in 1711, the Arbat was home to 3 churches and 216 homes.[2]

---

1. I. A. Bunin, *Sobranie sochinenii* (Moscow, 1987), 1:203 ("Moskva").
2. S. O. Shmidt, "Arbat v istorii i kul'ture Rossii," in *Arbatskii arkhiv*, vyp. 1, ed. S. O. Shmidt (Moscow, 1997), 20–26; N. A. Geinike, N. S. Elagin, E. A. Efimov, and I. I. Shitts, *Po Moskve: progulki po Moskve i eia khudozhestvennym i prosvetitel'nym uchrezhdeniiam* (Moscow, 1917; reprint, Moscow, 1991), 254; Im. Levin, *Arbat: odin kilometr Rossii* (Moscow, 1993), 6; P. V. Sytin, *Iz istorii Moskovskikh ulits (ocherki)* (Moscow, 1952), 282; O. Shmidt, *Arbat* (Moscow, 1990); Vladimir Murav'ev, *Ulochki-shkatulochki,*

Fire destroyed the Arbat in 1739 and 1812. After the latter catastrophe, the neighborhood was rebuilt according to the tastes of the empire (*ampir*) school, which advocated neoclassical structures like the Bolshoi Theater, the Manège (an indoor equestrian academy), and the Moscow University building on Mokhovaia Street. The empire buildings proved immensely popular among wealthy merchants and aristocrats in the decades following the Napoleonic Wars, and the Arbat quickly became one of Moscow's most exclusive addresses, a Russian Faubourg Saint-Germain. Writing in 1840, one memoirist hinted at the neighborhood's lively social life: "By the time the residents of the Arbat . . . are going to bed, those in Zamoskvorech'e [an artisanal district across the river] have already arisen."[3]

During these years, dozens of notable cultural figures settled in the neighborhood. Aleksei Khomiakov, one of the founders of the Slavophile movement, lived near Sobach'e Square. His home was the site for many of the intellectual debates that figured prominently in what the memoirist Pavel Annenkov called the "remarkable decade" in the history of the Russian intelligentsia, the 1840s. After his wedding in 1831, Alexander Pushkin, Russia's most beloved writer, lived briefly in an apartment near the western end of Arbat, his only Moscow address of note. Even though Pushkin had much deeper roots in St. Petersburg, later residents attached a great deal of significance to his presence in the neighborhood. In the late 1990s, a statue of the poet and his bride was placed at the western end of Arbat, outside the building where they had once lived. Okudzhava even argued that the neighborhood had a formative impact on Pushkin, even though Pushkin never mentioned it in his poetry and prose. In the Arbat, Okudzhava wrote, "there are no meaningless places, there is just Arbat—a district, a country, a living and trembling history, our culture, what is in our souls—and over several centuries it has had an invisible but beneficial impact on our moral lives . . . and on many of our famous predecessors, chief among whom is Alexander Sergeevich."[4]

moskovskie dvory (Moskva, vozvrashchennye imena) (Moscow, 1997), 72–74; Ia. M. Belitskii, *Zabytaia Moskva* (Moscow, 1994), 7–57; Ia. M. Belitskii and G. N. Glezer, *Moskva neznakomaia* (Moscow, 1993), 271–78; Sergei Romaniuk, *Iz istorii Moskovskikh pereulkov* (Moscow, 1998), 343–455; and I. A. Zhelvakova, *Togda v Sivtsevom* (Moscow, 1998).

3. Levin, *Arbat*, 7. On the Arbat's exclusivity, see Shmidt, "Arbat v istorii i kul'ture Rossii," 31.

4. Bulat Okudzhava, "Net zadvorok u Arbata," in *Arbatskii arkhiv*, 140. For a similar argument, see Viacheslav Meshkov, " 'U Simeona,' ili 'Arbat i Povarskaia,' "*Arbatskie vesti* 11 (June 2003): 4. For an account of Pushkin's time in Arbat, see S. T. Ovchinnikova, ed., *A. S. Pushkin, Moskva, Arbat: Letopis' zhizni A. S. Pushkina s 5 dekabria 1830 goda po 15 maia 1831 goda* (Moscow, 2001).

Mikhail Lermontov, who lived on Malaia Molchanovka Street, wrote about the Arbat in his 1836 novel *Princess Ligovskaia*. Nikolai Gogol spent his final years in a building near Arbat Square, now marked with a statue of the writer that once stood on Gogolevskii Boulevard. Anton Chekhov moved to the neighborhood in the late 1870s after finishing school in Taganrog on the Sea of Azov. He set his short story, "Terrible Night," on Mertvyi Lane, a few blocks south of Arbat Street. Mikhail Bulgakov put the flight of his heroine in *Master and Margarita* in the backstreets of Arbat, and used the Spasskii House, the residence of the American ambassador that Bulgakov visited in 1935, as the site of the climactic devil's ball. Boris Pasternak put the residence of the Zhivago family on Sivtsev Vrazhek, which parallels the Arbat a few blocks to the south. In later years, the writers Nikolai Glazkov, Aleksei Arbuzov, Boris Iampol'skii, and many others contributed to the neighborhood's unique cultural associations by invoking it in their works. When the soprano Nina Dorliak was asked in 1993 why the Gnesin family had located their famous music school in the Arbat a century earlier, and about the unique "Arbat style" that made the neighborhood attractive, she responded that there was "just something" about the neighborhood, "a special spirit" that reflected the sophistication and worldliness of its residents. Like Dorliak's native St. Petersburg, Russia's "window onto Europe," the Arbat was outward looking in its cultural and intellectual orientation.[5]

By the turn of the century, the Arbat was one of the most affluent areas of Moscow. According to the 1897 census, one out of every six residents was a member of the nobility, by far the highest ratio in the city.[6] The Arbat also boasted the lowest number of inhabitants per apartment, and a majority of women, an unusual characteristic in a rapidly industrializing city, and one that may reflect the high number of female servants employed in wealthy homes.[7] A history of Moscow published in the 1950s described the Arbat as a "Junker" stronghold during the upheaval of 1917, a contemptuous comparison between the neighborhood's residents

5. Nina Dorliak, "'Ia ochen' liubila Arbat . . . ,'" interview by Sigurd Ottovich Shmidt, in *Arbatskii arkhiv*, 301.
6. *Pervaia vseobshchaia perepis' naseleniia Rossiiskoi imperii 1897 goda* (St. Petersburg, 1904), 23:20–23.
7. Robert W. Thurston, *Liberal City, Conservative State: Moscow and Russia's Urban Crisis, 1906–1914* (New York, 1987), 22; and Statisticheskii otdel Moskovskoi gorodskoi upravy, *Perepisi g. Moskvy 31 ianvaria 1902 g.* (Moscow, 1902–4), 31.

1. *Arbat Street at the Beginning of the Twentieth Century,* by Mikhail Germashev (1868–1930). Germashev's painting looks west along Arbat Street toward Smolensk Square. The columned building on the right of the street, typical of the nineteenth-century empire style, was destroyed by a bomb in the Second World War. The bell tower on the right was part of the Church of the Revelation of St. Nicholas the Miracle-Worker, built in 1689. It was demolished in the early 1930s. Reproduced courtesy of the Museum of the History of Moscow.

and the militaristic and reactionary aristocracy of Prussia.[8] Even during the 1920s, relatively freewheeling by Soviet standards, entrepreneurs, speculators, and "high-born" ladies congregated at the baccarat, roulette, and *chemin de fer* tables at the Hotel Prague on Arbat Square. At an "inner circle" table, the pot for a single game could exceed 25,000 American dollars. The Arbat's high rollers were sometimes joined by foreigners like Walter Duranty, the Moscow correspondent for the *New York Times* and infamous apologist for Stalinism, and Walter Benjamin, the German-Jewish philosopher who traveled to the Soviet Union in 1926 to pursue a woman and see firsthand the merits of a planned society.[9]

8. I. N. Vasin and G. P. Makarov, "Pobeda sotsialisticheskoi revoliutsii i ustanovlenie sovetskoi vlasti v Moskve," in *Istoriia Moskvy,* vol. 6, bk. 1, ed. D. V. Diagilev, S. M. Kovalev, G. D. Kostomarov, and R. N. Mordvinov (Moscow, 1959), 102.
9. Walter Duranty, *I Write As I Please* (New York, 1935), 145–46; and Walter Benjamin, *Moscow Diary,* ed. Gary Smith, trans. Richard Sieburth (Cambridge, Mass., 1986), 108.

The Arbat's trappings of wealth and power did not sit well with the new Soviet government. The official assault on the neighborhood's status began soon after the revolution, when municipal authorities expropriated the homes of the wealthy, divided them into communal apartments, and redistributed them to workers and communists according to need. The population of the elegant Filatov apartment building, now opposite the Vakhtangov Theater, ballooned from 200 to 3,000. More than a dozen churches in the neighborhood were destroyed during these years to make way for housing for newly privileged persons: Moscow policemen, Central Committee staffers, Central Executive Committee staffers, and many others. Among the demolished churches were four seventeenth-century wood and stone structures named for Saint Nicholas the Miracle-Worker, the Arbat's unofficial patron saint. During the late 1930s, the Kremlin Polyclinic was built atop the rubble of an aristocratic mansion on Sivtsev Vrazhek Lane. The Church of the Holy Trinity on Arbat Street was destroyed to make way for the offices of the Organization for Proletarian Tourism. After the war, the seventeenth-century Church of the Holy Mother of Rzhev on Vorovskii (Povarskaia) Street was razed to accommodate the new Supreme Court building. Both Smolensk and Arbat Squares were subjected to repeated rounds of demolition, as the narrow, crowded streets of aristocratic and bourgeois Moscow were reshaped into the efficient thoroughfares of the communist future. Arbat Street became a "military-transport road" and a "secure street," the route that Stalin took from the Kremlin to his dacha at Kuntsevo. NKVD agents sealed the attics on buildings fronting the street, and forbade residents from hanging their laundry from windows and having overnight guests. Dozens of RVKs, the popular acronym for secret policemen with their "hands in pockets" (*ruki v karmanakh*) walked the street. And the Hotel Prague became a "special cafeteria" for Stalin's personal security force. It would not reopen its doors to the public until 1954.[10]

Stalinist terror also changed the Arbat. Igor Zinoviev, one of the interview subjects in Marina Goldovskaia's 1993 documentary film about the Filatov apartment building, *House of Knights*, recalled living in constant

---

10. D. E. Trushchenko, *Prestizh tsentra: gorodskaia sotsial'naia segregatsiia v Moskve* (Moscow, 1995), 79, 86; S. K. Romaniuk, *Moskva. Utraty* (Moscow, 1992), 174–204; Mariia Semenova, "Tri Nikoly," *Arbatskie vesti* 21 (November 2001): 4; idem, "Nikola na kur'ikh nozhkakh," *Arbatskie vesti* 23 (December 2001): 4; idem, "Khramy bylo povarskoi," *Arbatskie vesti* 1 (January 2003): 4; "Toptuny," *Arbatskie vesti* 3 (February 2001): 4; and L. M. Roshal', "Arbat kak istoricheskii istochnik," in *Mir istochnikovedeniia (sbornik v chest' Sigurda Ottovicha Shmidta)*, ed. A. D. Zaitsev (Moscow, 1994), 441–42.

fear during the 1930s. Of aristocratic descent, Zinoviev's family lived in an eleven-room apartment before it was seized by municipal authorities and subdivided into communal apartments. The Silver Age (1890–1920) poet Nina Komarova, who wrote under the surname Khabias, lived on Denezhnyi Lane (Vesnin Street) until she was arrested in September 1937. Her first husband was an officer in Admiral Aleksandr Kolchak's anti-Bolshevik White forces during the Civil War, a family tie she was never able to suppress. Komarova disappeared for good in Turkmenistan near the end 1943. The poet Marina Tsvetaeva lived at several different addresses in the Arbat before going into exile in the West in 1922. After returning in 1939, her husband, Sergei Efron, was executed; her daughter, Ariadna, was imprisoned. In 1955, after her release, Ariadna sought out her childhood home on Borisoglebskii Lane: "My first footstep! My first way, I know you not by sight, but by heart. You waited for me!" While in prison, the poet Daniil Andreev wrote "Old House," an ode to his childhood home on Malyi Levshinskii Lane. Barred from residence in Moscow after his first arrest in 1934, the poet Osip Mandelstam and his wife, Nadezhda, were frequent visitors to their former residence, the writers' cooperative on Furmanov Street (Nashchokinskii Lane), where their friends Viktor and Vasilisa Shklovskii and Mikhail Bulgakov still lived. After the arrest of her third husband and son in 1935, the poet Anna Akhmatova traveled from Leningrad to the Arbat to grieve with the Mandelstams, perhaps suspecting that their freedom was in jeopardy as well. Indeed, Osip died in the gulag in 1938.[11] At the height of the Great Purges in 1937–38, 177 residents of the Arbat were arrested, summarily executed, and buried alongside more than 20,000 others at the Butovskii proving ground outside of Moscow. This was the toll from

11. On Komarova, see Viacheslav Meshkov, "'Po gorbatomu Arbatu, Denezhnyi 7 . . . ,'" *Arbatskie vesti* 2 (February 2001): 4. On Tsvetaeva, see idem, "'Byl trevozhen Arbat . . . ,'" *Arbatskie vesti* 4 (February 2001): 4; and S. O. Shmidt, "Dva Arbata Mariny Tsvetaevoi," in *Tvorcheskii put' Mariny Tsvetaevoi. Pervaia mezhdunarodnaia nauchno-tematicheskaia konferentsiia (7–10 sentiabria 1993 g.)*, ed. O. G. Revzina (Moscow, 1993), 7–8. On Andreev, see Viacheslav Meshkov, "'Gde besshumny i nezhny pereulki Arbata . . . ,'" *Arbatskie vesti* 9 (May 2001): 3. On the writers' cooperative, see Nadezhda Mandelstam, *Hope against Hope*, trans. Max Hayward (New York, 1999), 349–53; Viacheslav Meshkov, "'Arbat predan'iami bogat . . . ,'" *Arbatskie vesti* 11 (June 2001): 4; Mikhail Bulgakov, *Manuscripts Don't Burn: A Life in Letters and Diaries*, ed. J. A. E. Curtis (Woodstock, N.Y., 1992), 172, 186, 195; and Belitskii, *Zabytaia Moskva*, 39–40. On Bulgakov's history in the Arbat, see Nataliia Saposhnikova's series of articles, "Bulgakov i prechistentsy" in *Arkhitektura i stroitel'stvo Moskvy* 9 (September 1989): 26–27; 2 (February 1990): 32–33; and 11 (November 1990): 13–15.

only one NKVD facility. Many other Arbat residents perished in the countless other facilities that were spread across the Soviet Union.[12]

The post-Stalin years were no less transformative for the Arbat. With few exceptions, the neighborhood was spared the grandiose reconstruction projects that gave Moscow wide radial streets and scenic river embankments during the Stalin period. This changed in the 1950s and '60s, when a mass exodus to single-family apartments in Moscow's peripheral regions began. Although exact figures are not available, data collected by the city's Architectural-Planning Administration suggest that the neighborhood's population stood at just under 100,000 persons at the end of the 1950s; it declined steadily thereafter to about 20,000 today.[13] As old pre-revolutionary structures emptied, they were often torn down and replaced with boxy, seven and eight-story, yellow-brick apartment buildings. While the old buildings crowded the sidewalks and hid internal courtyards—thus creating the sense of coziness and distance from the rest of Moscow that Ivan Bunin noticed at the turn of the century—the new buildings were built in the center of lots and surrounded by landscaping, much like the new neighborhoods on the outskirts of Moscow. The destruction of the Arbat's streetscape peaked in the early 1960s, when entire blocks were razed to accommodate Novyi (New) Arbat, a gargantuan project a few blocks north of Arbat Street. It included a radial street with three lanes of traffic in each direction, wide pedestrian walkways, parking, and an ensemble of glass, steel, and concrete skyscrapers. For a city where private automobiles were still a rare luxury, Novyi Arbat was an extraordinary investment in the prevention of future traffic jams.

This was only the beginning of the Arbat's physical transformation. In 1984 and 1985, the Architectural-Planning Administration realized a decade-old plan to turn old Arbat into a pedestrian mall. Urban planners claimed that the creation of an Arbat "historical district" (*zapovednik*) that was free of traffic would produce a "new level of urban culture, interaction . . . and leisure." Urban planners drew comparisons to a similar

12. This figure is culled from E. A. Bakirov and V. P. Shantsev, eds., *Butovskii poligon. 1937–1938 gg. Kniga pamiati zhertv politicheskikh repressii*, vols. 1–8 (Moscow, 1997–2004). A list of people from the Arbat who perished is available at the website of Memoria-Pamiat', a neighborhood organization dedicated to preserving their memory. See http://www.arbat-info.ru/org-memoria.html.
13. Tsentral'nyi arkhiv nauchno-tekhnicheskikh dokumentov g. Moskvy [hereafter TsANTDM], f. 655, o. 1, d. 2453, ll. 17, 25. For a firsthand account of the reconstruction of the Arbat during these years, see Vladimir Potresov, *Arbat nashego detstva: fotografii Aleksandra Potresova (1902–1972)* (Moscow, 2006).

pedestrian mall in Munich, which had impressed Soviet visitors during the 1972 Olympics, and estimated that up to 60,000 people would visit the Arbat on holidays and weekends.[14] Few expected that this figure would prove conservative. As Mikhail Gorbachev's glasnost transformed the Soviet Union, the "new, old Arbat" became something that neither political leaders nor long-time residents especially liked. Beginning in 1987, punks, hippies, "intellectual bums," addicts, runaways, and tens of thousands of young people made the Arbat into their personal "Mecca." It was a kilometer-long *tusovka*, a friendly, informal gathering.[15] Moscow police estimated that more than 30,000 people were on the street at any given moment; on holidays and weekends, 100,000 people visited the Arbat every hour. Young people came from across the Soviet Union to witness the spectacle; inspired by what they saw, many created "micro-Arbats" at home. The situation was so extraordinary that worried city officials issued "temporary" regulations in August 1987 to quiet the street, allegedly because "the public was still learning to live in the conditions of democracy." But ridding the Arbat of its youth salon was an impossible task in the new political climate. Newspapers railed against the regulations. The Komsomol, the acronym for the Union of Communist Youth, sponsored a series of discussions so young people could question the constitutionality of the regulations and grill the municipal officials who had helped draft them. Under popular pressure, municipal officials relaxed the regulations in the spring of 1988 and enforced them only sporadically thereafter.[16] When the rock star Viktor Tsoi died in 1990, grieving fans created an impromptu shrine on Krivoarbatskii Lane. They called the wall they covered with graffiti "Necrophilia." In later years, the rock band Liube celebrated the youth of Arbat in its anthem against the war in Chechnya: "Behind us are Russia, Moscow, and Arbat."

Like nearly every underground crosswalk and street corner in Moscow, the Arbat pedestrian mall became the site of spontaneous capitalism after 1991. During the dire years of economic "shock therapy," when Boris Yeltsin's government impoverished the vast majority of Russians by floating prices and devaluing the currency, the pedestrian mall was an open-air marketplace, where Muscovites sold stamps and coins, pirated CDs, clothing, antiques, books, and "deficit" items of all sorts.

14. "Arbat. 16 rakursov odnoi ulitsy," *Arkhitektura SSSR* 4 (April 1986): 33, 35.
15. Sergei Rumiantsev, "Progulki po Arbatu," *Moskva* 7 (July 1995): 145–46; and Snork [pseudonym], "Peshekhodnaia zona," interview by Anna Rudenko, *Na dne* 35, no. 2 (February 1998), http://www.pressa.spb.ru/newspapers/na_dne-35-art-6.html.
16. "Akh Arbat, moi Arbat," *Iunost'* 8 (August 1988): 8–13.

The crosswalk under Arbat Square became one of the city's chief pet markets, even though there was an established pet store farther down Arbat. Chalk artists displayed caricatures of Western pop stars like Bruce Springsteen and Johnny Hallyday in front of the Hotel Prague, which had been transformed into a fancy restaurant. They hoped to convince foreign tourists that it was worth a few dollars to sit for a portrait. Street musicians and hucksters entertained passersby with Beatles' songs and shell games. And everywhere there were lacquer boxes, supposedly from the masters of Palekh, a village in Ivanovo oblast east of Moscow, and *matreshki,* the nesting dolls that seemed to constitute post-Soviet Russia's chief export. In the mid-1990s, municipal officials eliminated much of the trade by enforcing street-vendor licenses. A McDonald's opened near Smolensk Square, then one of several in Moscow. It pledged not to serve alcohol since so many young people congregated on Arbat. In the late 1990s, dozens of restaurants and stores, many with Western labels and prices, opened and closed their doors as Muscovites exercised their new power as consumers. Like the 1920s, when Sergei Esenin, an icon among Soviet youth, read his poetry to crowds of admirers in Arbat pubs, the neighborhood was again home to a lively nightlife. The Arbat Blues Club opened in January 1993 to a crowd of foreigners and young Russian professionals.[17] A Hard Rock Café followed a decade later. On Novyi Arbat, the Angara restaurant catered to Mafiosi, prostitutes, and bureaucrats with lucrative government connections. It required customers to pass through a metal detector before entering. And across from the Smolensk metro station, near the western terminus of Arbat Street, John Bull Pub offered Bass Ale on tap and the English Premiership on television.

In the backstreets south of the pedestrian mall, buildings were renovated to Western standards, or razed entirely and replaced with new structures built in the "Luzhkov style," the retrospective and kitschy glass and steel architecture preferred by Moscow's mayor. Their tenants were *biznesmeny* and the multinational corporations that employed them. Architects drew up still unrealized plans to put the Novyi Arbat thoroughfare underground, and to replace the dated and decrepit skyscrapers that lined it with larger, more modern structures. Real-estate brokers were always happy, of course, to advertise the Arbat's reputation as a community of artists and writers for the few prospective buyers who could afford the neighborhood's skyrocketing prices.

17. Michael Urban, *Russia Gets the Blues: Music, Culture, and Community in Unsettled Times* (Ithaca, N.Y., 2004), 72–74.

One of the newest attractions on the Arbat is Georgii Frangulian's monument to the poet Bulat Okudzhava, the neighborhood's most famous native son. Born in Moscow in 1924 to a Georgian father and Armenian mother, devoted communists who had come from Tbilisi for work and study, Okudzhava spent much of his childhood playing in the Arbat courtyards. After moving to Nizhnii Tagil in the Urals in 1934, where his parents had been elected to positions in the local party organization, Okudzhava learned firsthand the tragedy of Stalinism. His father was executed in 1937 as a German and Japanese spy; his mother survived nearly two decades in the gulag. As a minor without parents, Okudzhava went to Tbilisi to live with relatives in 1940. Before he finished secondary school, he enlisted in the army, and served first in a mortar platoon, and then after being wounded in an air strike, as a radio operator. After the war, Okudzhava enrolled in a pedagogical program at Tbilisi State University. Still barred from residency in Moscow as a relative of "enemies of the people," he found his first teaching job in Shamordina, a village in Kaluga oblast southwest of the capital. In 1956, the year his parents were rehabilitated, Okudzhava published his first volume of poetry, *Lirika* (Lyric Poetry). He also returned to Moscow, where he found work as an editor. Okudzhava made his mark during these years as one of the key figures in the development of the "author's song" genre of poetry: like fellow bards Vladimir Vysotskii and Aleksandr Galich, Okudzhava put much of his verse to music, accompanying himself on a seven-string guitar. Okudzhava ran afoul of authorities in the 1960s when his songs were deemed overly pessimistic, and also when he signed letters in support of the dissidents Andrei Sinyavsky and Aleksandr Solzhenitsyn. In the early 1970s, he was nearly kicked out of the party after writing an introduction for the work of an émigré writer that was published abroad. Yet Okudzhava was never saddled with the dissident label. His poetry and prose—about youthful love, the passing of childhood and time, the old intelligentsia as a moral compass for the present, and the camaraderie and casualties of war—generally stayed away from politically charged topics that were certain to cause trouble. Most of all, he focused on the past and present of his native Arbat, a place that seemed to embody the history and fate of the intelligentsia like no other.[18]

18. Okudzhava describes his family history in *Uprazdennyi teatr: semeinaia khronika* (Moscow, 1995). A shorter biography can be found in idem, *65 pesen/65 songs*, ed. Vladimir Frumkin (Ann Arbor, Mich., 1980), 170.

2. Bulat Okudzhava in Yalta, 1966. From *Bulat Okudzhava: ego krug, ego vek* (Moscow: Sol', 2004). Used with permission of Olga Vladimirovna Okudzhava.

Frangulian's bronze monument stands at the intersection of Arbat Street and Plotnikov Lane, near the apartment building where Okudzhava lived in the 1920s and '30s. It depicts a middle-aged Okudzhava strolling through an archway, his hands in his trouser pockets, apparently lost in thought. Behind Okudzhava is a second archway, and in between, a table and a bench—the trappings of an Arbat courtyard. Because the monument is at street level, passersby can walk through the archways, sit on the bench in the courtyard, and reflect on the fact that Frangulian depicted Okudzhava leaving. Visitors who are old enough may recall Okudzhava's 1959 poem, "Arbat Courtyard," where he used departure from the courtyard as a metaphor for his passage to adulthood, and the "warm pockets" of memory where he soothed his "cold hands." A few may even remember that Okudzhava never returned to live in the Arbat

3. Georgii Frangulian's monument to Bulat Okudzhava at the intersection of Plotnikov Lane and Arbat Street. Photograph by Andrey Shlyakhter.

neighborhood, and that his feelings about the Arbat turned negative in the 1960s. But only the most astute will wonder whether Frangulian's monument was meant to commemorate Okudzhava's connection to the Arbat, or like Okudzhava himself, criticize what the Arbat had become.[19]

Okudzhava's poetry helped define a sense of uniqueness in the Arbat that was not readily apparent to outsiders. Compared to similar cities in Europe and North America, Moscow was characterized by a relatively low degree of residential segregation. Measured by conventional criteria like class and estate, the Arbat was no exception. Even at its aristocratic zenith in the late-nineteenth century, the Arbat municipal ward was home to more than four hundred manufacturing establishments and small workshops. The affluent Prechistenka ward to the south had a similar number.[20] Given the Soviet government's commitment to egalitarianism, and its penchant for redrawing municipal boundaries to avoid the appearance of segregation, the few distinct social enclaves and neighborhoods that existed before 1917 seemed to disappear almost entirely. Yet the sociologist Gerald Suttles has argued that "reputational content and ethos of local culture" are factors that shape the cognitive maps and corporate identities of city dwellers.[21] Like New York's Greenwich Village in the early part of the twentieth century, that self-consciously

19. On Frangulian's monument, see Mikhail Ul'ianov, "'Tut vsegda bylo uiutno . . . ,'" *Arbatskie vesti* 6 (March 2001): 3; and "I pravnuki zabudut slovo 'dvor,'" *Arbatskie vesti* 2 (January 2002): 2. In an interview on the radio station Ekho Moskvy on May 8, 2002, Okudzhava's daughter claimed that the monument would help combat the "grime and tastelessness" associated with present-day Arbat. See http://echo.msk.ru/guests/5120.
20. On social segregation in the tsarist period, see Joseph Bradley, *Muzhik and Muscovite: Urbanization in Late Imperial Russia* (Berkeley and Los Angeles, 1985), 52–60, 231–34. On social segregation after 1917, see Timothy J. Colton, *Moscow: Governing the Socialist Metropolis* (Cambridge, Mass., 1995), 502–18; and R. Anthony French, *Plans, Pragmatism, and People: The Legacy of Soviet Planning for Today's Cities* (Pittsburgh, 1995), 135–50. On the peculiar forms of segregation in socialist cities, see Jens Dangschat, "Social Disparities in a 'Socialist' City: The Case of Warsaw," *International Journal of Urban and Regional Research* 11, no. 1 (1987): 37–60; and Ivan Szelenyi, *Urban Inequalities under State Socialism* (New York, 1983), 8.
21. Gerald D. Suttles, *The Social Construction of Communities* (Chicago, 1972), 13. On the construction of place-based identity, see Timothy Oakes, "Place and the Paradox of Modernity," *Annals of the Association of American Geographers* 87, no. 3 (1997): 509–31; Victoria E. Thompson, "Telling 'Spatial Stories': Urban Space and Bourgeois Identity in Early Nineteenth-Century Paris," *Journal of Modern History* 75, no. 3 (September 2003): 523–66; Elena Iarskaia-Smirnova and Pavel Romanov, "At the Margins of Memory: Provincial Identity and Soviet Power in Oral Histories, 1940–53," in *Provincial Landscapes: Local Dimensions of Soviet Power*, ed. Donald J. Raleigh (Pittsburgh, 2001), 299–329; and Scott Spector, *Prague Territories: National Conflict and Cultural Innovation in Franz Kafka's Fin de Siècle* (Berkeley and Los Angeles, 2000), 1–35.

Bohemian "republic of dreams," the Arbat was not distinguished by characteristics like ethnicity and class that were easily quantifiable.[22] Nonetheless, Okudzhava framed the neighborhood's past in ways that captured "the common experience that defines group identity."[23] He referred to the Arbat as his "religion" and "fatherland." It was something that shaped his morality and soul.

Sigurd Shmidt, a prolific historian of medieval Russia and one of the central figures in the development of "local studies" (*kraevedenie*) as a scholarly field, identified a similar affinity among his Arbat neighbors. He claimed that they were united by a certain "socio-cultural commonality" that was devoid of "haughtiness." In the Arbat of his childhood in the 1920s and '30s, one heard "the speech patterns of old Moscow, taught in pre-revolutionary gymnasia," yet found the children of professors playing with the children of doormen. It is important to note that Shmidt, born in 1922, counted himself among the former group. His father, Otto, was a famous arctic explorer and a respected scientist. In 1933–34, Otto Shmidt led the ill-fated Cheliuskin expedition, whose members had to be airlifted off the polar cap when their ship became icebound.

Many of the neighborhood's residents called themselves *arbattsy* (Arbatites), an identity that the writer Andrei Belyi coined in the memoir he wrote in the early 1930s.[24] They were certain that their surroundings were unique in the cultural geography of Moscow. They imagined a core neighborhood around Arbat Street, a world of "intricate lanes and alleys, courtyards and gardens . . . roads and winding bricks that we knew by heart, and everything, everything with its smell and color and intonation," and a peripheral region—*priarbat'e*—connected to the core by history and proximity that stretched to Herzen (Bol'shaia Nikitskaia) Street on the north, Kropotkinskaia (Prechistenka) Street on the south, and Marx Avenue (Mokhovaia Street) on the east.[25]

Residents of the Arbat still invoke the neologism *arbatstvo*, a word that combines Arbat with *bratstvo* (brotherhood) to describe the neighborhood's

22. Ross Wetzsteon, *Republic of Dreams: Greenwich Village, the American Bohemia, 1910–1960* (New York, 2002), 1–14.
23. Kathleen E. Smith, *Mythmaking in the New Russia: Politics and Memory during the Yeltsin Era* (Ithaca, N.Y., 2002), 7.
24. Sigurd Ottovich Shmidt, *Put' istorika: izbrannye trudy po istochnikovedeniiu i istoriografii* (Moscow, 1997), 331; idem, "Neistrebimoe arbatstvo," interview by Arutian Amirkhanian, *Kuranty*, September 24, 1993, 9; and Viacheslav Meshkov, "'Krepis', Arbatets, v trudnoi . . . ,'" *Arbatskie vesti* 7 (April 2001): 7.
25. Bulat Okudzhava, "Akh Arbat, moi Arbat—ty moe otechestvo . . . ty moe prizvanie," in *Arbatskii arkhiv*, 142.

longstanding ties with the intelligentsia.[26] Okudzhava attributed author-
ship of the word to his elementary school classmates. He initially thought
that *arbatstvo* was indicative of a cultural and moral continuity between
past and present in the neighborhood, an important theme in his early
poetry. Writing about his executed father in 1957, for instance, he maintained that "There are no, no deaths among old Arbat children, just those
who had to sleep, and those who could not." Similarly, in his famous
"Little Song about the Arbat" (1959), Okudzhava wrote that "no one
could ever come to the end of you."[27] *Arbatstvo* designated residents of
the Arbat as the heirs to the idealism of earlier generations of artists and
writers. It imbued the landscape of their daily lives with past cultural
achievements, transforming it into what the geographer Yi-Fu Tuan called
"time made visible."[28]

In the early 1960s, however, in the midst of the Novyi Arbat demolition, Okudzhava began to rethink *arbatstvo*. He saw it as a relic of the
past that lacked a referent in the present, memory ruptured from context.
This shift was evident in Okudzhava's increasingly melancholy poetry
about the neighborhood, which explored themes like the irreversibility
of time, the victims of modernization, and the "days in Moscow when
the Arbat still existed."[29] In 1988, he told an interviewer that the destruction of the Arbat began during the Stalin period, when the secret police
targeted the intelligentsia, "those so-called eggs that had to be broken to
make an omelet," and continued in the 1950s and '60s, when the neighborhood's "unique atmosphere" and "external look" were lost. "The
Arbat is gone," he claimed, "and will not come back." Immanuil Levin,
who was born in 1923, and who, like Okudzhava and Shmidt, spent his
childhood playing in the Arbat courtyards, was similarly downbeat.
"Modern Arbat does not know *arbatstvo*," Levin wrote in a popular

26. Sigurd Ottovich Shmidt, interview by author, March 23, 1998; idem, "Arbatstvo
rifmuetsia s bratstvom," interview by T. Sergeeva, *Moskovskaia pravda*, April 24, 1993, 5;
and Boris Gennadievich Bushmelev, interview by author, April 4, 1998.
27. Bulat Okudzhava, "Menia vospityval Arbatskii dvor," interview by Mikhail Pozdniaev
(1988), in *Arbatskii arkhiv*, 145; idem, *Stikhi, rasskazy, povesty* (Ekaterinburg, Russ., 1998), 32
("'O chem ty uspel peredumat' . . . ,'"); and idem, *65 pesen/65 songs*, 54–55 ("Pesenka ob
Arbate").
28. Yi-Fu Tuan, *Space and Place: The Perspective of Experience* (Minneapolis, 1977), 179. On the
intersection of place and memory, see Michael G. Kenny, "A Place for Memory: The Interface
between Individual and Collective History," *Comparative Studies in Society and History* 41,
no. 3 (July 1999): 420–37; and Jay Winter, *Sites of Memory, Sites of Mourning: The Great War in
European Cultural History* (Cambridge, 1995), 8.
29. Bulat Okudzhava, "Vspominanie o Dne Pobedy," in *Arbatskii arkhiv*, 133–34.

post-Soviet guidebook to the neighborhood. *Arbatstvo* was "one of the first and most hard-hit victims of Stalinism"; what remained after the Great Purges was finished off by war and urban renewal.[30]

The writer Anatolii Rybakov also contributed to the pessimistic view of the Arbat's fate. Born into a secular and affluent Jewish family in 1911 near Chernigov, a city in north-central Ukraine, Rybakov moved to a communal apartment at 51 Arbat, the largest residential building along the street, in 1919. In an interview just before his death in 1998, Rybakov noted that his parents and sister, atheists and social-democrats who spoke French (but not Yiddish) at home, easily adjusted to the "Arbat milieu." As a teenager, Rybakov studied with many of the children of the new Soviet elite at Moscow's famous Experimental-Model School.[31] After graduation, he worked briefly in a chemical factory—perhaps to bolster his own credentials as a worker, since his father had been a factory director before the revolution—and then, in 1930, enrolled at the Moscow Institute of Transportation Engineers. Rybakov told the story of his expulsion from the institute and his arrest by the OGPU for counterrevolutionary propaganda in the first volume of the fictional trilogy about Stalinism, *Children of the Arbat*. Like Sasha Pankratov, the trilogy's protagonist, Rybakov was sentenced to three years exile along the Angara River in Siberia. Upon completion of his sentence, he was denied the right to live where "passport regimes" were in effect, cities like Moscow and Leningrad that required residency permits. After the war began, Rybakov participated in the defense of Moscow and fought his way to the gates of Berlin. In 1946, despite special restrictions governing residency on the Arbat (because it was the route that Stalin took to his dacha), Rybakov received permission to return to his family's old apartment. His wife and son had been living there since returning from wartime evacuation in Central Asia. Rybakov claimed that he charmed the local NKVD functionary in charge of residency permits by helping him repair his Opel. It also helped that Rybakov's apartment had a view of the courtyard rather than the street. In the postwar years, Rybakov made his mark as a writer of adventure stories for

---

30. Bulat Okudzhava, "Menia vospityval arbatskii dvor," 151–52; Levin, *Arbat*, 5; and idem, "Voina byla za shkol'nym porogom," in *Arbatskii arkhiv*, 410–17. For similar appraisals of the Arbat's fate, see Shmidt, "Arbat v istorii i kulture Rossii," 116; idem, "Neistrebimoe arbatstvo," 9; Roshal', "Arbat kak istoricheskii istochnik," 441; and Belitskii, *Zabytaia Moskva*, 50–51.
31. Although he doesn't mention Rybakov, Larry E. Holmes has written a history of the model school. See *Stalin's School: Moscow's Model School No. 25, 1931–1937* (Pittsburgh, 1999).

adolescents. His first novel for adults, *Drivers,* won the Stalin Prize in 1951. In 1958, Rybakov began writing *Children of the Arbat,* an autobiographical novel that treated the neighborhood as a symbol of the crushed innocence and idealism of the first Soviet generation. After it was rejected for publication in 1967, Rybakov's manuscript circulated among a small group of friends and potentially sympathetic editors until 1987, when it was finally published to domestic and international acclaim. The second and third installments in the trilogy came out in the 1990s.[32]

Although they were separated by thirteen years, Okudzhava and Rybakov had similar life trajectories. Both of their families were newcomers to Moscow and sympathetic to the Soviet government. Both spent many happy days playing in the Arbat courtyards. Both had their naiveté about the regime shattered at young ages by terror. And later in life, in the 1950s and '60s, both cast the Arbat as a casualty of Soviet power. Their pessimistic view of the Arbat's fate, and its corollary, the supposed disjuncture between the neighborhood's past and present, were by no means insignificant. They underlay the myth of the Arbat that emerged in the 1950s and '60s and that was widely disseminated among the Soviet intelligentsia, often through bootlegged recordings of Okudzhava's songs and samizdat editions of his work. The myth drew on the popular obsession with the past that arose during the thaw. According to Sigurd Shmidt, the Arbat was nothing less than a "symbol . . . of the Moscow intelligentsia . . . and a monument to the value of respect and a warm heart for the past."[33] The myth situated an intellectual and cultural paradise in the Arbat that existed before Stalin; it tallied what had been lost in the intervening years; and it explained the neighborhood's supposed demise in terms of its longstanding association with the Russian and Soviet intelligentsia.

To be sure, the Arbat myth was unusual in the Soviet context. Unlike core Soviet myths that originated in the revolution, the campaigns of the First Five-year Plan, and the Second World War, and that were articulated at the encouragement or behest of authorities, the Arbat myth did not legitimize socialism or mobilize the public.[34] Nonetheless, it functioned

32. Anatolii Rybakov, *Roman-vospominanie* (Moscow, 1997), 79–93, 130–32; idem, "Zarubki na serdtse: poslednee moskovskoe interv'iu," *Druzhba narodov* 3 (March 1999), http://magazines.russ.ru/druzhba/1999/3/rybak.html.

33. Shmidt, *Put' istorika,* 331, 338.

34. Amir Weiner argues that historians need to look beyond the "highly stylized" Soviet state when considering the articulation and dissemination of myths. See "The Making of a Dominant Myth: The Second World War and the Construction of Political Identities within the Soviet Polity," *Russian Review* 55, no. 4 (October 1996): 640. On myths that originated in 1917, see Frederick C. Corney, *Telling October: Memory and the Making of the Bolshevik Revolution* (Ithaca, N.Y., 2004).

like its more prominent counterparts. It consisted of a set of "unexamined assumptions" that helped persons "explain, cope with, and evade" events that were confusing and morally ambiguous.[35] The myth lent meaning to two experiences in particular. First, it treated the fate of the Arbat under Stalin as a synecdoche for the fate of the intelligentsia. The tendency to substitute a part for the whole is evident in the writings of both Rybakov and Okudzhava. Rybakov argued that the neighborhood embodied *"intelligentnost',"* literally, the quality of being a member of the intelligentsia. The Arbat he knew as a child had a thousand diversions: the Art, Carnival, Prague, and *Ars* movie theaters; street peddlers from China who sold exotic toys; privately owned bookstores that traded in treasures from the West and the past; studios where avant-garde artists displayed their work; and restaurants where the poets Vladimir Mayakovsky and Sergei Esenin held court. Similarly, Okudzhava claimed that the destruction of the Arbat was proof that authorities deemed the intelligentsia to be "not only unnecessary and superfluous, but dangerous as well." He used the Arbat courtyards, his childhood playground and a subject he returned to repeatedly, as a symbol of what his generation lost: friends, family members, and the innocence of youth. These were places of "happiness and laughter," where Lenka Korolev, the Arbat's most popular boy, ruled as a just and benevolent "king" before perishing in the war.[36] The myth, therefore, was partly a rhetorical strategy: it was possible to say things about the Arbat that were impossible to say about the intelligentsia. The myth was also a defense mechanism. Michael David-Fox has observed that efforts to engage the past through the culture of the present invariably entail both remembering and forgetting.[37] The Arbat myth was no exception. In the context of the thaw, where questions of guilt and complicity were omnipresent, the myth privileged memories of an intelligentsia that opposed Stalinism and suffered as a

35. Peter Heehs, "Myth, History, and Theory," *History and Theory* 33, no. 1 (February 1994): 3; and Aaron J. Cohen, "Oh, That! Myth, Memory, and World War I in the Russian Emigration and the Soviet Union," *Slavic Review* 62, no. 1 (Spring 2003): 70. Svetlana Boym argues that myths were ubiquitous in the Soviet Union, but "rarely interpreted critically." See *Common Places: Mythologies of Everyday Life in Russia* (Cambridge, Mass., 1994), 4.
36. On Rybakov, see Levin, *Arbat*, 5; and Rybakov, *Roman-vospominanie*, 34–35. On Okudzhava, see Vitalii Amurskii, *Zapechatlennye golosa: Parizhskie besedy s russkimi pisateliami i poetami* (Moscow, 1998), 90; and Bulat Okudzhava, *Chaepitie na Arbate: stikhi raznykh let* (Moscow, 1997), 27 ("Korol'"), 54 ("'Na arbatskom dvore . . .'"). For a similar account of the Arbat in the 1920s and '30s, see Ivan Arianovich Saposhnikov, "Ulitsa detstva," interview by Mariia Semenova, *Arbatskie vesti* 23 (December 2003): 7.
37. Michael David-Fox, "Cultural Memory in the Century of Upheaval: Big Pictures and Snapshots," *Kritika* 2, no. 3 (Summer 2001): 604, 611.

result, and downplayed memories of an intelligentsia that was a prime beneficiary of Stalinism.[38]

Second, the Arbat myth reflected the ways in which the intelligentsia experienced the thaw. The focus of memory may be the past, but it is an action that occurs in and is shaped by the present. Two of the chapters that follow show how the physical changes in the Arbat in the 1950s and '60s, themselves products of the political and cultural imperatives of the thaw, reinforced the sense of decline that was central to the myth. All of the chapters show that similar processes of re-imagining the past and making sense of Stalinism were widespread in the Arbat. When Okudzhava and Rybakov cast the Arbat of their childhoods as a lost paradise, they were doing the same thing as many other Soviet citizens, who were counting the victims of Stalinism and searching for alternate political and cultural models in the pre-Stalinist past. All of them found encouragement in the de-Stalinization reforms, which began haltingly in 1953, and in Khrushchev's unexpected denunciation of Stalin in 1956. The latter event, especially, made it possible for Soviet citizens to speak openly about Stalinism as an individual and collective trauma. In a context where the past Arbat seemed distant and unreachable—separated, as it was, from the present by the brutality of Stalinism—nostalgia was all but inevitable. The émigré scholars Petr Vail' and Aleksandr Genis have argued that Okudzhava's lost Arbat was part of a romantic idealization of the "road to nowhere" that was common in Soviet literature during the 1960s. The "road to nowhere" located individual freedom in the act of journeying to the Soviet Union's intimate, far-flung, and in the case of the Arbat, historical locales. It emphasized journey rather than destination, because the latter was often unreachable.[39] Like the "road to nowhere," the Arbat myth was a commentary on present realities. It reflected awareness about what had been lost under Stalin, but also the sense that the lost Arbat was impossible to recreate. It is not hard to imagine the development in a different context of a "restorative" Arbat myth that would have presented the neighborhood as the embodiment of the eternal values of the intelligentsia, and that would have undergirded efforts to reconstitute the neighborhood after the trauma of Stalinism. But in the context of the thaw, the Arbat myth was "reflective,"

---

38. On the latter, see Sheila Fitzpatrick, *The Cultural Front: Power and Culture in Revolutionary Russia* (Ithaca, N.Y., 1992), 1–15.

39. Petr Vail' and Aleksandr Genis, *60-e: Mir sovetskogo cheloveka* (Ann Arbor, Mich., 1988), 105, 116–17.

a gloomy meditation on what the Arbat had once been and why it was no more.[40] As one of the interview subjects in the documentary *House of Knights* put it, the Arbat "is the memory of what can never be repeated."

The emergence of the Arbat myth during the thaw offered an image of a past Arbat that still shapes the way residents and outsiders understand the neighborhood. More than three decades after the myth first appeared in the writings of Okudzhava and Rybakov, it resonates in Sigurd Shmidt's local studies and Immanuil Levin's tourist guidebook. It informs public discussions about the meaning of Georgii Frangulian's monument to Okudzhava, and many stories I heard from lifelong residents. Why the myth took root in the 1950s and '60s, and why it made sense, had a lot to do with the way the Arbat intelligentsia experienced the thaw. In the chapters that follow, I step away from the myth in order to look at the Arbat's experienced thaw. Our tour begins at the Gnesin Music-Pedagogy Institute.

40. I have borrowed the restorative/reflective binary from Svetlana Boym's discussion of the different types of nostalgia. See *The Future of Nostalgia* (New York, 2001), 49–51.

CHAPTER TWO

A Cult of Personality and a "Rhapsody in Blue"

In 1895, the sisters Evgeniia and Mariia Gnesina, recent graduates of the Moscow Conservatory, opened a children's music school a few blocks north of the Arbat on Gagarinskii Lane, near Sobach'e Square. Their idea originated in the social circles of pre-revolutionary Arbat. Evgeniia Gnesina regularly hosted a group of friends that included the composers Alexander Scriabin and Sergei Rachmaninov, and the director of the Moscow Conservatory, Vasilii Safonov. They played chamber music and discussed the latest in culture and politics. With the encouragement of Konstantin Stanislavsky, a lifelong friend who later became the cofounder of the Moscow Art Theater, Evgeniia convinced her younger sisters, Mariia and Elena, to back her plans for a private music school. According to the composer Iulii Veisberg, their undertaking took considerable pluck: "When . . . several young sisters, girls who were fresh from the benches of the conservatory, opened a small music school, their capital consisted solely of their youthfulness, talent, and enthusiasm." In truth, the Gnesin sisters had more at their disposal than Veisberg let on. During its first years, the school's faculty included the composers Reinhold Glière and Eduard Langer. Many other prominent musicians and cultural figures lent their support by enrolling their own children.[1]

1. M. E. Rittikh, *Istoriia muzykal'nykh uchebnykh zavedenii imeni Gnesinykh* (Moscow, 1981), 7–11.

The Gnesins built a solidly progressive reputation during the school's formative years. During the Revolution of 1905, Evgeniia's younger brother, the composer Mikhail Gnesin, served as a liaison between revolutionary forces in St. Petersburg and the Moscow Conservatory, where discussions about a student strike were underway. In Moscow's Krasnopresn'ia district, the site of fierce street fighting northwest of the Arbat, Gnesin students helped build barricades, apparently with the tacit approval of teachers. The Gnesins also made certain that their school was accessible to poor students by waiving or reducing tuition for nearly half the student body. The Gnesins' reputation for progressive, egalitarian education helped the school survive the upheaval of 1917 and prosper in subsequent years. Contrary to many friends who went into emigration after the Bolsheviks seized power, the Gnesins remained in the Arbat. They continued to host "musical evenings" well into the 1930s, until it finally became too dangerous to do so. Their social circle soon encompassed a younger generation of musicians and artists: the pianist Sviatoslav Rikhter, who grew up on the Arbat; his wife, the soprano Nina Dorliak; and her mother, Kseniia Dorliak, who taught with the Gnesins, and who as a young woman sang, in Paris, Prague, and Berlin, the roles of Elsa in Richard Wagner's *Lohengrin* and Brünnhilde in the Ring Cycle. The circle also included Rikhter's teacher, Genrikh Neigaus, who lived on Trubnikovskii Lane; the composer Vissarion Shebalin; the stage director Ruben Simonov, who would later become the artistic director of the Vakhtangov Theater; the pianist Konstantin Igumnov, who lived on Plotnikov Lane; the writer Boris Pasternak; and many others. In 1977, Vladimir Soloukhin, a writer who figured prominently in the historical preservation movement, wrote that it was impossible to imagine Moscow without the Gnesins. He might have said the same about the Arbat and the Gnesins.[2]

By 1944, the Gnesin Music Academy comprised three prestigious programs: the original Children's Music School, a secondary-level Music Gymnasium, and the university-level Music-Pedagogy Institute. In 1946, the latter two programs moved from their crowded quarters on Sobach'e Square, where one of the Gnesin sisters, Elena, still lived, to a new building on Vorovskii (Povarskaia) Street, a few blocks to the north. By then, the academy had produced a lengthy list of famous alumni, including the composer Aram Khachaturian, and the longtime chief of the Union of

2. Ibid., 107; and Nina Dorliak, "'Ia ochen' liubila Arbat . . . ,'" interview by Sigurd Ottovich Shmidt, in *Arbatskii arkhiv*, vyp. 1, ed. S. O. Shmidt (Moscow, 1997), 299–300.

Composers, Tikhon Khrennikov.[3] Although the university-level Pedagogical Institute was a less glamorous destination than the Moscow and Leningrad Conservatories, where the curriculum was oriented toward performance, the competition for one of its thousand-odd spots was fierce.[4] Many of the institute's teachers were prominent figures in their fields and helped determine the content of music curricula in schools across the Soviet Union. This stature meant that the institute's affairs often had repercussions that extended far beyond its walls.

The hazards of institutional notoriety became evident in the mid-1950s, during the years surrounding the Twentieth Party Congress, when Gnesin teachers found themselves at the frontlines of the struggle to make sense of the Stalinist past. Teachers recognized that de-Stalinization necessitated curricular change and opened new topics to scholarly analysis. This was especially true in the fields of music history and theory, where the existing curriculum had been shaped in powerful ways by the *zhdanovshchina*, the vitriolic campaign against Western culture that the party's chief ideologue, Andrei Zhdanov, waged from 1946 to 1948.[5] In 1953, under pressure from outside officials, teachers debated a proposal to provide students with greater "creative independence," a euphemism for individual research and informal seminars. In 1954 and 1955, they reintroduced modern Western composition into the curriculum, the very sort of music that Zhdanov had skewered after the war. And after the Twentieth Party Congress, they began to reevaluate Soviet music that party leaders had denounced as formalist before 1953. These curricular initiatives were necessarily tentative, however, and in some cases temporary, because Khrushchev did not curtail the authority of the xenophobic decree from the *zhdanovshchina* that governed

3. Rittikh, *Istoriia*, 11–12, 19–51; Boris Schwarz, *Music and Musical Life in Soviet Russia, 1917–1970* (New York, 1972), 393; and Tsentral'nyi arkhiv literatury i iskusstva Moskvy [hereafter TsALIM], f. 306, o. 1, d. 3, ll. 4–6.
4. Rossiiskii gosudarstvennyi arkhiv literatury i iskusstva [hereafter RGALI], f. 2329, o. 2, d. 990, l. 56; and Rittikh, *Istoriia*, 99–100.
5. After 1953, similar changes were underway in other scholarly fields as well. On historical analysis, see John Keep, "Sergei Sergeevich Dmitriev and His Diary," *Kritika* 4, no. 3 (Summer 2003): 719–22; and Roger D. Markwick, *Rewriting History in Soviet Russia: The Politics of Revisionist Historiography, 1956–1974* (New York, 2001), 38–72. On the sciences broadly, see Paul Josephson, *New Atlantis Revisited: Akademgorodok, the Siberian City of Science* (Princeton, N.J., 1997). On cybernetics, see Slava Gerovitch, *From Newspeak to Cyberspeak: A History of Soviet Cybernetics* (Cambridge, Mass., 2002). On ethnography, see Yuri Slezkine, *Arctic Mirrors: Russia and the Small Peoples of the North* (Ithaca, N.Y., 1994), 337–85. On the humanities and social sciences broadly, see Walter Z. Laqueur and George Lichtheim, *The Soviet Cultural Scene, 1956–1957* (New York, 1958), 65–236.

activities in the musical sphere until 1958, more than two years after he denounced Stalin at the Twentieth Party Congress. Even though Stalin was in disgrace, his decree on music remained valid, at least in theory. In reality, the perceived authority of the decree was tied to the prevailing political winds. During periods of reform, few teachers at the Gnesin Institute thought the decree was anything more than a minor nuisance; during periods of retrenchment, disregarding the decree could be perilous.

In their struggle to reconcile past and present, Gnesin teachers confronted one of the chief paradoxes of the thaw: despite its name, de-Stalinization was neither systemic in scope, nor coherent in implementation. Khrushchev did not overturn a moral universe and replace it with something different. Instead, he denounced Stalin but not Stalinism. He destroyed some parts of the old regime, preserved others, and dealt with the ensuing inconsistencies in an ad hoc manner. To counter criticism at the highest levels of the party, he spent the latter part of 1956 reining in the very reforms he unleashed earlier in the year. Consequently, activities that were encouraged at the Gnesin Institute during the spring were discouraged during the fall. Stalin may have been a cancer on the body politic, but few Gnesin teachers could say for certain which tissues were malignant. Even Khrushchev, the Soviet Union's chief oncologist, changed his diagnoses with unnerving frequency.

Discussions about curricular reform were always linked with concerns about student welfare. While teachers at the Gnesin Institute realized how risky it could be to pursue the logic of de-Stalinization to its end, students were more intrepid. Beginning in 1953, they saw de-Stalinization as a license to explore the music of George Gershwin and Igor Stravinsky. Like the Viennese *Jungen* who rebelled against the failed liberalism of their fathers in the 1870s, Gnesin students challenged the necessity of Marxist-Leninist theory in a music school, and ridiculed teachers whom they perceived as overly deferential to the party line.[6] They kindled teachers' fears of a "fathers and sons" schism, named for Ivan Turgenev's 1862 novel about the nihilism of a generation bred on science and radical politics. Teachers saw in their students the spirit of Evgenii Bazarov, Turgenev's young antihero who mocked the patronizing liberalism of the provincial gentry. Like Okudzhava and Rybakov, many teachers had suffered personally under Stalin. Yet they

6. Carl E. Schorske, *Thinking with History: Explorations in the Passage to Modernism* (Princeton, N.J., 1998), 141–56.

feared that students were challenging their authority because of their perceived complicity in the injustice and obscurantism of Stalinism.

Teachers' concerns revolved around guilt for the past, another issue that party leaders did a poor job explaining.[7] At the Twentieth Party Congress, Khrushchev—to protect his own political and moral authority—attempted to preempt discussions of guilt by placing all blame for the cult of personality and unjust repressions on Stalin and Beria. After the unsuccessful "antiparty group" coup in June 1957, he added Georgii Malenkov, Viacheslav Molotov, and Lazar Kaganovich, his rivals for supreme power, to the list of the guilty. Teachers were convinced that the institute's disciplinary problems were a sign that students were unpersuaded by the official line. Whether students actually held teachers accountable for the sins of the past is unclear. That many teachers felt guilty in the presence of students is undeniable. By nature, gnawing guilt is always self-ascribed.

Teachers at the Gnesin Institute were not alone in their fears of a generational schism. Official concern that Soviet youth had ceased to be the most active participants in the construction of socialism, as they were commonly portrayed in the 1920s and '30s, arose in the postwar years and was a recurring issue in the politics of the 1950s and '60s. It invariably surfaced during periods of ideological retrenchment, such as during the international upheaval of late 1956, when the Central Committee identified Soviet youth as a special risk group, and after the modern-art debacle at the Manège in December 1962, when Khrushchev rejected, at great length, assertions that the Soviet Union suffered from a "father and son problem" (thus confirming, ipso facto, that young people were a point of concern).[8]

Contrary to the vacillating attention that party leaders paid to it, youthful rebellion was a constant theme in the culture of the thaw. In large cities like Moscow, Leningrad, and Sverdlovsk, young *stiliagi*—so-called fashion hunters—became everyday fixtures in cafes, pubs, and hotels that catered to foreigners. Rock-and-roll pioneers like Bill Haley and Chuck Berry found a devoted, if mostly underground following among Soviet youth. During the late 1950s and early '60s, literary Young Turks like

7. On guilt for Stalinism, see Nanci Adler, *The Gulag Survivor: Beyond the Soviet System* (New Brunswick, N.J., 2002), 122–24.

8. On Soviet youth in the prewar years, see Anne E. Gorsuch, *Youth in Revolutionary Russia: Enthusiasts, Bohemians, Delinquents* (Bloomington, Ind., 2000), 15–22. Khrushchev's denial of a "fathers and sons" problem can be found in "Khrushchev Speaks Again," in *Khrushchev and the Arts: The Politics of Soviet Culture, 1962–1964*, ed. Priscilla Johnson and Leopold Labedz (Cambridge, Mass., 1965), 155.

Evgenii Yevtushenko and Okudzhava read to standing-room-only crowds of young admirers thrilled by their unconventional poetry. In Moscow scores of young poets gathered nightly below the statue of Vladimir Mayakovsky on Gorky Street to share their work with the public, a practice so unstructured that apprehensive officials eventually put an end to it. In universities and technical schools across the Soviet Union, tens of thousands of students joined voluntary folk and nature protection brigades, finding in them alternate, unofficial foci for their time and energy.[9]

To many observers, these activities marked the emergence of a critically-minded "thaw generation" that was galvanized by the supposedly liberal political climate, alienated from the state, and committed to further reform.[10] To teachers at the Gnesin Institute, however, they were symptomatic of the incongruence of de-Stalinization. It was an article of faith among Gnesin faculty, and indeed, a guiding principle of Soviet pedagogy, that curriculum mattered; students were the products of what they were taught.[11] After 1953, as political reform made the institute's music history and theory curriculum obsolescent, student disciplinary problems reached crisis proportions. From 1956 to 1958, the curriculum was patently contradictory: it parroted Khrushchev's denunciation of the cult of personality at the same time that it affirmed the authority of a decree that represented the worst of Stalinist xenophobia. When teachers tried to tackle the inconsistency directly, that is, to reinterpret Stalin's

9. Hilary Pilkington, *Russia's Youth and Its Culture: A Nation's Constructors and Its Constructed* (London, 1994), 64–71; Elena Zubkova, *Russia after the War: Hopes, Illusions, and Disappointments, 1945–1957*, trans. Hugh Ragsdale (Armonk, N.Y., 1998), 109–16; S. Frederick Starr, *Red and Hot: The Fate of Jazz in the Soviet Union* (New York, 1982), 239; Timothy W. Ryback, *Rock around the Bloc: A History of Rock Music in Eastern Europe and the Soviet Union* (New York, 1990), 9–10; Douglas R. Weiner, *A Little Corner of Freedom: Russian Nature Protection from Stalin to Gorbachev* (Berkeley and Los Angeles, 1999), 312–39; Juliane Fürst, "The Arrival of Spring? Changes and Continuities in Soviet Youth Culture and Policy between Stalin and Khrushchev," in *The Dilemmas of De-Stalinization: Negotiating Cultural and Social Change in the Khrushchev Era*, ed. Polly Jones (London, 2006), 135–53; and idem, "The Importance of Being Stylish: Youth, Culture and Identity in Late Stalinism," in *Late Stalinist Russia: Society between Reconstruction and Reinvention*, ed. Juliane Fürst (London, 2006), 209–30. For first-hand accounts of youth culture after the war, see Yevgeny Yevtushenko, *A Precocious Autobiography*, trans. Andrew R. MacAndrew (New York, 1963), 98, and Liudmila Polikovskaia, *My predchuvstvie . . . predtecha . . . : ploshchad' Maiakovskogo, 1958–1965* (Moscow, 1997).

10. Ludmilla Alexeyeva and Paul Goldberg, *The Thaw Generation: Coming of Age in the Post-Stalin Era* (Pittsburgh, 1993); and Robert D. English, *Russia and the Idea of the West: Gorbachev, Intellectuals, and the End of the Cold War* (New York, 2000), 49–115.

11. Larry E. Holmes, *Stalin's School: Moscow's Model School No. 25, 1931–1937* (Pittsburgh, 1999), 77–107.

decree in the spirit of the Twentieth Party Congress and create a more coherent narrative of the Stalin period, they were stopped by party officials who thought that reform was veering out of control. The result, teachers feared, was a curriculum that fostered the very generational schism that Khrushchev would later deny. Students thought that teachers were complicit in perpetuating the cult of personality and were determined to explore on their own the Western music that was forbidden to them. Curriculum was the place where the Stalinist past intersected and shaped the present.

THE SONS REBEL

In February 1953, a month before Stalin's death, an anonymous critic in the journal *Sovetskaia muzyka* (Soviet Music), the official voice of the Union of Composers, criticized the faculty at the Gnesin Institute for failing to abide by the 1948 Central Committee decree on Vano Muradeli's opera *Great Friendship*, which had marked the peak of the *zhdanovshchina* in the music world. Beginning in 1946, Andrei Zhdanov, on Stalin's orders, orchestrated a broad attack on the intelligentsia for catering to the West and for indulging in a host of "formalist" sins. Two years later, Zhdanov took Muradeli to task for ignoring the lessons of the party's 1936 denunciation of Dmitrii Shostakovich's opera *Lady Macbeth of the Mtsensk District*, the implication being that *Great Friendship* was too modern for Soviet tastes. He also censured Shostakovich, Dmitrii Kabelevskii, Sergei Prokofiev, and Khachaturian for mistakes ranging from "formalism" to "anti-democratic tendencies" in their composition. In the aftermath of the attack, composers were encouraged to look for inspiration in folk music, the supposed antithesis of modern Western composition. Works by contemporary Western composers and Soviet composers implicated in the *Great Friendship* affair were pulled from repertoires. Popular genres like jazz and variety (*estrada*) were purged of Western influences and their shady performers. Even the saxophone was outlawed.[12]

12. Schwarz, *Music and Musical Life*, 213–68; Alexander Werth, *Musical Uproar in Moscow* (London, 1949); Sheila Fitzpatrick, *The Cultural Front: Power and Culture in Revolutionary Russia* (Ithaca, N.Y., 1992), 210–13; Starr, *Red and Hot*, 204–34; Francis Maes, *A History of Russian Music: From Kamarinskaya to Babi Yar*, trans. Arnold J. Pomerans and Erica Pomerans (Berkeley and Los Angeles, 2002), 308–17; Kiril Tomoff, "Uzbek Music's Separate Path: Interpreting 'Anti-Cosmopolitanism' in Stalinist Central Asia, 1949–52," *Russian Review* 63, no. 2 (April 2004): 212–40; and idem, *Creative Union: The Professional Organization of Soviet Composers, 1939–1953* (Ithaca, N.Y., 2006), 97–121.

The *Sovetskaia muzyka* article was in many ways surprising. Faithful to the wording of the Central Committee decree, it denounced all instances of "formalism, the alien influence of cosmopolitanism, and bourgeois nationalism" at the Gnesin Institute. But charges that the Gnesin faculty had ignored landmarks in the Soviet musical canon were limited to just a handful of works, and these charges were buried beneath a four-page list of more prominent transgressions. More important was the critic's sense that the institute's curriculum had become superficial and, paradoxically, overly regimented. The critic argued that many of the institute's textbooks were "antihistorical" (a charge that was also lodged against Muradeli's opera) because they emphasized only the stereotypes of individual composers. Student familiarity with Mikhail Glinka was limited to a few trite phrases regarding his role in the emancipation movement and the "progressive character of his work." Textbooks distilled Frédéric Chopin's life into his activities on behalf of the Polish nationalist movement and his interest in folk melodies. Faculty members compounded these shortcomings by glossing over delicate topics like the worldview and philosophical problems of Richard Wagner. The result was a "passive attitude" among students, who were bored by the curriculum and not engaged in any "concrete analysis of musical works." The critic recommended a vaguely defined course of independent study and research, especially for students beyond the first year of study. He encouraged faculty to allow students to pursue their own interests, like the expedition to the countryside to collect folklore that a worried administrator aborted in the fall of 1952. And he suggested that students devote less time to studying their instruments of specialty, and more time to developing the broad musical background and pedagogical skills essential to their success as teachers.[13]

The institute's academic council met on February 21, 1953, to discuss the charges and offer solutions. In typical fashion, virtually every speaker acknowledged the validity of the criticism and accepted responsibility for deficiencies. The quality of education at the institute had dropped precipitously, council members admitted. Students tended to fare poorly on the standardized exams required by the government. Even upon graduation, many appeared ignorant of the most fundamental aspects of music. Yet it was not clear how these problems might best be remedied. A formalistic, Western repertoire was easy to fix; student ennui was a

13. "O vospitanii molodykh muzykovedov," *Sovetskaia muzyka* 2 (February 1953): 7–13.

different issue altogether. Most council members agreed that faculty members had to demand more than rote memorization, especially in the fields of music history and theory. "One ought not reduce all [student] work to copying lectures," one teacher remarked. "It's necessary to discuss the texts of the lectures, but it's also necessary to discuss scholarly problems and resolve specific issues so theorists will not lose touch with broad creative problems."[14]

It is easy to see in the *Sovetskaia muzyka* criticism how political and cultural phenomena typically associated with the thaw—like the development of greater individual and institutional autonomy—sometimes antedated Stalin's death. Stalinism, after all, was far from monolithic, and some political imperatives, like the desire for young people to be enthusiastic participants in their education and in Soviet life more broadly, undermined others, like the need for ideological conformity. If the *Sovetskaia muzyka* criticism was at all startling, however, Gnesin faculty members did not show it. Yet they may have wondered whether student ennui was really contrary to the spirit of the 1948 Central Committee decree, or a product of it. It is clear that the critic's remedy—greater independence for students—was wholly contrary to the way that the *Great Friendship* affair was normally interpreted at the institute. Only three weeks earlier, the academic council met to mark the fifth anniversary of the decree. According to one faculty member, the decree obligated teachers to exercise greater control over their students. A closely supervised seminar was fine, but independent study was incompatible with the ideological vigilance required by the Central Committee.[15] Even the institute's scholarly work had to be evaluated in light of its effect on students. Viktor Krasnoshchekov, a specialist in choral music, pointed out that the forthcoming work of a prominent musicologist at the Moscow Conservatory, Sergei Skrebkov, might lead students to believe that the type of polyphony—the combination of two or more melodic voices—present in Russian folk music (*podgolosochnyi sklad*) was an "offshoot" of the Western variety that developed during the Renaissance, the very sort of "cosmopolitan" mistake that the Central Committee sought to prevent.[16]

14. RGALI, f. 2927, o. 1, d. 105, l. 103.
15. RGALI, f. 2927, o. 1, d. 105, ll. 14–15.
16. RGALI, f. 2927, o. 1, d. 104, ll. 68–69; and d. 105, ll. 26–28. Thanks to Kiril Tomoff for explaining *podgolosochnyi sklad*. Krasnoshchekov was probably referring to the second edition of Skrebkov's *Uchebnik polifonii* (Moscow, 1956). The first edition was published in 1951.

On December 22, 1953, the academic council again convened to review a proposal for curricular reform. The discussion hinged on the same question that *Sovetskaia muzyka* had raised ten months earlier: was it possible to eliminate rote memorization and excessive oversight from the curriculum, on the one hand, and maintain ideological conformity, on the other? Most faculty thought that greater student autonomy would reinforce ideological development in the long term, as students realized on their own the merits of the party line. But few could agree what greater autonomy entailed. Some sought to resurrect the perceived informality of the pre-revolutionary Moscow Conservatory, where Nikolai Rubinstein, a world famous pianist, treated students as colleagues rather than subordinates. Others put stock in the institute's moribund Student-Scholar Society (NSO), hoping that it would inculcate a sense of "independence" among its members. Until council members could decide on a concrete agenda, Iu. V. Muromtsev, the new director of the institute, told teachers that the onus of reform would fall on them; they would have to decide on their own how to foster amorphous ideals like "creative individuality" in the classroom. Socialist realism, Muromtsev argued, allowed for a "diversity of schooling." It was now time to "give more freedom to the student."[17]

Muromtsev, a graduate of the Moscow Conservatory, was the administrative director of the Stanislavsky Opera Studio before Elena Gnesina invited him to become her deputy in 1946. Despite personal connections with the Gnesins—he had studied piano with them as a child—this was surely a demotion. It may be the case that Muromtsev was forced out of the opera studio, not an unusual occurrence during the *zhdanovshchina*. After Elena Gnesina retired to the honorary post of artistic director in 1953, Muromtsev served as rector of the institute until 1970, when he became the administrative head of the Bolshoi Theater.[18] In his new position, Muromtsev discovered that a rising tide of student disorder complicated the "search for new paths" in the music history and theory curriculum. At an academic council meeting in April 1954, one longtime faculty member remarked that he could not "remember a year when it was so bad, when there were such catastrophic conditions in regard to discipline." The party bureau devoted two meetings

17. RGALI, f. 2927, o. 1, d. 114, ll. 9, 24–25; d. 116, l. 71; and d. 120, l. 5.
18. Rittikh, *Istoriia*, 93.

during the spring of 1954 to disciplinary problems, usually an issue it deferred to the Komsomol.[19] By the end of the year, disciplinary problems were so widespread that they brought efforts to reform the curriculum to a halt. It had simply become impossible for teachers to promote greater independence in the classroom when they could not get control of students.

Student disciplinary problems provoked hours of worried discussion at the Gnesin Institute, yet assessments of the specific dimensions of the crisis—and even what constituted a disciplinary problem—varied widely. Faculty members complained about musical jargon that "lessened the dignity of the Russian language," about a pandemic of "careerist tendencies," about male students' penchant for bragging about their amorous conquests, about high truancy rates, about the large number of students who "strutted around" in new clothes and fashionable shoes, and about a general sense of laziness and conceit. Charges of hooliganism, a legal category that encompassed disorderly conduct, vandalism, and other antisocial behaviors that young, intoxicated men were apt to display, were also common in the classroom. Party members criticized a group of students whose "laughter, foolishness, shouting, heckling of teachers, making sounds on musical instruments, and unacceptably rude tone of voice" disrupted class and demoralized teachers. Muromtsev condemned a piano student who had shoved the institute's doorman against a wall, which spoke poorly of his "attitude . . . toward a comrade with less education."[20]

Student behavior outside of the classroom was also an issue. In the spring of 1954, several students were expelled for playing in a cinema orchestra, forbidden because variety entertainment supposedly reinforced bad musical habits and brought students into contact with disreputable persons. Another teacher admitted that a majority of students in his department moonlighted in similar groups. Several months later, a student was given a two-year suspended prison sentence for unspecified "amoral conduct." Another student was disciplined for being rude to employees at a movie theater while drunk. Most faculty members recognized that disciplinary problems were not unusual in a university, but many worried that they were far worse at the Gnesin

19. RGALI, f. 2927, o. 1, d. 116, l. 97; and Tsentral'nyi arkhiv obshchestvennykh dvizhenii Moskvy [hereafter TsAODM], f. 4081, o. 1, d. 11, ll. 28, 68.
20. TsAODM, f. 4081, o. 1, d. 11, ll. 2, 28–29; RGALI, f. 2927, o. 1, d. 116, ll. 74–76, 97; and d. 121, l. 14.

Institute than elsewhere.[21] One council member, V. L. Kubatskii, conducted his own investigation.

> I thought, what was the cause of this? I decided to check out the situation in different . . . universities. I went and began to observe how students behave themselves, how they walk in the corridors, and how they conduct themselves at school. When I'm at this institute, I avoid walking in the corridor because I'm afraid I'll be hurt by students who are running.
>
> I admit that there are very nice students, remarkable young men and women who show themselves well. I speak bitterly about a small, but, it seems, extraordinarily dangerous group. In a [typical] university, students sit in concentration during the lectures, and when they leave the auditorium, walking in groups of three and four, they discuss the topic of the lecture. . . . Nothing like this happens in our institute.[22]

By 1954 the institute's disciplinary problems had begun to attract the attention of outside officials. In March, the newspaper *Trud* (Labor) ran a feuilleton about a Gnesin student who showed up at a police station in the middle of the night in a "fashionable coat, checkered shirt, and colorful tie" to check on a female friend who had been assaulted (and presumably raped) after consorting with several strangers outside the Metropol Hotel. The anonymous author implied that the young woman got what she deserved, since she and her *stiliagi* friends had eschewed conventional Soviet morality for the "easy life" of restaurants and dance music. Later in the year, *Vecherniaia Moskva* (Evening Moscow) and *Vestnik vyshei shkoly* (Higher Education Herald) panned the quality of ideological work at the institute, making explicit the link between pedagogical content and student discipline.[23] This publicity augmented the sense that disciplinary problems had reached crisis proportions; it also helped cloud the line that divided childish mischief from more serious offenses. When a student missed a recital, he "ruined" the work of the collective. When a student failed to attend class, he "inflicted harm upon the government." The student who drove his own car to class was guilty of philistinism. The daily circus in the institute's dormitory, where

21. RGALI, f. 2927, o. 1, d. 116, ll. 88, 93; and TsAODM, f. 4081, o. 1, d. 12, l. 12.
22. RGALI, f. 2927, o. 1, d. 116, l. 98.
23. "V noch' pod voskresen'e . . . ," *Trud*, March 31, 1954, 3; "Uluchshat' prepodovaniia obshchestvennykh nauk v vuzakh," *Vecherniaia Moskva*, October 1, 1954, 2; and I. A. Vedernikov, "Likvidirovat' nedostatki v rabote," *Vestnik vyshei shkoly* 8 (August 1954): 4–7.

students were "under the influence, lying about on beds, and not doing anything," portended the development of more serious work-discipline problems after graduation.[24]

There were other problems that required less creativity to interpret. In October 1954, the party bureau reprimanded the former secretary of the institute's Komsomol for baptizing his son. Even though the student accused his wife's family of baptizing the child without his consent, and apologized for his lack of vigilance at home, his contrition was complicated by the fact that he had become a martyr of sorts among his peers. He received more applause at a subsequent Komsomol meeting than the director of the institute. Another student got a similar reaction from Komsomol members when party officials tried to discipline him for "drinking, cheating on exams, and working in a church." There were Komsomol members who were trying to "justify his actions," one party member raged. "With a diploma in his pocket, he will spread ideas foreign to us; by justifying [him] . . . we are justifying any sort of work." Another party member noted that students in his dialectical-materialism course had also questioned the seriousness of the student's transgressions.[25]

The scattered interest in religion was accompanied by an open indifference to the required Marxism-Leninism and socialist-realist theory courses, and the current-events discussion groups (*politchasy*). On average, both the rates of attendance and the exam scores in these courses were lower than for the institute as a whole, as students avoided what they considered boring and unimportant. During the fall of 1954, students in the orchestra department told visiting officials from the Ministry of Culture that socialist-realist theory was a waste of time. Several months earlier, the same students ran afoul of the party bureau for challenging the necessity of "politics" in a music school. In November 1955, students in a choral music course mounted a similar offensive against the current-events discussion groups: "they announced that they do not need *politchas.*"[26] In January 1954, students in a music history course tried to ask their teacher, Margarita Rittikh, difficult questions so she would make an ideological blunder and get fired. When Rittikh proved too adept, students filed a complaint with the administration that Rittikh had "incorrectly explained material covered during the course, and that her

---

24. TsAODM, f. 4081, o. 1, d. 11, ll. 24, 29; RGALI, f. 2927, o. 1, d, 116, ll. 77–80; and d. 119, ll. 66–67.
25. TsAODM, f. 4081, o. 1, d. 11, ll. 67–68, 131–33.
26. RGALI, f. 2927, o. 1, d. 115, l. 7; d. 116, l. 76; TsAODM, f. 4081, o. 1, d. 11, ll. 70, 177; and d. 12, l. 45.

work . . . was unsatisfactory."[27] Because students knew that existing punishments were inconsequential, they offered patently disingenuous excuses for skipping classes. They openly ridiculed teachers who confronted them about their truancy. And they spent their time in class reading, writing letters, and whispering with friends.[28]

A meeting of the institute's Komsomol on October 26, 1955 brought the issue of student discipline to a head. The purpose of the meeting was to elect the officers for the coming academic year, an occasion solemn enough that several persons from the party bureau and administration attended. Given the institute's national stature, representatives from the Komsomol Central Committee and the municipal district party committee were also present. The meeting got off to a poor start when Muromtsev criticized several students who left early to go to work. It degenerated further when dozens of students jeered E. V. Mel'nikova, the chair of the Marxism-Leninism department and one of the institute's least popular teachers. When Muromtsev rose to defend Mel'nikova, "one part [of the audience] demanded quiet, and the other part, after 8–10 seconds, began to hiss."[29] For teachers, the debacle laid bare the full extent of the institute's disciplinary problems. At a joint meeting of the academic council and party organization on November 1, Muromtsev somberly recounted the events: "I have to say that our youth, the majority of the Komsomol members—unfortunately it is necessary to say this straightforwardly—showed themselves to be disorganized, poorly educated, politically immature, and a morally unstable mass, with even the tendency toward hooliganism." The affair was made worse by the fact that it occurred in the presence of important outsiders, one of whom described the meeting as the most chaotic he had ever witnessed. Even more troubling was the fact that the offenders were the very students who were supposed to be the most exemplary.[30]

Muromtsev called on teachers to punish the students responsible for the chaos on October 26, and to ask whether they were culpable as well. The Komsomol representative at the meeting also demanded a purge of the Komsomol ranks. But the academic council and party organization chose not to levy any punishment, since issues concerning cause and blame for disciplinary problems rarely elicited any consensus. The

27. TsAODM, f. 4081, o. 1, d. 11, ll. 91–92. For a similar case in Taganrog, see Laqueur and Lichtheim, *The Soviet Cultural Scene*, 209–10.
28. RGALI, f. 2927, o. 1, d. 119, l. 66; and d. 127, ll. 18–19.
29. RGALI, f. 2927, o. 1, d. 127, ll. 3–4.
30. RGALI, f. 2927, o. 1, d. 127, ll. 2, 4.

majority of teachers readily admitted that the Komsomol meeting reflected poorly on their tutelage, but they were reluctant to bear full responsibility. The most egregious disciplinary violations usually merited a visit with the institute's in-house psychiatrist, an implicit acknowledgment that some types of behavioral disorders were beyond the power of teachers to cure. Teachers also deflected blame by portraying the problems as part of a national crisis and the product of upbringing, and they found scapegoats in vulnerable colleagues like Mariia Iudina, a teacher in the piano department who took a special interest in the music of unconventional composers like the Austrian-American modernist Arnold Schoenberg, who developed a method of twelve-tone (dodecaphonic) composition, and his young Soviet disciple, Andrei Volkonsky.[31]

It was impossible, however, for teachers to deflect all responsibility from themselves. During 1954 and 1955, they devoted special attention to the Marxism-Leninism department, which evoked the worst in students because the teaching was often done by persons who were not musicians and lacked credibility in the eyes of students. As early as February 1954, the party organization urged the department to incorporate more than the works of Stalin into its classes, linking, for the first time, an obsolescent curriculum with the rising tide of disorder. But most teachers and administrators still associated disciplinary problems with excessive laxness, and simply wanted to change a climate that allowed students to act with impunity. As Muromtsev observed, "whether it's the case that they have scared us, or whether it's the case that we incorrectly understand our tasks, students . . . have us by our necks. And instead of straightening them out, our position is not brave enough—'just so it doesn't get any worse.'"[32]

THE CONTRADICTORY YEAR, 1956

The institute's disciplinary problems did not get worse after the Komsomol meeting in October 1955. But more teachers and administrators came to agree with the party organization. Curriculum had a direct bearing on student discipline; simply cracking down on the worst offenders did not improve aggregate student behavior. Teachers' volte-face had a

31. RGALI, f. 2927, o. 1, d. 11, ll. 116, 133; d. 117, l. 41; and d. 142, ll. 32–33.
32. TsAODM, f. 4081, o. 1, d. 11, l. 25; d. 116, ll., 99, 104; RGALI, f. 2927, o. 1, d. 116, l. 103; and d. 119, l. 17.

lot to do with the Twentieth Party Congress, an earthshaking event that changed many things at the institute. The congress revitalized efforts to reform the institute's curriculum. It provided opportunities for teachers to look critically at the past. And it introduced into the institute a discourse of victimhood and guilt that would have important repercussions for the way teachers viewed themselves and their students.

The crucial event at the Twentieth Party Congress was Khrushchev's denunciation of Stalin, the so-called secret speech. Read to 1,400 shocked delegates on February 25, 1956, the last day of the congress, the speech was an undeniable watershed in Soviet history. Over the course of four hours, Khrushchev demolished the reputation of a man whom many had considered infallible. He detailed Stalin's triumph over the principle of collective leadership, his "willfulness" vis-à-vis the party, and his persecution of its innocent members. He questioned Stalin's role in the death of Sergei Kirov, the Leningrad party chief whose 1934 assassination was used as an official justification for mass terror. He condemned Stalin's passivity in the wake of the 1939 Molotov-Ribbentrop pact, which pledged ten years of nonaggression between Nazi Germany and the Soviet Union. And he enumerated the most egregious examples of self-promotion that lay at the heart of Stalin's cult of personality. Khrushchev also called on party members to extirpate Stalin's cult "decisively, once and for all" by criticizing what remained of it in Soviet life, by resurrecting the old practice of criticism/self-criticism within the party, and by restoring the "Leninist principles of Soviet socialist democracy." What these steps entailed, exactly, and what their repercussions would be, were clear to no one, least of all Khrushchev himself.[33]

Despite Khrushchev's disingenuous plea not to "let this matter get out of the party," Soviet citizens quickly learned of the gist, if not the details of his speech. To prevent the spread of false rumors, the Central Committee Presidium decided shortly after the congress to share the text

---

33. N. S. Khrushchev, *The Crimes of the Stalin Era: Special Report to the 20th Congress of the Communist Party of the Soviet Union*, ed. Boris I. Nicolaevsky (New York, 1962). On the circumstances surrounding the speech, see V. P. Naumov, "K istorii sekretnogo doklada N. S. Khrushcheva na XX s"ezda KPSS," *Novaia i noveishaia istoriia* 4 (July–August 1996): 147–68; idem, "Bor'ba N. S. Khrushcheva za edinolichnuiu vlast'," *Novaia i noveishaia istoriia* 2 (March–April 1996): 10–31; Iu. V. Aksiutin and O. V. Volubuev, *XX s"ezd KPSS: novatsii i dogmy* (Moscow, 1991), 214–23; V. V. Zhuravlev, ed., *XX s"ezd KPSS i ego istoricheskie real'nosti* (Moscow, 1991), 37–66; William Taubman, *Khrushchev: The Man and His Era* (New York, 2003), 270–99.

of the speech with all party and Komsomol members, government workers, and foreign communist officials. The party organization at the Gnesin Institute met on March 16 to discuss Khrushchev's revelations about Stalin. The meeting came nearly three weeks after the congress, a late enough date that several persons complained the delay was fueling rumors. Only thirty-five of the institute's fifty-seven party members attended, a striking absence rate given the significance of the congress. It is not clear how much party members already knew. The transcript of the meeting does not indicate whether those who were present listened as Khrushchev's speech was read aloud (a chore that was handled by multiple readers in other locales), or whether the bureau permitted party members to familiarize themselves with a printed copy beforehand.[34] Whatever the case, the subsequent discussion suggests that the bureau was uncomfortable addressing the same issues as the secret speech— Stalin's mistakes during the war, his repression of innocent party members, and his penchant for self-promotion. Instead, the keynote speaker, Konstantin Rozenshil'd, a teacher in the music history and Marxism-Leninism departments and one of the few faculty members without a degree in music, began by tallying the impact of Stalin's cult on Soviet composers, who with a few exceptions had written "no songs with good music" about Lenin, but many about Stalin. Rozenshil'd then trained his sights on the authoritarian proclivities of the institute's administration and on a colleague who had once denounced him. Another speaker reminded Rozenshil'd that the party bureau had its own history of tyranny, and that all party members were culpable for denunciations they knew were baseless. Aleksandr Iokheles, the chair of the piano department, claimed that an "inhumane" party bureau had nearly fired one teacher because she allowed her students to perform the discredited work of Shostakovich and Maurice Ravel. Even after 1953, the bureau expelled a student from Kishinev, the capital of Moldova, after receiving an anonymous denunciation about her in the mail. "This formal approach is an echo of the past," Iokheles concluded, "but it . . . is still very much alive."[35]

The meeting was striking for its tranquility, especially in comparison with the sometimes trenchant discussions that occurred elsewhere as

---

34. For an account of a similar party meeting, see Fedor Burlatsky, *Khrushchev and the First Russian Spring: The Era of Khrushchev through the Eyes of His Adviser* (London, 1991), 64.
35. TsAODM, f. 4081, o. 1, d. 13, ll. 14–16.

party members pointed fingers at each other and their leaders.[36] There were no questions about the role of Khrushchev in the purges. There were no demands that Khrushchev return "all power to the soviets." Nor were there any nostalgic comments about Stalin's "achievements." Instead, party members tried to eradicate the cult of personality from their everyday affairs. It was exactly the type of discussion that Khrushchev hoped to provoke: it underscored Stalin's malevolence, but did not challenge national power structures. Only at the end of the meeting did one party member hint at the problems that Khrushchev's secret speech would cause in the coming months. Was it still possible, she asked, to teach Leninism with Stalin's writings?[37]

The dissemination of congress materials began immediately among the institute's nonparty faculty. On March 14, bureau members met to review the institute's discussion groups, where faculty were familiarizing themselves with a sanitized version of the congress under the tutelage of so-called party propagandists. Their study was complicated by the official secrecy that surrounded Khrushchev's speech: the cult of personality was appropriate for discussion with nonparty members; Stalin's specific mistakes and repressions were not. The initial results of the discussion groups were not promising, as ambiguity at higher levels manifested itself as confusion at lower levels. One bureau member complained that high party officials had failed to explain the congress in an intelligible way during citywide orientation sessions. Propagandists, in turn, complained that the bureau had not offered sufficient guidance. The bureau could only refer the propagandists to a number of model seminar outlines that had been published in the March issue of *Partiinaia zhizn'* (Party Life).[38] Even among persons who were privy to the secret speech, few were able to grasp its repercussions on their own; even fewer were willing to risk interpreting it for others without guidance from above.

The institute's students were also obligated to familiarize themselves with the congress. A Ministry of Higher Education decree on February 29

36. Zubkova, *Russia after the War*, 185–90; N. A. Barsukov, "Oborotnaia storona 'ottepeli' (istoriko-dokumental'nyi ocherk)," *Kentavr 4* (1993): 129–43; Aksiutin, *Khrushchevskaia "ottepel'*," 154–98; idem, "Popular Responses to Khrushchev," 177–208; Taubman, *Khrushchev*, 285–87; and T. A. Sivokhina and M. R. Zezina, *Apogei rezhima lichnoi vlasti, "ottepel'," povorot k neostalinizmu: obshchestvenno-politicheskaia zhizn' v SSSR v seredine 40-x–60-x gody* (Moscow, 1993), 14–20.
37. TsAODM, f. 4081, o. 1, d. 13, l. 17.
38. TsAODM, f. 4081, o. 1, d. 13, ll. 119–22.

required the institute to incorporate congress materials into its Marxism-Leninism and *politchasy* curricula by March 12. This was not an easy task, especially given the confusion surrounding the work with teachers. According to E. V. Mel'nikova, a teacher in the Marxism-Leninism department, students lodged numerous complaints with the administration about the way teachers dealt with the congress. Some students criticized teachers for ignoring the congress altogether; others wondered why teachers failed to link it with the "problems of the institute." While it was appropriate for party members to look for evidence of the cult in their scholarly lives, the same, apparently, was not true for students. The reluctance to incorporate the congress into coursework reflected fears—often justified—that students would draw their own, impolitic lessons from the congress. After discussing the cult of personality in a Marxism-Leninism class, for instance, several students asked about Khrushchev's culpability for Stalinism and the wisdom of the party line. Others said they would no longer allow themselves to be sullied by Soviet power, and refused to participate in the institute's occasional field trips to factories and collective farms. Officials called this form of shirking *beloruchki* (white hands), since students who remained at home did not have dirty, callused hands like their more patriotic classmates. Yet shirkers did not have to be familiar with Lady Macbeth to conclude that white hands were clean hands, free of the blood of a repressive regime.[39]

According to Muromtsev, the problems that plagued the dissemination of congress materials in class were symptomatic of students who failed to understand the importance of the congress, and thus "withdrew from this important work."[40] Yet the opposite may also have been true. Students understood all too well the significance of the congress, and thus rebelled against the guidelines that governed the discussions in the Marxism-Leninism and *politchasy* classes. By early spring, both teachers and students had ample opportunity to familiarize themselves with the congress outside the highly regimented setting that the party bureau tried to provide. In March, the journal *Partiinaia zhizn'* codified the link between Stalin's cult and the "perversion of party principles and party democracy . . . violations of revolutionary legality . . . [and] unfounded repression." Later that month, *Pravda* began a series of essays attacking persons who were manipulating the speech for "antiparty"

---

39. RGALI, f. 2927, o. 1, d. 131, ll. 22, 24–25. On the *beloruchki* phenomenon, see Laqueur and Lichtheim, *The Soviet Cultural Scene*, 207.
40. RGALI, f. 2927, o. 1, d. 131, l. 29.

purposes.[41] The upshot of this publicity was the growth of two strikingly dissimilar discursive spheres at the institute. In those locales that were explicitly devoted to the congress—the *politchasy* classes, the party meetings, and the teacher/propagandist study groups—the range of possibilities for discussion was narrow. But in a host of more ordinary locales—the academic council, the music history and theory classes, and the Student-Scholar Society—teachers and students were able to explore more thoroughly the repercussions of the congress.

This latter development was evident in renewed attempts to reform the institute's history and theory curriculum. In March 1956, the academic council reviewed the manuscript of a music history textbook that the history and theory faculty had written before the Twentieth Party Congress. The authors hewed closely to the Zhdanov line. They emphasized Khachaturian's "mistakes" in the Union of Composers and the "great harm" that Muradeli inflicted on Soviet music, both points of criticism in the 1948 Central Committee decree. Their only reference to Vissarion Shebalin, another target of the 1948 decree, was that he was a "composer-formalist." They claimed that the international success of Shostakovich's *Lady Macbeth of the Mtsensk District* proved that it was unsuitable for Soviet audiences. And they underscored the opera's "crude naturalism" (code for overt sensuality), and claimed that Shostakovich was often "grotesque for the sake of grotesque." According to Mirra Bruk, an expert on the compositions of Georges Bizet, and lead editor of the textbook, these were the truths revealed by "historical documents." Bruk had good reason to toe the official line. Her husband had perished under Stalin, and she had been singled out for criticism during the anti-Semitic campaign against "cosmopolitans" in the late 1940s.[42] In the wake of the Twentieth Party Congress, however, many thought that Bruk's truths were unbefitting a serious textbook. One council member told the editors that it was "awkward to talk this way about Shostakovich now," and that it did not "correspond to reality." Editors' criticism of Shostakovich's Fifth Symphony seemed especially misguided. It premiered to official acclaim in 1937 and was widely understood as Shostakovich's repentance after the *Lady Macbeth* disaster.

41. "V chem vred kul'ta lichnosti," *Partiinaia zhizn'* 5 (1956): 17; "Pochemu kul't lichnosti chuzhd dukhu Marksizma-Leninizma?" *Pravda*, March 28, 1956, 2–3; and "Kommunisticheskaia partiia pobezhdala i pobezhdaet vernost'iu Leninizmu," *Pravda*, April 5, 1956, 2–3.
42. My thanks to Katerina Clark for news of Bruk's husband. Additional data on Mirra Bruk is available in Rittikh, *Istoriia*, 172; and Tomoff, *Creative Union*, 169n51.

It was subjected to minor criticism only at the height of the *zhdanovsh-china* in 1948.[43] Other council members encouraged the editors to empha-size Khachaturian's strengths as a composer and to avoid claims that did "not sound believable."[44] A similar discussion occurred a month later, when the history and theory faculty met to revise a three-volume textbook before it went to press. Iurii Keldysh, the chief editor of the textbook, called on his coauthors to eliminate the "clear one-sidedness" that marred the text. He noted that one article dismissed Alexander Scri-abin for his flirtation with "decadence." Another used "thickly one-sided tones" to describe the music of Igor Stravinsky.[45] For Keldysh, rectifying past scholarly mistakes was not without peril. Like Bruk, he was tar-geted during the anti-cosmopolitan campaign in 1949 for his role in the collaboratively authored, two-volume *History of Russian Music* (1940), which traced the Western influences on Russian composition. Yet in 1947, Keldysh presciently renounced these views by criticizing his former collaborators in print, thus mitigating the impact of his own censure, and clouding distinctions between guilt and innocence.

These meetings were more than exercises in rewriting history. Many Gnesin teachers associated the tendentious tone and meaningless abstractions of Stalinist scholarship with problems in the classroom. At the meeting of the history and theory faculty in April 1956, Mikhail Pekelis, who as chief editor of the *History of Russian Music* textbook was also targeted for criticism in 1949, claimed that "indiscriminate condem-nations" of modern, Western composition only pushed students "in the opposite direction" by encouraging them to explore on their own forbid-den music.[46] Pekelis's concerns were partly personal. Contrary to Keldysh, he refused to repent fully for his "cosmopolitan" scholarship and was undoubtedly hurt by his former collaborator's desertion and criticism.[47]

Six months later, Gnesin faculty met again to discuss plans to restruc-ture the "aesthetic education" of students. At issue was the meaning of realism and whether the current curriculum provided students with sufficient tools to identify and understand realist music. The initial reports were not promising. According to Vladimir Razumnyi, an accom-

43. Schwarz, *Music and Musical Life*, 173.
44. RGALI, f. 2927, o. 1, d. 123, ll. 65–66, 70, 87.
45. RGALI, f. 2927, o. 1, d. 427, ll. 4–5.
46. RGALI, f. 2927, o. 1, d. 427, ll. 19–20.
47. On Pekelis, Keldysh, and the criticism of musicologists in 1949, see Schwarz, *Music and Musical Life*, 250–53; and Tomoff, *Creative Union*, 152–88.

plished scholar of socialist-realist theory, not a single student had given a "convincing answer" on a recent examination to the question of "what is realism?" Instead, students had become skilled at rearticulating a confusion that existed in their course materials. Razumnyi claimed that students who searched for the definition of "realism" in a popular Soviet music dictionary found only a counter-reference to the entry for "socialist realism," which was defined as "the highest stage in the development of [the still undefined] realism." Even many of the institute's teachers were unsure how to define realism. During the anti-Western paranoia of the *zhdanovshchina*, one of the institute's musicologists coined the phrase "high-Pushkin style" to distinguish nineteenth-century Russian classics from their Western counterparts. Now, several years after Stalin's death, the same musicologists treated all nineteenth-century classics as realist, regardless of whether they were Russian or foreign. "We have widened our definition of realism to the point that everything good is realism," Razumnyi argued, "and everything bad is from the Evil One—it's formalism. As a result, students do not obtain a concrete understanding of realism." Seven months after she defended the Stalinist line as historical truth, Mirra Bruk, perhaps deciding that the political changes of the previous months were permanent, told her colleagues that it was now time to restore empiricism to musicology.[48]

Razumnyi and others feared that the confusion surrounding realism left students vulnerable to what one speaker called the "wide opening of doors to the abroad." Razumnyi thought that students were too sharp to be persuaded by the obfuscated tendentiousness of the current curriculum. Like many of his colleagues, however, he feared that students lacked the erudition to evaluate contemporary Western music objectively. The challenge confronting reformers was to create a curriculum that would effect "internal conviction" in students, but not by "way of prohibition," which, as Pekelis and others argued, tended to make things worse. Instead, the new curriculum had to provide students with a "true perspective" that would allow them to discern on their own the superficiality of contemporary Western culture.[49] At a joint Marxism-Leninism and history and theory departmental meeting in the fall of 1956, Pekelis urged teachers to speak honestly in class about their own culpability for the scholarly sins of Stalinism.

48. RGALI, f. 2927, o. 1, d. 453, ll. 1, 11, 21–23.
49. RGALI, f. 2927, o. 1, d. 453, ll. 22–23.

Students are waiting for a truthful word. They know that over the course of many years we have knowingly passed off bad work as good, and they regard this not as an error, but as a falsehood. We tried to smarten up . . . works that were interesting and necessary in terms of thematics, but indisputably bad in terms of artistic value. In the process, we undermined students' confidence in themselves and in pedagogical work. We need to talk about this with great clarity to correct our mistakes.[50]

During the latter half of 1956, the permissive approach to curricular reform spawned by the Twentieth Party Congress—the eschewal of restrictions in view of the righteousness of the argument—came under pressure as students began to flirt more openly with Western music and culture. During the period between Stalin's death and the Twentieth Party Congress, only the Central Committee's denunciation of the sexual misconduct of Georgii Aleksandrov, a philosopher and former Agitprop chief who had allegedly run a bordello out of his apartment, provoked a round of complaints about student interest in Gershwin's *Rhapsody in Blue*, American jazz, and foreign clothing.[51] In the spring of 1956, attitudes toward modern Western culture were relaxed enough that the history and theory departments sponsored a roundtable discussion on Stravinsky's ballet *Petrushka*, which Khrennikov denounced as "decadent" during the *Great Friendship* affair, and Gershwin's musical, *Porgy and Bess*. The latter discussion was provoked by Everyman Opera, a traveling American troupe that premiered *Porgy and Bess* in Leningrad and Moscow in late 1955 and early 1956. According to Truman Capote, who accompanied the troupe on the Leningrad leg of the tour, Soviet audiences were overwhelmingly enthusiastic, even though they were shocked by the sensuousness of songs like "I Ain't Got No Shame," which were "too aptly titled, too graphically illustrated, for Russian tastes."[52] (Undoubtedly, Soviet audiences remembered that Shostakovich nearly lost his head when *Lady Macbeth* was criticized for too much sexual content.) The Gnesin Institute scheduled a similar discussion of Gustav Mahler—a less controversial figure, to be sure—for the summer

---

50. RGALI, f. 2927, o. 1, d. 453, l. 24.
51. TsAODM, f. 4081, o. 1, d. 12, ll. 12–17. On Aleksandrov's sexual misconduct, see Z. Vodop'ianova, G. Ivanov, and L. Shishkova, "Elochka i drugie liudoedki," *Nastoiashchee* (May 1999): 5–7; and Dmitrii Shepilov, *The Kremlin's Scholar: A Memoir of Soviet Politics under Stalin and Khrushchev*, trans. Anthony Austin, ed. Stephen V. Bittner (New Haven, Conn., 2007), 80.
52. Truman Capote, *The Muses Are Heard* (New York, 1956), 175.

of 1956.[53] On July 2, however, *Pravda* printed the Central Committee decree: "On Overcoming the Cult of Personality and Its Consequences." The decree marked the most prominent attempt yet to clear the popular confusion concerning Stalin, and to direct further discussion through acceptable channels. It warned that international enemies were manipulating the denunciation of Stalin to discredit socialism and embarrass the Soviet Union. In September, after the institute convened for the new academic year, the secretary of the party bureau read aloud a Central Committee letter on the same topic during a party organization meeting. The letter warned party members to be on guard for students who listened to the BBC, and to watch closely over those who had traveled abroad.[54] At the Gnesin Institute, of course, the latter group was small. A few older students had served in Eastern Europe during and after the war. But the group was potentially growing, since the institute encouraged students to compete in international competitions. Apparently, the Central Committee letter was meant to transform the way that faculty thought about student disciplinary problems. During an academic council discussion in October, Muromtsev asserted that there "are many reasons that might complicate work with youth as a whole, but the root . . . is not in our own country." He cited the case of a student who refused to participate in Marxism-Leninism and *politchas* discussions by arguing that the American violinist "[Isaac] Stern plays well, and he has not studied any of this."[55] The riots in Poznan, Poland, during the summer of 1956, when workers took to the streets to demand higher wages and greater national autonomy, and in Hungary during the fall, when tens of thousands of students, nationalists, and soldiers fought the Red Army in the narrow streets of Budapest, reinforced fears that disciplinary problems were linked to excessive exposure to Western culture. During an institute-wide meeting on December 7, Muromtsev urged faculty to listen carefully to students, since their growing familiarity with Western culture and recent international crises had engendered many questions. "Some of the young people incorrectly assess the surrounding events, and are subject to pressure coming from the West. . . . The older generation remembers the revolution and even tsarism. Young people, not knowing the past, do not properly evaluate the surrounding events and see only the bad aspects of our life."[56]

53. RGALI, f. 2927, o. 1, d. 131, ll. 25–26.
54. TsAODM, f. 4081, o. 1, d. 13, ll. 48–49.
55. RGALI, f. 2927, o. 1, d. 137, ll. 65–65, 68–69.
56. TsAODM, f. 4081, o. 1, d. 13, l. 177.

Discussion about the relationship between disciplinary problems and Western culture continued in a smaller setting on December 28, when the party organization met to discuss the "closed" Central Committee letter: "On Strengthening the Political Work of Party Organizations among the Masses, and Preempting the Attacks of Hostile Anti-Soviet Elements." The letter represented the most significant attempt yet to rein in the public discussion of Stalinism in light of events in Eastern Europe. It was so acerbic that post-Soviet prosecutors included it as evidence in the unsuccessful trial of the Communist Party. Using language reminiscent of the terror of 1937, the letter encouraged communists in the courts and state-security agencies to show special vigilance in "the search for hostile elements." Like the Central Committee decree the previous summer, it claimed that persons were taking advantage of domestic "difficulties and deficiencies" to slander the Soviet Union and spread provocative rumors.[57] Because it identified students as a special risk group, the letter empowered teachers who were not thrilled with the direction of curricular reform after the Twentieth Party Congress. Referring to the letter, Konstantin Rozenshil'd accused his colleagues of standing aside while students experimented freely with Stravinsky and the German modernist composer Paul Hindemith. He also condemned the notion, then popular among students and even some teachers, that Soviet citizens were "so ideologically hardened and educated" that they could "listen to whatever they desire." Underscoring the suddenly frosty political climate, another party member wondered about the loyalty of three students who had spent time in the gulag.[58]

Nearly four years after Stalin's death, attempts to reform the institute's curriculum had once again ground to a halt, this time amid fears of Western culture. In the wake of the Central Committee letter, party members reaffirmed the centrality of the 1948 decree on *Great Friendship* in the institute's curriculum. They denounced the "dangerous hullabaloo" surrounding Shostakovich's Eighth Symphony, a dark, seemingly defeatist wartime composition that was attacked as formalist in 1948. And they prescribed a large dose of Peter Tchaikovsky, Mikhail Glinka, and Modest Mussorgsky for students interested in Gershwin and Stravinsky. A similar backlash was underway at Moscow State University, Leningrad's

---

57. Rossiiskii gosudarstvennyi arkhiv noveishei istorii [hereafter RGANI], f. 89, perechen' 6, dokument 2. For analysis of the letter and its repercussions, see Erik Kulavig, *Dissent in the Years of Khrushchev: Nine Stories about Disobedient Russians* (New York, 2002), 16–34.
58. TsAODM, f. 4081, o. 1, d. 13, ll. 78–80.

Herzen Pedagogical Institute, and scores of other schools and universities across the Soviet Union, where students were expelled and even arrested for expressing sympathy for the Hungarian revolutionaries, and for organizing themselves into seemingly subversive organizations to discuss and criticize the Soviet intervention.[59] At the end of 1956, it was hard for Gnesin teachers to avoid the impression that the Twentieth Party Congress was not the beginning of a new party line, but an aberration in the old.

REEVALUATING THE *ZHDANOVSHCHINA*

The clampdown at the end of December underscored the perils of reforming the institute's curriculum without clear signals from above. Many teachers thought that the Twentieth Party Congress spelled the end of the *Great Friendship* era. They spoke of deemphasizing the denunciation of Khachaturian and Shostakovich, and of reevaluating modern, Western music, and Soviet music that party leaders had tagged as formalist. The new curriculum promised to be more empirical and international, and less ideological. As Mirra Bruk argued in the fall of 1956, it was time to get rid of the "amateurishness" in Soviet musicology, where every book began with a quotation from Stalin.[60] Yet the Central Committee letter seemed to reinforce the very decree that teachers had come to think of as obsolete. Stalin was in disrepute, but his xenophobic decree on music was not. For many, the lesson of 1956 was that no curricular reform was possible until the party addressed this apparent contradiction.

Notwithstanding full-fledged reform, there were opportunities in 1957 for students who were interested in the outside world. The Second All-Union Congress of Composers, which ran from March 28 to April 5, put a damper on the anti-Western paranoia caused by the unrest in Eastern Europe. The congress was significant for its eschewal of the militancy that characterized its predecessor in 1948. Presided over by the

59. Naumov, "Bor'ba N. S. Khrushcheva za edinolichnuiu vlast'," 18; Zubkova, *Russia after the War*, 197–98; and Taubman, *Khrushchev*, 302–3. On youth disturbances after 1953, see Vladimir A. Kozlov, *Mass Uprisings in the USSR: Protest and Rebellion in the Post-Stalin Years*, trans. and ed. Elaine McClarnand MacKinnon (Armonk, N.Y., 2002), 136–62; and Samuel H. Baron, *Bloody Saturday in the Soviet Union: Novocherkaask, 1962* (Palo Alto, Calif., 2001), 14–16.
60. RGALI, f. 2927, o. 1, d. 453, l. 22.

Central Committee secretary Dmitrii Shepilov—a thoughtful man who had helped Zhdanov draft the decree on *Great Friendship* a decade earlier and who later expressed sadness about his role—the congress endorsed a policy of "Leninist flexibility" in music. It also denounced the "mechanical leveling" of contemporary Western culture, despite Shepilov's warning that American rock-and-roll and jazz induced "wild orgies of cavemen" and the "basest emotions and sexual impulses."[61] Preparations for the Sixth International Festival of Youth and Students, which Moscow hosted in late July and early August, reinforced the moderate line of the composers' congress. Planners expected that the festival would draw more than 30,000 foreign students, many from hostile Western countries.[62] The institute's academic council revealed plans in May for increased foreign-language study, and for student research on unspecified "foreign themes" so that students could interact intelligently with their foreign guests. The Gnesin auditorium was one of many sites scattered across the city that were designated for jazz, pop, classical, and folk music performances, even though party members worried that the quality of the institute's instruments made them unsuitable for use in the presence of foreigners. Students were also a point of concern. Because their interaction with foreigners would be unsupervised, students had to be coached how to answer "very diverse questions of an ideological-religious character, everyday-life questions, and questions connected with the cult of personality." Even more important, they had to answer these questions in a manner that did not seem "defensive or aggressive." To this end, the institute scheduled a series of lectures on the meaning of the festival, the importance of revolutionary vigilance and behavior, Soviet-Yugoslavian relations, and the condition of the working class abroad.[63] According to a municipal party official, the point was not to misrepresent Soviet life, but to admit shortcomings like poor living conditions, and to explain to foreign guests why they persisted.[64]

There were also other problems that hampered festival planning. Administrators initially hoped that students would bear the brunt of the institute's share of festival work. In November 1956, the institute

61. Schwarz, *Music and Musical Life*, 299–307; and "Shepilov's Speech at the Congress of Soviet Composers," *Current Digest of the Soviet Press* 9 (May 8, 1957): 17. Shepilov's views on rock-and-roll are quoted in slightly different form in Starr, *Red and Hot*, 249. On Shepilov and Zhdanov, see Shepilov, *The Kremlin's Scholar*, 101–3.
62. "Stranichki festival'noi zhizni," *Vecherniaia Moskva*, July 27, 1957, 1.
63. RGALI, f. 2927, o. 1, d. 139, l. 91; and TsAODM, f. 4081, o. 1, d. 14, ll. 25, 120.
64. TsAODM, f. 4, o. 113, d. 23, l. 40.

proposed a series of student recitals and concerts to raise money for a discretionary fund that it could use to stage some of the festival's musical events. In the spring of 1957, it reduced class times and instituted more liberal attendance policies so students could participate directly in the planning activities. In May, however, it became clear that these plans would go unrealized. According to Muromtsev, many of the institute's students had taken advantage of the new attendance policies to skip class altogether. Another critic castigated the institute's Komsomol as a "dead thing," and indicated that students' unwillingness to participate in planning spoke to "the absence of a close tie" between generations: "The unique problem of 'fathers and sons' has arisen, despite the fact that it should have no place in our society."[65]

Because party leaders had so often treated Western culture as either a symptom or the principal cause of moral decay among Soviet youth, the youth festival aggravated longstanding fears of a "fathers and sons" schism.[66] Yet when faced with young people from the West and their jazz and pop music, teachers and administrators reacted not with confidence honed by ideological certainty, but with embarrassment over their insularity. Their fears were aggravated by official paranoia about jazz-induced sexual promiscuity, and by warnings that "spies" had poisoned the food and water supplies at previous youth festivals in Warsaw and Bucharest.[67] Their response was not illogical; it reflected the tension that was at the core of efforts to reform the institute's curriculum after 1953. Was it possible to create students who were knowledgeable and worldly, and simultaneously reinforce the ideological convictions required by the party? The initial wave of de-Stalinization made the youth festival possible, but subsequent efforts to limit public discussion of Western culture and Stalin's cult raised questions about how Soviet citizens were supposed to interact with their foreign guests. The institute's students then made the situation worse by refusing to behave in what their teachers considered an appropriate way. Many students, it seemed, just wanted to be left alone.

Teachers also saw evidence of students' apathy in their response to Khrushchev's call to realize through "public work" (volunteer work) the "bond between literature, art, and the life of the people." Renewed calls

65. RGALI, f. 2927, o. 1, d. 137, l. 21; and TsAODM, f. 4081, o. 1, d. 14, ll. 15, 113.
66. Kristin Roth-Ey, "'Loose Girls' on the Loose?: Sex, Propaganda, and the 1957 Youth Festival," in *Women in the Khrushchev Era,* ed. Melanie Ilic, Susan E. Reid, and Lynne Atwood (New York, 2004), 90–91.
67. TsAODM, f. 4, o. 113, d. 23, ll. 6, 40.

to "public work" grew out of a series of meetings that Khrushchev held with prominent writers and artists during the spring and summer of 1957 to dispel some of the political and cultural confusion that had arisen during the previous year.[68] It was no secret that nearly all students disliked "public work." Even teachers sometimes dismissed its importance. During the summer of 1957, most students managed to avoid the supposedly obligatory trip to work on a collective farm by taking advantage of various exemptions. Moreover, students who did go were often rude or patronizing toward their peasant hosts. One student who fell ill returned to Moscow without telling his hosts. Several of his healthy friends later did the same. Another student feigned incompetence until his hosts sent him home. "He played the fool . . . and acted like an idiot, and when an opportunity came for them to send him home, they did so without complaint." Still another student told collective farmers that the Soviet division of labor provided for "collective farmers to work with vegetables and potatoes" and for musicians "to work with music." Even during the academic year, many students refused to perform in the free concerts that the institute staged for the public. Several students told their teacher that it was "an act of sabotage to perform outside [for the public], that it was party fantasy, and that no one needed it."[69]

Khrushchev's endorsement of "public work" did little to make it more appealing to students. In fact, it may have done the opposite. During a class discussion in the fall of 1957 on Khrushchev's meetings with artists and writers, one student asked why Khrushchev was again meddling in affairs he knew little about. The same was true of Shostakovich's programmatic music, particularly the officially acclaimed Eleventh Symphony (*The Year 1905*), which Shostakovich finished in 1957 to mark the fortieth anniversary of the October Revolution. Students saw the supposed political transparency of the Eleventh as a sign that Shostakovich had turned his back on artistic innovation. "He is the type of musician who goes lower and lower," one student claimed, "and just as he turns to a historical-revolutionary theme, he comes to naught." Some of this dissent had even appeared in the institute's student newspaper, where a recent issue included a scathing review of Shostakovich's new work.

68. N. Khrushchev, "Za tesnuiu sviaz' literatury i iskusstva s zhizn'iu naroda," *Pravda*, August 28, 1957, 3–4; Zubkova, *Russia after the War*, 199; Roy Medvedev, *Khrushchev: A Biography*, trans. Brian Pearce (Garden City, N.Y., 1984), 101; and Wolfram [Vol'fram] Eggeling, *Politika i kul'tura pri Khrushcheve i Brezhneve. 1953–1970 gg.* (Moscow, 1999), 84–88.
69. RGALI, f. 2927, o. 1, d. 142, ll. 7, 12–14.

Teachers feared that official approbation caused students to engage in "excessive carping" (*kritikanstvo*). Official condemnation, on the contrary, seemed only to peak their interests. In the fall of 1957, Gnesin students, like many other Soviet citizens, rallied around *Not by Bread Alone*, Vladimir Dudintsev's landmark novel about the arbitrariness of the Soviet bureaucracy, which had been published by *Novyi mir* (New World) during the previous year. The overwhelmingly positive response to *Not by Bread Alone* by Soviet citizens illustrated, in Elena Zubkova's words, a newfound "readiness for a fight," and a widely-held desire to eradicate the "Drozdovs," named for the novel's bureaucratic villain, from Soviet life. For many Gnesin students, *Not by Bread Alone* was a masterpiece precisely because Khrushchev and other officials had denounced it. In fact, the official criticism was proof of Dudintsev's artistic integrity. The reputation of the Austrian-American modernist Arnold Schoenberg also flourished among students, in no small part because of the official hostility toward his work.[70]

By the fall of 1957, teachers and administrators were openly reluctant to punish students who were convinced that the official line was wrong. Most thought that students had the "right" to criticize any musical or artistic work, and that punishing them for voicing personal opinions was counterproductive, since it only tended to reinforce student views. "I disagree that it is forbidden for students to speak critically about a given work," Muromtsev told the academic council. "This is an echo of the cult of personality, and it cannot have a place in our work."[71] Less than a year after opponents of curricular reform used the "closed" Central Committee letter to restore the primacy of the 1948 decree on *Great Friendship,* the academic council endorsed the necessity of a free exchange of ideas, even if those ideas were politically awkward. Council members, of course, were not acting in a disinterested way, since they also stood to benefit from a lively academic climate. In February and March 1958, the institute hosted two workshops on the appropriateness in Soviet music of polytonality, the use of more than one key at a time. Even though *Sovetskaia muzyka* had posed the same question in 1957, polytonality was still mildly taboo, since it was associated with Shostakovich's first opera *Nose*, which was later labeled as formalist. Sergei

70. RGALI, f. 2927, o. 1, d. 142, l. 20. On Dudintsev, see Zubkova, *Russia after the War*, 193–95; and Karl Edward Loewenstein, "The Thaw: Writers and the Public Sphere in the Soviet Union, 1951–1957" (Ph.D. diss., Duke University, 1999), 296–327.
71. RGALI, f. 2927, o. 1, d. 142, ll. 21, 30, 53.

Skrebkov, a professor at the Moscow Conservatory who had taught at the Gnesin Institute before being fired during the anti-cosmopolitan campaign in 1948, cited the ice-battle scene in Prokofiev's score for the film *Aleksandr Nevskii* and to parts of Shostakovich's Piano Sonata no. 2 to argue that polytonality could serve as "a sharply characteristic means of expressiveness."[72]

The more permissive atmosphere at the Gnesin Institute was not without its critics. E. V. Mel'nikova, the chair of the Marxism-Leninism department and the primary object of abuse at the infamous Komsomol meeting in October 1955, wondered why it was necessary to allow students to criticize in the name of academic freedom, only to condemn them for the content of their criticism. "Does this mean that it's possible to say that this or any other student who has expressed a harmful view on music can have his own opinion about musical issues? This is incorrect and not useful."[73] At the beginning of June 1958, however, *Pravda* helped erase whatever misgivings persisted at the institute when it published the Central Committee decree of May 28, "On the Correction of Mistakes in the Evaluation of the Operas *Great Friendship, Bogdan Khmel'nitskii,* and *From All One's Heart,*" under an explanatory article entitled "The Path of Soviet Music—the Path of National Character and Realism." The decree reaffirmed "the positive role" that the 1948 decree on *Great Friendship* played, but it also attacked Stalin's "subjective approach" to music and his "unsubstantiated and unjustified" denunciations of different works. Ten years after the *zhdanovshchina,* party leaders admitted that Muradeli's *Great Friendship* was not an "example of formalism." Nor were Shostakovich, Prokofiev, and Khachaturian "representatives of the antidemocratic, formalistic trend in music." Party leaders also overturned the party's 1951 denunciation of Konstantin Dan'kevich's *Bogdan Khmel'nitskii* and German Zhukovskii's *From All One's Heart,* citing its "subjectivity" and "one-sided evaluation."[74] The 1958 decree marked the first time since Stalin's death that the Central Committee formally corrected itself in the cultural realm. Tikhon

---

72. S. Skrebkov, "O sovremennoi garmonii," *Sovetskaia muzyka* 6 (June 1957): 74–84; V. Berkov, "Eshche o politonal'nosti," *Sovetskaia muzyka* 10 (October 1957): 84–87; S. Skrebkov, "Otvet V. Berkovu," *Sovetskaia muzyka* 87–89; and RGALI, f. 2927, o. 1, d. 486, ll. 5–9.
73. RGALI, f. 2927, o. 1, d. 142, ll. 45–46.
74. "Ob ispravlenii oshibok v otsenke oper 'Velikaia druzhba,' 'Bogdan Khmel'nitskii' i 'Ot vsego serdtsa,' postanovlenie TsK KPSS ot 28 maia 1958 goda," and "Put' sovetskoi muzyki—put' narodnosti i realizma," *Pravda,* June 8, 1958, 3 and 3–5, respectively.

Khrennikov, the chief of the composers' union, later claimed that he convinced Khrushchev that it was unjust for the most prominent Soviet composers, "the leading lights of world music," to live with the stigma of 1948.[75] Khrennikov's account suggests that Khrushchev wanted to counter the bad publicity that the 1948 decree generated, especially outside of the Soviet Union. He might have added the confusion it caused at home.

The institute's party organization met in an open session on June 13 to discuss the decree with the help of Vladimir Feré, a Moscow Conservatory professor, composer, and People's Artist of Latvia. Feré admitted what the Gnesin faculty had long known: after the Twentieth Party Congress, the persistence of the 1948 decree caused a great deal of uncertainty among students, some of whom began to "doubt the rectitude of the party's leadership in art." Feré imagined himself as a skeptical student: "If there are false assessments about the most concrete things, then maybe there is something false in the most important thing, the base." Feré also argued that many Soviet citizens misunderstood the purpose of the 1948 decree. He recalled working as a party propagandist in factories during the late-Stalin period. Workers frequently asked him about the fate of Muradeli and the other targets of the decree. They wondered whether "antidemocratic" was synonymous with "enemy of the people," and whether Stalin had imprisoned or executed the luminaries of Soviet music. At establishments like the Gnesin Institute and the Moscow Conservatory, the 1948 decree was even more corrupting. Student composers and musicologists, wary of the fate of Muradeli, approached their work reluctantly, and squandered the innovativeness of youth. Moreover, students who believed the decree to be a mistake displayed a "scornful, arrogant attitude toward the tastes and demands of the people," and shared an "unhealthy, exaggerated interest . . . in Western music." Like Pekelis and Razumnyi in 1956, Feré feared that the strict curricular regime that accompanied the 1948 decree kindled student interest in forbidden topics. He urged the institute's teachers and administrators to initiate a genuinely open discussion with students about all varieties of music, and to do so without the overly cautious regard for the opinion of higher authorities.[76]

75. On the decree, see Zhuravlev, *XX s"ezd KPSS*, 335–39; M. R. Zezina, *Sovetskaia khudozhestvennaia intelligentsiia v 1950-e–60-e gody* (Moscow, 1999), 206–10; Eggeling, *Politika i kul'tura*, 92–95; and Schwarz, *Musical Life*, 311–12.
76. TsAODM, f. 4081, o. 1, d. 15, ll. 32–33, 43–44.

It seems to me that the result of this decree should be the wide expansion of public criticism. This criticism should be careless of authorities and persons. In this way, we can move our criticism beyond the cult of personality. We should not wait for an evaluation from above, but we ourselves should evaluate the works of our musical art.[77]

After Feré finished speaking, Muromtsev underscored the "serious mistakes" that teachers had made in their history and theory classes since 1948, and he urged all who were present to renounce "the naked administering of art," where works that were on the Ministry of Culture's "black list" were forbidden for students to perform or discuss. Other speakers shared their memories of 1948, and joked about students who "look at us with suspicion, say that we are old men, reactionaries, and that we have not discovered America."

Contrary to the period following the Twentieth Party Congress, this optimistic rhetoric was finally accompanied by a thorough review of the music history and theory curriculum. In June, Mikhail Pekelis announced that he had secured permission to rework the curriculum "independently" of federal authorities. He hoped to submit two manuscripts—one on Soviet music and one on Western music since 1789—to the State Musical Press before the end of the year. Until the new texts were available, Konstantin Rozenshil'd encouraged teachers to "pay more attention to the study of contemporary, progressive music in foreign countries" in their classes. The institute also began to place greater emphasis on research and publication to encourage the codification of the new curriculum. In accordance with a July 1957 Ministry of Higher Education decree, the institute implemented competitive hiring for all department heads and teachers "to raise the quality of scientific, scholarly-educational, and methodological work" at the institute. To create positions for ambitious young scholars, the institute offered its faculty members five-year contracts, after which a "competition commission" would determine whether they were still the most qualified candidates.[78]

Pekelis's hope that curricular reform would be complete by the end of 1958 was overly optimistic. Debate on the proper balance between Stalin's mistakes and Soviet achievements, between Western modernism and socialist realism continued well into the 1960s. At the end of 1958, reform was slowed by an unpopular Central Committee decree that required

77. TsAODM, f. 4081, o. 1, d. 15, l. 42.
78. RGALI, f. 2927, o. 1, d. 15, ll. 52, 54, 58; d. 24, ll. 28–29; d. 144, l. 87; and d. 156, l. 46.

university students to have practical work experience, typically in a factory, before graduation. During the following year, curricular reform took another detour when the Central Committee reprimanded the Gnesin Institute for replicating, contrary to its mission, the performance-oriented curriculum of the Moscow Conservatory.[79] Nonetheless, the Central Committee decree in 1958 was an important turning point for the institute. By voiding Stalin's decree on music, it cleared up much of the confusion that marked the period following the Twentieth Party Congress. It also produced a more coherent narrative of the Stalin period. Teachers and administrators once again began to incorporate modern Western music and Soviet music that party leaders had denounced as formalist into the curriculum. By doing so, they hoped to ameliorate the institute's disciplinary problems. This was a project that met with mixed results. In coming years, students continued to sing in church choirs, wear Western fashions, play jazz in their spare time, and praise the artistic merits of Boris Pasternak and Evgenii Yevtushenko, even when the party did otherwise.[80] After 1958, however, few teachers thought these problems constituted a crisis; no one thought they were symptomatic of a flawed curriculum. The 1958 decree freed the institute's curriculum from Stalinism, and in the process, disengaged it from student behavior.

In truth, the link between the institute's curriculum and the behavior of its students was never concrete. It was a causal relationship that teachers and administrators perceived, but could not prove. They thought that Stalinism persisted in what Feré called the "prohibitive methods" of the classroom, even as the thaw opened up new worlds of Western culture to students and revealed to them the Soviet Union's checkered past. They feared that this incongruence produced students who were profoundly skeptical of the intentions of teachers, whom they held responsible for perpetuating the obscurantism of Stalinism in the classroom. When discussing disciplinary problems, teachers were actually relying on a common rhetorical trope of the 1950s and '60s: the characterization of persisting deficiencies in Soviet life as "survivals" (*perezhitki*) of Stalinism. The institute's curriculum was a "survival;" disciplinary problems were a symptom; and curricular reform was the cure.

79. On factory work, see RGALI, f. 2927, o. 1, d. 149, ll. 2–11; d. 152, ll. 11–48; Donald Filtzer, *Soviet Workers and de-Stalinization: The Consolidation of the Modern System of Soviet Production Relations, 1953–1964* (Cambridge, 1992), 73–74; and Zhuravlev, *XX s"ezd KPSS*, 294–329. On the Central Committee investigation, see RGALI, f. 2927, o. 1, d. 156, ll. 1–58.
80. TsAODM, f. 4081, o. 1, d. 15, ll. 92–94; d. 16, ll. 14, 45, 153; and d. 18, l. 94.

Teachers and administrators invoked disciplinary problems in an instrumental manner, but their concerns about a "fathers and sons" schism were heartfelt. At moments when disciplinary problems peaked, teachers feared that students had become hostile to them; during more tranquil periods, they worried that the curriculum was too stodgy and ideological to appeal to students who were familiar with atonal composition and American jazz. This type of generational conflict has long been one of the central themes in analyses of the thaw: those who came of age in the 1950s and '60s rebelled against the conventions of the generation they thought responsible for Stalinism.[81] Yet the experience of the Gnesin Institute suggests that the guilt of the fathers was largely self-ascribed. After the Twentieth Party Congress, party members reminded each other that they all bore responsibility for remaining silent in the face of repressions they knew to be unjust. In the fall of 1956, Mikhail Pekelis urged his colleagues to confess to students their own responsibility for the tendentious tone of Stalinist musicology. In fact, with the exception of a student who wondered about Khrushchev's culpability for Stalinism, few teachers reported that the sons held the fathers accountable for their actions prior to 1953. Rather, the fathers felt guilty in the presence of the sons. Curricular reform promised to mitigate their guilt.

Teachers did not have to be Stalinists to be saddened by some aspects of the thaw. Stalin's death and the reforms that ensued brought Stravinsky and Gershwin—good things, to be sure—but also an overly critical attitude among students about all things Soviet, and painful questions about the past. Who, during the darkest days of the *zhdanovshchina*, could have predicted that teachers would one day rue excessive Western culture? Who, during the anti-Semitic campaign against "cosmopolitans," could have known that persons who had personally suffered under Stalin would one day question their own complicity? These were wholly unexpected developments. It is not illogical that one response to upheaval of this sort is nostalgia for the pre-Stalinist past. But that is a topic best saved for the next two chapters.

81. Nancy Condee, "Cultural Codes of the Thaw," in *Nikita Khrushchev,* ed. William Taubman, Sergei Khrushchev, and Abbott Gleason (New Haven, Conn., 2000), 160–66; and Starr, *Red and Hot,* 239. For an attempt to conceptualize the impetus behind Khrushchev's reforms in generational terms, see Martin Malia, *The Soviet Tragedy: A History of Socialism in Russia, 1917–1991* (New York, 1994), 320.

Raining on Turandot

Nostalgia for the 1920s was a central component of thaw culture. It was fueled by the generational schism that the previous chapter explored: cultural figures who felt complicit in the injustices of Stalinism naturally looked at the 1920s as a more innocent age, devoid of the moral complexities of the recent past and present. If they were in their thirties and forties at the time of Stalin's death, of the same generation as Rybakov and Okudzhava, the 1920s corresponded with their childhood and teenage years, which helped reinforce the perception that it was an age of innocence. But even for those who were older and younger, there were ample reasons to look at the first Soviet decade with nostalgia. When Khrushchev called for the restoration of "Leninist principles" to Soviet politics, a euphemism for the end of terror and the eradication of Stalin's cult, he unwittingly conjured seductive images of a benevolent pre-Stalinist past. The 1920s, after all, were Soviet but not Stalinist years, a crucial distinction in a society struggling to fission the two. Artists and writers responded to Khrushchev's call by casting the 1920s as an era of artistic vitality, tolerance, and openness to the outside world. Young economists saw the limited market economy of NEP (Lenin's New Economic Policy) as a potential cure for chronic shortages and inefficiencies, a presumption that Brezhnev's head of government, Aleksei Kosygin, would test in the mid-1960s, and Gorbachev in the late 1980s.[1]

1. Moshe Lewin, *Stalinism and the Seeds of Reform: The Debates of the 1960s* (Armonk, N.Y., 1991), 300–333.

And the rehabilitation of scores of disgraced cultural figures from the 1920s and early '30s marked the outward face of an inward search for alternate political and cultural models. Yet the pre-Stalinist past was not always retrievable, at least in toto. Stalinism was too transformative for it to be otherwise. Many persons looked to the 1920s for models for the present; not everyone was able to recover what they found.

This was the principal lesson of the Arbat's most famous bout of restorative nostalgia: the 1963 revival of Carlo Gozzi's fairytale, *Princess Turandot*, at the Vakhtangov Theater. The original *Turandot* was the crowning achievement of Evgenii Vakhtangov, Konstantin Stanislavsky's disciple at the Moscow Art Theater (MKhAT), and one of the most influential figures in early Soviet theater. It was a central event in the cultural life of the Arbat in the 1920s, and oft-cited proof of vitality of NEP culture and the inventiveness of early Soviet theater. Its revival in 1963 was widely cast as a triumph of the thaw. At the final rehearsal, Ruben Simonov, the theater's artistic director since 1939, argued that *Turandot* represented "not only the rebirth of a performance, but the rebirth of the underlying atmosphere" that gave rise to it.[2] He would soon discover that sanguine predictions are easier made than realized.

In truth, the underlying atmosphere of the original *Turandot* was more trying than many cared to admit. The play grew out of an often troubled experiment that began in 1913 when a group of aspiring teenage actors asked Evgenii Vakhtangov to lead a studio where they could study Stanislavsky's method acting. Vakhtangov agreed, and the Mansurovskaia Studio was born. It was named for its location on Mansurovskii Lane, not far from Vakhtangov's home in the Arbat. To the dismay of students, Vakhtangov set low expectations: he promised only that students would become better people, not better actors. He was a famous despot. An official history of the Vakhtangov Theater notes that its founder was both "cruel and gentle," and that his "insults . . . were forever remembered as lessons." In 1919, twelve students, apparently feeling otherwise, left the Mansurovskaia Studio to protest Vakhtangov's disregard for their professional success. Nonetheless, the results of Vakhtangov's experiment were impressive. His first production, Boris Zaitsev's *Lanin Estate*, opened to positive reviews in March 1914. A string of future successes drew talent from other studios and schools, including many persons who would later become famous: the actor and pedagogue Boris

2. Abri Amaspiurants, *Printsessa Turandot 63* (Moscow, 1996), 10. See also, Vasilii Lanovoi, *Letiat za dniami dni* (Moscow, 2003), 132.

Shchukin, the director Ruben Simonov, and the actors Iurii Zavadskii and Boris Zakhava. In 1920, Vakhtangov's studio became the Third Studio of MKhAT, an imprimatur that made it possible to move to the theater's present location at 26 Arbat Street. Inspired by the independent success of Vsevolod Meyerhold, one of Vladimir Nemirovich-Danchenko's students at MKhAT, Vakhtangov despised his new subordination to MKhAT. He dismissed "Stanislavsky's dead theater" and spoke of the potential of his own "imaginative realism" (*fantasticheskii realizm*), an ironic style that emphasized elements of the grotesque rather than the naturalistic detail that was common in Stanislavsky's plays. Vakhtangov hoped that *Princess Turandot* would convince critics that he had surpassed the achievements of his former teachers at MKhAT.[3]

Turandot premiered on February 28, 1922. It was the third and final play that Vakhtangov directed in the studio's new residence on the Arbat. According to Ruben Simonov, a former Vakhtangov student who was present at the original in 1922, and who presided over the revival in 1963, Vakhtangov was clearly showing symptoms of cancer at the last rehearsal on February 23; he rested in a chair in the sixth row, and occasionally ascended the stage to give directions. Vakhtangov took a taxicab home that evening and never returned to the theater. On opening night, he asked Iurii Zavadskii, who played the principal role of Calaf, to read a letter warning the audience that cast members were still students, and that some were performing their first roles. *Turandot*, Vakhtangov wrote, should be considered "laboratory work" rather than a polished play. Yet when the curtain came down after the first act, there were cries of bravo. During the subsequent curtain call (which was highly unusual because there were no curtain calls according to MKhAT tradition), the cast noticed Stanislavsky and Nemirovich-Danchenko, rival titans of the Russian theatrical world, applauding with their hands outstretched. The second act had to be delayed so Stanislavsky could drive to Vakhtangov's apartment and personally congratulate him. "In the life of the Moscow Art Theater, there are few such victories, such accomplishments," Stanislavsky told Vakhtangov's wife by telephone after the play had finished. "I am proud of such a student, if he is my student. Tell him, 'Please wrap up in the blanket as if it were a toga, and sleep with the sleep of a conqueror.'" Vakhtangov died on May 29, 1922. The chair in the sixth row

3. W. L. Turner, "Vakhtangov: The Director as Teacher," *Educational Theatre Journal* 15, no. 4 (December 1963): 320; and I. L. Sergeeva and M. R. Litvin, *Teatr imeni Evg. Vakhtangova* (Moscow, 1996), 7–11.

where he supervised his final rehearsal was left permanently empty as a memorial to the artist who never witnessed his masterpiece.[4]

The revival of *Princess Turandot* premiered on April 21, 1963, too late to mark the fortieth anniversary of its first appearance, and the hundredth anniversary (according to the Julian calendar) of Stanislavsky's birth in December 1862. When the theater's artistic council asked Ruben Simonov to choose between timeliness and an original interpretation of Vakhtangov's masterpiece, Simonov opted for the latter.[5] In order that there would be no doubt that he intended the new version of *Turandot* to be every bit as significant as the original, Simonov ordered artists to stencil two dates on the stage curtain: 1922 and 1963. Simonov's desire to retrace his teacher's footsteps reflected the Vakhtangov Theater's diminished stature. Despite the perquisites of institutional prominence—comfortable salaries and annual performances abroad—and despite Simonov's constant reassurances that the Vakhtangov remained "the best theater," the center of theatrical creativity had shifted elsewhere. Anatoly Smeliansky, a manager at MKhAT and a prominent theater critic during the Brezhnev years, mentions the Vakhtangov only in passing in his survey of Soviet theater after Stalin. He notes that the Vakhtangov was a "relatively safe" venue with a first-class cast. By the mid-1960s, it was best known as the incubator of a prodigious young talent who got away. In 1963, after staging a smash production of Bertolt Brecht's *The Good Person of Szechwan* with a cast of student actors, Iurii Liubimov left the Vakhtangov to preside over the new Taganka Theater. Liubimov quickly transformed it into one of the Soviet Union's most creative stages. The Taganka enjoyed the sort of international acclaim that the Vakhtangov had known in the 1920s.[6]

The Taganka was not the only Soviet theater that attracted enough critical attention during the thaw to challenge the supremacy of old stalwarts like MKhAT and the Vakhtangov Theater. The same was true of Moscow's Malyi Theater, which, in 1956, found a hit in Leo Tolstoy's peasant tragedy, *The Power of Darkness;* of Leningrad's Bolshoi Drama Theater, which, in 1956, became the home of the talented director Georgii Tovstonogov; and, especially, of Moscow's new Sovremennik (Contemporary) Theater, which, under the leadership of Oleg Efremov, scored a

4. Ruben Simonov, *Stanislavsky's Protégé: Eugene Vakhtangov,* trans. Miriam Goldina (New York, 1969), 168–70, 181, 191.
5. Amaspiurants, *Printsessa Turandot 63,* 98.
6. Anatoly Smeliansky, *The Russian Theater since Stalin,* trans. Patrick Miles (Cambridge, 1999), 6, 30.

long series of inventively staged hits. Although the Sovremennik was formally a MKhAT studio, its atmosphere was anything but. According to Efremov, the Sovremennik was a reminder of what MKhAT "used to be like": egalitarian, vibrant, and daring. In 1959, it premiered Evgenii Shvarts's *The Naked King,* an adaptation of Hans Christian Andersen's fairytale, "The Emperor's New Clothes." Audiences understood that it was a parable about the collective delusions of Stalinism. Even Khrushchev, after he was ousted from power in 1964, reputedly fell in love with the play. Many of the Sovremennik's productions were banned during these years; similar to students at the Gnesin Institute who rallied around Arnold Schoenberg's music because party officials had condemned it, cast members took the frequent censures as a sign that they were doing things right. Like many prominent theater companies, the Sovremennik benefited from growing contacts with the West. The Berliner Ensemble, the Comédie Français, and the Théâtre National Populaire made trips to Moscow and Leningrad in the 1950s.[7] Prominent domestic companies also began to journey abroad, first to the peoples' democracies in Eastern Europe, and then to points farther west. The result was a genuine blossoming of Soviet theater. Even amid the relatively dynamic culture of the thaw, theater was a bright spot. Yet for the most part, the Vakhtangov was not a participant. Simonov hoped to remedy that.

From the start, Simonov saw *Turandot* as a way out of the theater's "dead end." During a meeting with actors before the beginning of production, Simonov spoke at length about the difficult material conditions in Moscow in 1920–21, when students subsisted on "copious" rations of bread and lentils. He told actors how Vakhtangov's students were inspired by their friendship for one another, by their idealism and confidence in the future of the young Soviet republic, and by their conviction that *Turandot* would be their lives' greatest achievement. Simonov explained Vakhtangov's democratic way of delegating responsibilities to a so-called "central organ," where two senior students chose a third, three chose a fourth, and so on until the committee had a membership of seven. And finally, Simonov described how Nemirovich-Danchenko invited eighteen of Vakhtangov's students to join the troupe at MKhAT after Vakhtangov's death. The offer of steady work at Russia's most acclaimed theater was no small matter, yet sixteen students, unwilling to sever ties with Vakhtangov's studio, declined. Simonov hoped that

7. Ibid., 7, 10–22.

Turandot would restore to the theater a similar sense of *studiinost'*, the casual, experimental, and egalitarian atmosphere of those heady days in the early 1920s, when anything seemed possible.[8]

Simonov's hopes for the theater went unrealized, but not because it was oxymoronic to encourage creativity in the present by copying what had been done in the past, or naïve to believe that established actors would forsake their privileges to return to the studios of their youth. Rather, the theater's "underlying atmosphere" proved more intractable than Simonov realized. Shortly after *Turandot* premiered, the Minister of Culture, Ekaterina Furtseva, ordered Simonov to begin work on *Rainstorm*, an ostensibly anti-Stalinist play by the obscure playwright Boris Voitekhov. She also tried to reassign the theater's administrative director, Isai Spektor, amid charges of abuse and conflict of interests. There was more to Furtseva's intervention than normal bureaucratic heavy-handedness. In both instances, she sided with individuals at the theater who had circumvented the normal chain of command by asking her for assistance. To Furtseva's many critics at the theater, the latter was evidence that not much had changed since 1953, and that habits honed by Stalinism were hard to break. It was one thing to restage a play; it was quite another to re-create an era.

THE PAST AND FUTURE OF IMAGINATIVE REALISM

Princess Turandot was written in 1762 for the *commedia dell'arte*, the improvisational, open-air theater that developed in sixteenth-century Italy. It tells the story of Prince Calaf of Astrakhan, and his love for the beautiful Turandot of Beijing. After Astrakhan was vanquished by the armies of King Carizmo, Calaf sought his fortune in China to save his impoverished parents, the former king and queen of Astrakhan. The play begins in Beijing, where an incognito Calaf unexpectedly runs into his former tutor, Barach. Barach tells Calaf about the evil schemes of Turandot, a "heartless creature" who "hates men," and who refuses the wishes of her father, Emperor Altoum, that she marry—often at great peril to the empire. Turandot offers to marry only a suitor who can answer three impossible riddles. Suitors who fail, as they all do, are decapitated, and their heads impaled on pikes as a warning to others. After seeing a picture of the stunning princess, a smitten Calaf undertakes the challenge.

8. Amaspiurants, *Printsessa Turandot 63*, 10–11.

Contrary to his predecessors, he correctly answers the riddles and saves his own life, but fails to win Turandot's love. Turandot begs her father to show mercy by allowing her to write new, more difficult riddles. Pained by his beloved's unhappiness, Calaf offers a compromise: if Turandot can discover his identity by the following day, he will forsake his claim to marriage. With the help of the devious Adelma, a Tatar princess who is a slave in the court of Altoum, and who is plotting her own marriage to Calaf as a way out of bondage, Turandot learns Calaf's name. After she triumphantly reveals it at court, however, she is so moved by Calaf's misery that she agrees to marry. In the final scene, Altoum informs Calaf that the usurper Carizmo has died, and Turandot begs the forgiveness of heaven and men for her unwillingness to marry.[9]

Evgenii Vakhtangov's production of the play was inventive for a number of reasons. He started with Friedrich Schiller's 1802 adaptation, the basis for Giacomo Puccini's opera, which substituted Gozzi's romantic comedy with epic drama. Unhappy with the initial results and skeptical whether the troupe could add anything novel to the oft-performed play, Vakhtangov proposed that the theater use Carlo Gozzi's original instead, which was "a fairy tale, a continuation of the folk-theater tradition, the theater of improvisation, born on the streets of Italy." He especially liked the unscripted interaction between audience and cast that was characteristic of the *commedia dell'arte*. After the first scene, the character Brighella, the master of Altoum's pages, chastised latecomers who were then taking their seats, and sometimes provoked arguments with witty spectators. Between the first and second acts, as the stage hands changed the scenery, Brighella and Truffaldino, the chief eunuch in Turandot's chamber, entertained the audience with a stand-up dialogue that differed every night. Some nights they made fun of theater critics and prominent personalities; other nights they satirized Soviet and foreign politics. Simonov recalled "brilliant successes" in these stand-up routines, but also "dreadful failures" when the jokes fell flat. Similarly, between the second and third acts, a tense moment in the plot, the stage hands pantomimed an abridged version of the play, thus foreshadowing the happy ending.

Vakhtangov also reveled in anachronisms. Even though the play was set in ancient Beijing, the props included a tennis racket (Altoum's

9. My synopsis of *Princess Turandot* draws on Albert Bermel and Ted Emery's translation. See Carlo Gozzi, *Five Tales for the Theatre*, ed. and trans. Albert Bermel and Ted Emery (Chicago, 1989), 125–84.

scepter), an accordion, and a camera. Costumes were more ridiculous than accurate: minor characters wore masks and exaggerated make-up; men wore formal tuxedos under their Chinese robes; and Boris Zakhava (who played Timur, Calaf's father) fashioned a long beard out of a wool pashmina. When an Italian composer failed to produce a musical score that Vakhtangov liked, he turned to Nikolai Sizov, a "sullen young man" and conservatory graduate who penned a score that was improvised and ironic. When Barach first appeared on stage, he hummed a tune from Nikolai Rimsky-Korsakov's opera *Sadko*. When Turandot arrived, she parodied a dance made famous by Isadora Duncan. Orchestral musicians fashioned harmonicas from combs covered with paper. Several decades later, Iurii Elagin, a violinist who played in the theater's orchestra during the 1930s, claimed that the music for *Princess Turandot* was nothing less than "a subtle forerunner, an inspired, tonal grouping for the modern, musical tonalities which were being born at the same time in a different corner of the world and which have since become known as jazz."[10]

In the strange logic of Soviet culture, Vakhtangov's inventions became more remarkable in hindsight. In 1940, the Vakhtangov Theater celebrated the one-thousandth performance of *Turandot*. Some were for audiences in Stockholm, Berlin, Tallinn, and Paris, where, according to Zakhava, the surprised reaction was always the same: "What? This was born in Soviet Russia?"[11] Yet the reaction to *Turandot* at home was far more equivocal. In the late 1920s, proletarian radicals in the literary world dismissed *Turandot* as "mystical" and "class alien." After the emergence of socialist realism as official dogma in the 1930s, even Vakhtangov's followers labeled *Turandot* as peripheral to his main contributions, a "scenic exercise not to be taken seriously." In this climate, it was easy to dismiss Vakhtangov's imaginative realism as "fantasticality," a word that was hard to square with anything that was conventionally realist. In the mid-1930s, Zakhava, then the director of the Vakhtangov's pedagogical studio, the precursor to the famous Shchukin Theatrical School, was forced to denounce nearly the entire repertoire of the

10. Simonov, *Stanislavsky's Protégé*, 173, 175–76, 178, 184; Turner, "Vakhtangov," 321; Nikolai A. Gorchakov, *The Theater in Soviet Russia*, trans. Edgar Lehrman (New York, 1957), 253–56; idem, *The Vakhtangov School of Stage Art* (Moscow, n.d.); P. A. Markov, *The Soviet Theater* (New York, 1972), 87–90; B. Zakhava, *Sovremenniki* (Moscow, 1969), 256–92; Ts. L. Mansurova, "Tvorcheskaia avtobiografiia," in *Pervaia Turandot: kniga o zhizni i tvorchestve narodnoi artistki SSSR Tsetsilii L'vovny Mansurovoi*, ed. N. I. Zakhava (Moscow, 1986), 26–29; and Juri Jelagin, *Taming of the Arts*, trans. Nicholas Wreden (New York, 1951), 30.
11. Boris Zakhava, *Vospominaniia. Spektakli i roli. Stat'i* (Moscow, 1982), 67.

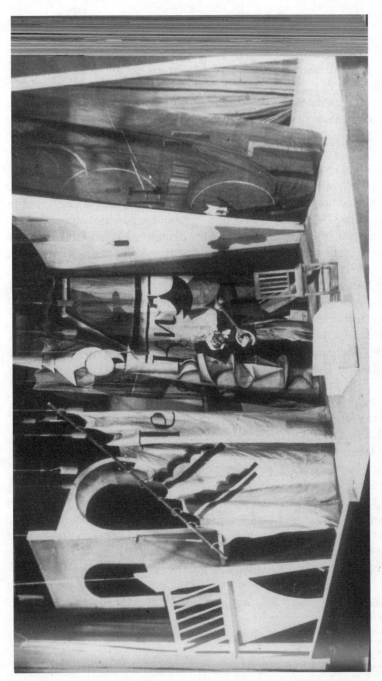

4. Scene from Evgenii Vakhtangov's production of *Princess Turandot*, 1920s.

theater as formalist. On the fifteenth anniversary of the theater's independence from MKhAT, one critic sarcastically asked how long the theater could survive on the "laurels of *Turandot*." He wondered, where was the "depth and realism" in the Vakhtangov's productions? From the vantage point of the early 1960s, the American critic W. L. Turner found it "depressing to contemplate the decay" of Vakhtangov's vision: "It was Boris Zakhava who complained of the unreality of the masks in [Brecht's] *The Caucasian Chalk Circle* when the Berliner Ensemble visited the Vakhtangov Theater [in 1957], though he had worn a Turkish towel around his chin for a beard . . . in *Turandot*." Many people at the theater would have heartily agreed.[12]

During the postwar period, when the whole Soviet theatrical world became "drug dependent," and only alcohol made it possible to maintain the "state of permanent optimism" demanded by socialist realism, conditions were no better for the experimental atmosphere promoted by Vakhtangov.[13] On November 19, 1945, the Vakhtangov Theater premiered Aleksandr Gladkov's *New Year's Eve*, a love story set during the war. The play was a hit that propelled its romantic hero, Andrei Abrikosov, to stardom. After a Central Committee decree on theater repertoire in August 1946, however, Gladkov's play was labeled a "grave repertory mistake," and pulled from the stage. In the ensuing weeks, Western plays like Edmond Rostand's *Cyrano de Bergerac* and Hervé's *Mam'zelle Nitouche;* Soviet plays that failed to display the requisite optimism in the socialist future; and anything else that veered from the strictest interpretations of socialist realism were targeted by the *zhdanovshchina*. Two of the theater's employees were fired for cosmopolitanism, an ideological deviation that suggested a lack of Soviet patriotism, and that was often applied to Jews who were thought to be overly sympathetic to Israel. Students at the Shchukin Theatrical School nearly got in trouble when they discussed writing a protest letter to Stalin in response.[14] The Vakhtangov Theater had a convenient excuse for minor criticisms: one of the first bombs to fall on Moscow during the war destroyed the theater, forcing the troupe into temporary exile in Omsk, a city in western Siberia, and then, until 1952, into inadequate quarters near Gorky Street.[15]

12. Gorchakov, *The Theater in Soviet Russia*, 262, 360; Simonov, *Stanislavsky's Protégé*, 145; Mikhail Ul'ianov, *Vozvrashchaias' k samomu sebe* (Moscow, 1996), 139; and Turner, "Vakhtangov," 321n21, 325.
13. Smeliansky, *The Russian Theater after Stalin*, 4.
14. Mikhail Ul'ianov, *Privorotnoe zel'e* (Moscow, 2001), 55–57.
15. TsAODM, f. 3954, o. 1, d. 1, l. 148.

However, the only response to criticism of the repertoire was to change it. According to the theater's official history, the Vakhtangov troupe made the best of it by staging good productions of bad plays, particularly Konstantin Simonov's thriller, *The Russian Question*, about an American journalist fired for telling the truth about the Soviet Union, and Aleksandr Fadeev's story of heroic partisans, *The Young Guard*.[16] The latter play was significant because Iurii Liubimov received a Stalin-Prize nomination for playing the lead role of Oleg Koshevoi. He later admitted that he was embarrassed to have benefited from Fadeev's "bad literature."[17]

Given the demise of Evgenii Vakhtangov's inventive brand of theater in the 1930s and '40s, it is not surprising that one of the most important events at theater after Stalin's death occurred off the stage. During the 1950s, Ruben Simonov and Nikolai Gorchakov, a Vakhtangov student who moved to MKhAT in 1924, tried to restore the reputation of their teacher by publishing lengthy autobiographical accounts that situated Vakhtangov squarely in the Stanislavsky tradition. Simonov, in particular, argued that it was time to reassert the "temporarily lost discipline of Vakhtangov's art" in Soviet theater to combat the "'sickness' of conformity." He differentiated Vakhtangov's emphasis on the "artist's fantasy" from "contrived fantasticalities that lead the artist away from truth." He cited Vakhtangov's last discussion with his student assistants, where he declared that "true reality on the stage" was "the product of the artist's great imagination." Summoning all the tropes of socialist-realist criticism, Simonov claimed that Vakhtangov was inspired by the October Revolution to challenge "naturalism, facelessness, and grayishness in art." *Turandot* was proof that he succeeded.[18]

Simonov's rehabilitation campaign was not altogether altruistic. Simonov had a long rivalry with Boris Zakhava, an original *vakhtangovets* who, even when it was dangerous to do so, was publicly dismissive of Vakhtangov's "woeful critics who can't see past their own nose."[19] Despite similar backgrounds in Vakhtangov's studio, Zakhava and Simonov had little in common. Born in Moscow in 1899, Simonov had studied with the famous bass Fedor Shaliapin, before transferring to Vakhtangov's studio

16. Sergeeva and Litvin, *Teatr imeni Evg. Vakhtangova*, 45–46.
17. Iurii Liubimov, *Rasskazy starogo trepacha* (Moscow, 2001), 184.
18. Gorchakov, *The Vakhtangov School*, 201; and Simonov, *Stanislavsky's Protégé*, 145–46, 199, 232. See also Mikhail Ul'ianov's undated essay, "Zagadki *Turandot*" in his collection, *Vozvrashchaias' k samomu sebe*, 133–41.
19. Zakhava, *Vospominaniia*, 70.

in 1920. Although best known as a director, Simonov was among only a small number of actors who were entrusted to play the role of Stalin in Stalin's presence, which he did in Nikolai Pogodin's *Man with a Gun* in 1938. Simonov was an accomplished guitarist, and a rabid soccer fan who sometimes cancelled rehearsal so that he could watch his beloved Spartak. Actors marveled at his friendly demeanor and his penchant for surrounding himself with beautiful women. By all accounts, Simonov was frightened by Soviet power into "unspoken conformism." Iurii Iakovlev, a longtime actor at the Vakhtangov Theater, wrote that Simonov "seemed defenseless in front of cultural *chinovniki* [a pejorative word for bureaucrats], and powerless to understand their logic." Similarly, Vladimir Etush, another longtime actor at the theater who liked Simonov but sided with Zakhava in their rivalry, claimed that Simonov perfected the art of "double morals" to preserve a "more or less peaceful life" at the theater. When Ekaterina Furtseva, the Minister of Culture, criticized Iurii Liubimov's early productions at the Taganka Theater, Simonov made no gestures toward professional solidarity or friendship: "I am in absolute agreement with you, Ekaterina Alekseevna, absolute agreement!" Simonov once admitted to Etush that he regularly performed conventional Soviet plays only so cultural authorities would leave him alone when he took up more daring works. Nonetheless, Simonov was not immune to extraordinary acts of bravery. It was widely rumored that he left Moscow in 1938 so he could avoid signing a letter denouncing Meyerhold. When his son Evgenii asked him about it, Simonov confirmed the rumor, but jokingly claimed that he would have refused to sign a positive letter about Meyerhold as well. Similarly, when authorities shut down Aleksandr Tairov's Kamernyi Theater in 1949, often a precursor to arrest, Simonov invited Tairov to join him at the Vakhtangov.[20]

In contrast to Simonov, Boris Zakhava was disgruntled with his role at the theater and confident in his political abilities to do something about it. Born in 1896 in a military family that had become wealthy in the Tula arms industry, Zakhava was educated at a classical school in Orel and at the Third Moscow Cadet School. Even in the 1970s and '80s, Zakhava's

20. Iurii Iakovlev, *Mezhdu proshlym i budushchim* (Moscow, 2003), 37–39; idem, *Al'bom sud'by moei* (Moscow, 1997), 126; Vladimir Etush, *I ia tam byl* (Moscow, 2002), 273–80; Mikhail Ul'ianov, *Rabotaiu akterom* (Moscow, 1987), 146–52; and A. Anastas'ev, "Ruben Simonov," and the collection of essays by Zavadskii, Mansurova, Ul'ianov, and twenty-three other actors who worked with Simonov in *Ruben Simonov: Tvorcheskoe nasledie. Stat'i i vospominaniia o R. N. Simonove,* ed. N. G. Litvinenko (Moscow, 1981), 5–12, 315–528.

privileged upbringing made the publication of his early memoirs impossible, and may have been the reason why he joined the party in 1943.[21] Zakhava helped convince Vakhtangov to open a studio in 1913 and was his assistant at the time of his death in 1922. He led the theater's pedagogical studio from 1925 to 1939, and then as an elder who was "respected and feared," turned down an offer to become the theater's artistic director so that he could take the helm of the Shchukin Theatrical School. As a "patriarch" of the theater, Zakhava considered himself to be Simonov's "equal," even though Simonov occupied the post of artistic director. Zakhava continued to direct plays at the Vakhtangov Theater in the 1950s, but was compromised by a string of mediocre productions, including an unsuccessful go at *Hamlet,* and by the sense among actors that his plays, though highly professional, were "a tad insipid . . . and simply boring." As he was approaching retirement, Zakhava married a young woman who encouraged him to be a more assertive defender of old ways. With his wife's help, Zakhava assembled a group of people who were unhappy with Simonov's stewardship of the theater, and who were "ready to use any occasion they could turn up to make their opposition public."[22]

Their opportunity came in 1959, when the Vakhtangov troupe met with Galina Zueva, a deputy Minister of Culture, before going abroad on tour. The meeting was supposed to be a mere formality, where Zueva and Simonov would deliver pep talks. "Cardinal issues," to be sure, were not on the agenda. After Simonov finished speaking, however, Zakhava looked at one of his allies, the actress Anna Orochko, asked if she were ready to begin, and then read a prepared text that was highly critical of Simonov. Zakhava claimed that the theater's repertoire did not conform to socialist realism, that Simonov ignored contemporary Soviet plays, that he was unfair in his distribution of roles to young actors, and that the theater was losing spectators. "Everyone sitting in the hall and in the presidium was struck dumb, confused, scared, and dismayed," Vladimir Etush wrote. "They saw themselves tossed out on the street, standing on the sidewalk with an outstretched hand." Zueva, it seems, was also surprised, since she immediately ended the discussion.[23] Accounts of what happened next vary. Etush claimed that Zueva ordered Simonov to convene a theater-wide meeting the next morning. When Etush arrived

21. Boris Zakhava, *Kadetskii korpus* (Moscow, 2000), 3.
22. Ul'ianov, *Privorotnoe zel'e,* 76; Etush, *I ia tam byl,* 295–301; and Iakovlev, *Mezhdu proshlym i budushchim,* 14–16.
23. Etush, *I ia tam byl,* 302–4.

at the meeting, he found several emergency vehicles parked outside, which he soon discovered were part of the coterie of Nikolai Mikhailov, the federal Minister of Culture, Aleksei Popov, the RSFSR Minister, and Dmitrii Polikarpov, the head of the Central Committee's Culture Department. Mikhail Ul'ianov, another longtime actor in the Vakhtangov troupe and a former Zakhava student, remembered a similar meeting, but claimed it took place after the traveling troupe returned from abroad. Iurii Liubimov recalled a smaller discussion that involved a carefully composed delegation from the Vakhtangov Theater and Polikarpov, who had been ordered by the Central Committee to resolve the dispute, and whose sympathies were clearly with Zakhava, a communist who had distinguished himself directing socialist-realist classics like Maxim Gorky's *Egor Bulychev and Others* and Fadeev's *The Young Guard*.[24]

There is no disagreement about the result of the conflict. Shortly after the meeting with cultural officials, Zakhava was fired, and assigned to a fulltime position as head of the Shchukin School. Liubimov claimed that Anastas Mikoian, a member of the Central Committee Presidium, played a decisive role. Mikoian was close friends with the architect Karo Alabian, who until his death in January 1959 was married to the actress Liudmila Tselikovskaia. Liubimov recalled that Polikarpov said something offensive to Tselikovskaia during the meeting at the Central Committee, and that his own "chivalrous feelings" for his future wife exceeded his "circumspection." Liubimov did not realize, apparently, that Tselikovskaia was more than capable of protecting her own honor as well as her friend Simonov. Among the casualties of the conflict were several longstanding friendships. Zakhava never forgave Liubimov for siding with Simonov, which he considered a personal "betrayal," since their acting styles were similar. Nor did he return to the Vakhtangov Theater before Simonov's death in 1968, despite the fact that the Shchukin School was just around the corner. Nonetheless, Zakhava did not retaliate against persons who spoke against him: if they had moonlighted as teachers at the Shchukin School before the controversy, they were welcome to do so afterward. Simonov was also gracious. Zakhava, after all, was not just another stage director, but one of the theater's founders. After some time had passed, Simonov, "understanding the cruelty of [Zakhava's] punishment," asked Etush how his former rival was doing.[25]

24. Ibid., 304–5; Ul'ianov, *Privorotnoe zel'e*, 76–77; and Liubimov, *Rasskazy starogo trepacha*, 200–201.
25. Liubimov, *Rasskazy starogo trepacha*, 201–2; and Etush, *I ia tam byl*, 305–6.

5. The Vakhtangov Theater on Arbat Street, 1970s.

It was in this context that Simonov began to lobby for a revival of
Princess Turandot, an idea he had publicly dismissed only a few years
earlier.[26] It is easy to understand Simonov's interest in the play: among
other things, it would establish him as Vakhtangov's principal heir, an
honor that had previously belonged to Zakhava. For decades, *Turandot*
had stood as an impossibly high benchmark, a mocking reminder that
youth and creativity go hand-in-hand. Iurii Iakovlev recalled that the
backstage walls at the theater were decorated with photos of the 1922
production, and that surviving cast members, understandably protec-
tive of the play, initially responded to Simonov's proposal with "some
kind of mystical horror." Yet Simonov not only convinced them to support
the revival, but to tutor new cast members. One notable exception was
Anna Orochko, who played Adelma in the original, and who sided with

26. Simonov, *Stanislavsky's Protégé*, 203.

Zakhava in 1959. Simonov allayed fears that a revival would denigrate the original by updating Vakhtangov's comedic elements to appeal to contemporary tastes. For the interludes, a crucial element in Vakhtangov's original production, he enrolled the help of Arkadii Raikin, a comic actor and director from Leningrad who excelled at "cabbage-pie shows" (*kapustniki*), satirical and self-deprecatory skits that Russian actors had traditionally performed for each other during Lent, when public performances and the consumption of meat were forbidden. Even during the Stalin period, *kapustniki* provided an irreverent, carefree, and private outlet for actors whose public performances were, by necessity, very different.[27]

Simonov's production of *Turandot* was a critical success, despite the fact that he became so anxious during rehearsals that he asked Vladimir Shlezinger, one of the theater's permanent stage directors, to lead them. "You rehearse it, and I will come and stage it," he told Shlezinger before leaving. For the background, Simonov had an artist create a phosphorescent image of the wedding-cake skyscraper on Smolensk Square, just a few blocks west of the theater, thus creating the outdoor atmosphere of the *commedia dell'arte*, and fulfilling Vakhtangov's wish that the theater serve as a "window onto Arbat." Raikin encouraged Iurii Iakovlev, who played Altoum's secretary, Pantalone, to speak in an accent so heavy that spectators would "understand only one or two words, not more." During one interlude, Pantalone did nothing but read in his ridiculous accent the lead (and typically exhortatory) article from the day's newspaper. It turned out to be one of the funniest moments in the play. The masked characters—Pantalone, Brighella, Truffaldino, and Altoum's high chancellor, Tartaglia—mimicked the iconic Dance of the Little Swans from Peter Tchaikovsky's ballet *Swan Lake*, sang the popular song "Moscow Nights," which was made famous by the International Festival of Youth and Students that Moscow hosted in 1957, and used several innocuous stage props as instruments. They referred to Calaf, played by Vasilii Lanovoi, as "His Highness Vas'ia," humorously suggesting that some cast members were jealous of Lanovoi. Simonov also maintained the improvisational character of Vakhtangov's original. After Brighella (Mikhail Ul'ianov) accidentally brushed against Pantalone's beard during one performance, Pantalone pretended he was an offended woman on a crowded trolleybus: "Good heavens! What are you touching?"

27. Iakovlev, *Al'bom sud'by moei*, 127; and Lanovoi, *Letiat za dniami dni*, 171. On *kapustniki*, see Smeliansky, *The Russian Theater after Stalin*, 21.

"The four of us," Iakovlev recalled, "Nikolai Gritsenko [Tartaglia], Mikhail Ul'ianov, and Maksim Grekov [Truffaldino], endlessly improvised things, forcing each other to get out of predicaments, to find witty answers to unexpected questions."[28]

The Vakhtangov Theater took its revival of *Turandot* on the road to Greece, Germany, Bulgaria, Romania, Czechoslovakia, and Austria, always performing in the language of spectators. Its success "grew from performance to performance," and was a transformative experience for many of the persons who were involved in the play. "Everything came together," Iakovlev recalled. "Everything worked out."

> I felt like I was an entirely different person. . . . The success of *Princess Turandot* signified our blood relationship with our predecessors, brought us together with Evgenii Bagrationovich [Vakhtangov] himself, and lent us courage in our search for the new, the unexpected, and at first glance, the unbelievable. As critics like to say, our old performances "ring" anew.[29]

But Simonov's expectations that *Turandot* would transform the theater's "underlying atmosphere" were more difficult to realize. Soon after *Turandot* premiered, the theater reluctantly began work on Boris Voitekhov's anti-Stalinist play, *Rainstorm*. Few could have anticipated the problems it would cause.

RAINSTORM

The Vakhtangov Theater, according to Anatoly Smeliansky, was always famous for its "special relationship with the center of power." Smeliansky probably had in mind the extensive patronage ties that the theater cultivated with political leaders in the 1930s.[30] Among all the fields of

28. Iakovlev, *Al'bom sud'by moei*, 128–32; idem, *Mezhdu proshlym and budushchim*, 57–59; Amaspiurants, *Printsessa Turandot 63*, 10; Sergeeva and Litvin, *Teatr imeni Evg. Vakhtangova*, 60; and Vasilii Lanovoi, *Schastlivye vstrechi* (Moscow, 1983), 106–33.
29. Iakovlev, *Mezhdu proshlym and budushchim*, 57; and idem, *Al'bom sud'by moei*, 130;
30. Smeliansky, *The Russian Theater since Stalin*, 30. Sheila Fitzpatrick has catalogued many of these relationships in *Tear off the Masks: Identity and Imposture in Twentieth-Century Russia* (Princeton, N.J., 2005), 190, 197. On informal patronage networks under Stalin, see Kiril Tomoff, *Creative Union: The Professional Organization of Soviet Composers, 1939–1953* (Ithaca, N.Y., 2006), 268–99.

cultural endeavor, theater artists were particularly well-positioned to create these relationships. Contrary to literature, which was usually a solitary endeavor for both writer and reader, the act of theatrical creation was a public affair. Even though Ruben Simonov "could not distinguish a district party secretary from an ordinary instructor," he was a gifted schmoozer, and was always curious to know who, among the dignitaries in the audience, he could "make into friends of the theater."[31] Moreover, the party's desire to maintain control over the staging guaranteed at least a modicum of interaction with cast members. It was common in the 1950s and '60s for prominent cultural officials to review performances with the theater's artistic council a day or two before opening. Their input, of course, was almost always unwelcome and often ridiculous. Before the 1962 premier of William Gibson's "Two for the Seesaw," for instance, Aleksei Popov, the RSFSR Minister of Culture, told the theater that it was inappropriate for the actress Iuliia Borisova to play the role of Gittel, an "American prostitute," because Borisova was a member of the Supreme Soviet, the Soviet Union's ornamental parliament. (It did not matter, apparently, that Gittel was actually a Bohemian dancer in New York.) The play was subsequently pulled from the repertoire under the pretext that the Sovremennik had already produced it. Similarly, before the 1965 premier of Leonid Zorin's "Dion," a play set in Rome at the time of Emperor Domitian, officials from the Ministry of Culture complained about a reference to Domitian's residence on Granatovaia (Pomegranate) Street. To their ears, it sounded too much like Granovskii Street, the location of an apartment building in Moscow where party leaders had lived before Khrushchev ordered the construction of a community of ornate Italianate villas in Lenin Hills.[32]

Despite the occasional nuisance, there were advantages to these contacts. Ekaterina Furtseva, the head of the Moscow Party Committee and a member of the Central Committee Presidium in the 1950s, was reputedly so impressed with the Vakhtangov's production of Shakespeare's *Two Gentlemen of Verona* that she took a special interest in the welfare of cast members. When Vladimir Etush, who played the role of Launce, heard about Furtseva's concern, he called her on the telephone, explained his cramped living conditions, and quickly received a new sixteen square-meter apartment in the Hotel Ukraine building. He later claimed

---

31. Sergeeva and Litvin, *Teatr imeni Evg. Vakhtangova*, 48; and Iakovlev, *Mezhdu proshlym i budushchim*, 39.
32. Iakovlev, *Al'bom sud'by moei*, 127; and Ul'ianov, *Privorotnoe zel'e*, 96.

he was reluctant to ask Furtseva for help until he heard that the film actor Mark Bernes had successfully done the same. Similarly, when the husband of the actress Valentina Bagrina, a high-ranking ministerial official, was arrested in the late 1940s, Andrei Abrikosov and Anatolii Goriunov secured a personal meeting with the head of the secret police, Viktor Abakumov, with whom the theater had longstanding ties.[33]

There appears to have been a mostly tacit code at the Vakhtangov Theater governing these sorts of interactions. It was acceptable for individuals to petition higher officials for material assistance and artistic latitude. And it was acceptable, of course, for cultural officials to review plays before their public premier. But it was unacceptable for individuals at the theater to take internal disputes to outside officials. Even among the friends of Boris Zakhava, for instance, there was a feeling that he should not have taken his dispute with Simonov to higher officials, because it was inappropriate for him to "throw trash out of the hut," a folk proverb that corresponds to Anthony Trollope's prohibition against washing dirty linens in public. Some even feared that Zakhava had jeopardized the existence of the theater by couching the dispute in ideological terms.[34] And finally, it was unacceptable for cultural officials to initiate the production of plays. According to a Ministry of Culture decree in August 1956, repertoire was the purview of artistic councils and party organizations at individual theaters. In principle, theaters were free to choose their repertoire from domestic and foreign plays that were approved for Soviet audiences by the All-Russian Theatrical Society. In reality, of course, there were a myriad of external pressures that affected repertoires. Nonetheless, cultural officials mostly honored the limited autonomy of theaters; they instructed theaters what not to perform, and let them decide what to perform.

Rainstorm was controversial because the latter two prohibitions governing contact between political officials and theater employees were violated. The play's author, Boris Voitekhov, had lived on the fringes of the Soviet theatrical world for several decades. Born in 1911, Voitekhov was perhaps best known at the Vakhtangov Theater as the second of Liudmila Tselikovskaia's five husbands. During the war, Tselikovskaia left Voitekhov to marry the actor Mikhail Zharov, initiating a famously bitter divorce. Voitekhov's credentials as a dramatist were modest.

---

33. Etush, *I ia tam byl*, 90, 145–46, 162–63. On the theater's ties with the secret police in the 1930s, see Jelagin, *Taming of the Arts*, 33, 44–47.
34. Etush, *I ia tam byl*, 302.

He wrote the play *Pavel Grekov*, which premiered in 1938, and reputedly co-wrote with the satirist Leonid Lench an unpublished and un-staged play about a Soviet official in charge of grain requisitioning in Tajikistan. According to one of Voitekhov's friends, the latter play nearly cost both writers their lives during the Great Purges. Voitekhov worked as a journalist during the war and wrote a series of famous dispatches for *Pravda* from Sevastopol.[35] Voitekhov's dispatches were the basis for a script he co-wrote for a 1944 film about the Germans' 250-day siege of Sevastopol. After the war, Voitekhov was the chief editor of the Komsomol journal *Smena* (Change) until he was arrested and sent to the gulag. After he was released and rehabilitated, Voitekhov became editor of a new weekly magazine called *RT*, which was devoted to Soviet radio and television broadcasting. Despite its seemingly mundane focus, Voitekhov used the journal as a forum for repressed writers from the Stalin period and future dissidents, which was probably the chief reason why his tenure ended after only twenty-eight issues.[36]

Voitekhov appears to have written the bulk of *Rainstorm* sometime between 1957, when the play's final scene occurred, and 1962, when the Pushkin Theater in Leningrad refused to perform it. The play was never published; it exists today only as an archival manuscript in four redactions that date from 1964–66. The differences between the redactions are substantial, particularly in the third act that was the target of most criticism. The play is set in 1946, 1953, and 1957, and tells the story of the Golovkin family. The family's patriarch, Zakhar Spiridonovich, is a political official, first the chairman of an oblast executive committee (a local governmental institution), and then the secretary of the oblast party committee and a member of the Central Committee. His family members are honest Soviet citizens who manage to preserve their faith in Soviet ideals despite Stalinism. They are a "living reproach" to the "ghosts of the past": persons who emerged from the Stalin era with "unclean consciences" because of their complicity in repression and bureaucratic arbitrariness.

The meaning of the play, barely opaque in the first two acts, is fully transparent at the end. The third act, set in a passenger terminal at a steamship port in June 1957, is structured around three overlapping discussions, each plainly didactic. The first involves the character Andrei,

<hr />

35. These were translated into English as *The Last Days of Sevastopol*, trans. Ralph Parker and V. M. Genne (New York, 1943).
36. Nikolai Mitrofanov, "Redaktsiia v dome Gogolia: Teni i siluety tridtsat' let spustia," in *Arbatskii arkhiv*, vyp. 1, ed. S. O. Shmidt (Moscow, 1997), 439–48.

an inveterate Stalinist and longtime secretary of a district party committee who recently learned that he was not re-elected to a seat on the oblast committee. Andrei attributes his political misfortune to the fact that he "did not change colors, and did not kick the banner" under which he lived his "entire life." He holds the "revisionist" Golovkin responsible for his fate, and warns that "there will be arrests. . . . And there will be executions" when Stalin rises from the grave. The second discussion, a counterpoint to the first, focuses on Gleb Il'ich Irmin, a Frenchman who has just arrived at the passenger terminal as a new Soviet citizen. When Irmin worriedly presents his new passport for inspection, his friends remind him to show it proudly, since it was forged in the fires of revolution. As Golovkin's daughter plays the "International" on a piano, the characters thank Kuz'mich, an old Bolshevik who will soon be celebrating the fiftieth anniversary of his entrance into the party. The final discussion involves Pliushchev, a longtime friend and aide to Golovkin, who confesses that he was once an informant for the secret police, and that he made up terrible lies about Golovkin and others to save his own life. As the curtain falls, Golovkin receives a letter from Moscow informing him that "careerists and schismatics have gathered an arithmetic majority" in the Central Committee Presidium, a reference to the unsuccessful coup against Khrushchev that the "antiparty group" staged in June 1957, and that he should fly to Moscow at once for an emergency Central Committee meeting. Before Golovkin departs, he forgives Pliushchev and explains the meaning of the play's title to Andrei, who believes that the events in Moscow have proven him right:

Do you understand what a rainstorm is? There is a rainstorm of nature. And now there is a different kind of rainstorm . . . a rainstorm that frees the soul, mind, and energy of man! . . .This rainstorm will wash away your arithmetic majority and the stain from our inheritance. . . . It will wash it away because our goal is not indigence, but rich communism, wealth . . . for everyone![37]

37. Ellipses, present in the original, designate dramatic pauses rather than elided material. Quoted materials in this and previous paragraphs were drawn from the second redaction of the play (RGALI, f. 2329, op. 25, d. 1148, ll. 55–77) from 1964. This material corresponds to a synopsis of the play that circulated in the Central Committee in January 1965 (RGANI, f. 5, o. 55, d. 106, ll. 195–99), and thus appears to have been the version that the Vakhtangov Theater produced. The first redaction of the third act of the play (RGALI, f. 2329, o. 25, d. 1147, ll. 56–79), which is also dated 1964, differs in only minor ways. In later redactions from 1965, Voitekhov substantially revised the final act, including the block quote (RGALI, f. 2329, o. 25, d. 1149, ll. 61–94; and d. 1150, ll. 61–92).

Even by the standards of socialist realism, *Rainstorm* was hokey. One of its critics referred to it as a "political play," which was a polite way of saying that it lacked the essential components of good drama: character development, a plot line, and dramatic tension. When the artistic council at the Vakhtangov Theater read the first redaction of the play in November 1963, only one member voted for production; the rest, though sympathetic to the play's political message, cited grave problems in the third act. In December 1963, however, for reasons that were then unclear, Furtseva ordered the theater to resume production of *Rainstorm,* promising that Voitekhov would rectify the problems that the artistic council had noted. In the spring of 1964, Voitekhov offered the theater a slightly revised version of the third act (the second redaction), and the theater premiered the play on May 6. After three performances that were universally judged as dreadful, the theater pulled *Rainstorm* from the stage, prompting Furtseva to summon administrators to discuss a new timeline for production. Simonov asked that *Rainstorm* be delayed until after the theater premiered Mikhailo Stel'makh's *Truth and Falsehood* in February 1965 so Voitekhov would have adequate time to make more thorough revisions. Furtseva instead ordered that the play be ready by October 31, 1964.[38]

Furtseva's insistence that the Vakhtangov Theater perform *Rainstorm* changed the nature of the theater's opposition to the play. Members of the artistic council had previously voiced doubts about the literary merits of the play; now Nikolai Timofeev, the secretary of the theater's party organization, complained that the "leadership of the federal Ministry of Culture does not aid normal creative work, which limits the theater's initiative and disorganizes its work schedule." On October 17, immediately after the Vakhtangov troupe returned from performances in Greece, the theater's party organization used Khrushchev's removal from power three days earlier as a pretext to again complain to the Ministry of Culture about the play. The theater, after all, had still not received Voitekhov's revisions to the third act (the third redaction). The ministry notified the theater that Voitekhov would finish the revisions by October 19, and indicated that the original schedule should be honored. Nonetheless, even at the final dress rehearsal for officials from the federal and RSFSR Ministries of Culture and the Central Committee on October 27, Voitekhov's revised script was absent, forcing the cast to read from the already discredited second redaction.[39]

38. TsAODM, f. 3954, o. 1, d. 8, ll. 131–37.
39. TsAODM, f. 3954, o. 1, d. 8, ll. 131–32.

By all accounts, the rehearsal on October 27 was a disaster. Two days later, Aleksei Popov, the RSFSR Minister of Culture, wrote a letter to the Central Committee describing the extraordinary discussion that occurred after the play, when cast members and administrators unanimously asked that Furtseva's order be annulled. The Central Committee representative at the rehearsal filed his own report on November 3, which detailed the play's unusual history, and unlike earlier criticisms, condemned Voitekhov's politics. In January 1965, Dmitrii Polikarpov, then the deputy director of the Central Committee's Ideological Department, notified Popov that the party supported his request to cancel the play and indicated that Furtseva "no longer insisted" on its production.[40] Clearly, Polikarpov was more concerned about the politics of *Rainstorm* than the autonomy of the Vakhtangov Theater. The idea that Khrushchev had been a defender of party unity against "careerists and schismatics" had become impolitic in the aftermath of his dismissal. The new political atmosphere did not escape critics at the Vakhtangov Theater. They cast Furtseva's interference as an example of "subjectivism," a word that Khrushchev's opponents in the Presidium used to describe his supposedly harebrained schemes. They claimed that Furtseva "behaved aggressively," that she was "unnecessarily insistent," and that she refused to take their concerns about the play seriously. Even though the theater's party members were obliged to criticize their meek opposition to Furtseva, they wanted to make sure that party officials understood that they had always opposed the play.[41] Similar sentiments could be found in the party organization at the Moscow Section of the Union of Writers, where *Rainstorm* came up in a discussion about Khrushchev's dismissal. "I know how Ekaterina Furtseva pressured the Vakhtangov Theater to stage this play, as some colleagues in literature are fond of patronage [*patronazh*]," one writer noted in November 1964. "What a terrible situation befell the theater on account of this play. But what could it do? Money was wasted and the play was rubbish." Like Khrushchev's subjectivism, *Rainstorm* was an example of meddling from above that made it difficult "for writers to think of themselves as communists."[42]

Given the Vakhtangov Theater's history, and its longstanding patronage relationships, it is not surprising that critics of *Rainstorm* saw Furtseva's advocacy as an example of patronage. They assumed that

40. RGANI, f. 5, o. 55, d. 106, ll. 193–99.
41. TsAODM, f. 3954, o. 1, d. 8, ll. 104–11.
42. TsAODM, f. 88, o. 45, d. 23, ll. 170–71.

Voitekhov had asked Furtseva for help finding a stage, and that Furtseva, thinking *Rainstorm* would polish the reputation of her boss, jumped at the opportunity. The truth was more complex and less flattering for a theater that thought itself innocent. A fuller account of the play's unusual history came out in March 1965, when the theater's party organization heard a complaint about Isai Spektor, the Vakhtangov's administrative director and the husband of the actress Iuliia Borisova. The complaint alleged that Spektor had exceeded "his prerogatives" by dictating the theater's "artistic policies," and that "at the head of the theater there should be artists, not administrators." Few persons would have disagreed with the latter assertion. The chief moral of *Rainstorm*, after all, was that officials should heed the "will of the collective." As Vladimir Shlezinger noted, "our error with *Rainstorm* lay in the fact that we were forced to perform it."[43] But whether Spektor was guilty of the same crimes as Furtseva was an entirely different question that plunged the theater into its worst crisis since Zakhava's firing in 1959.

Shlezinger was the first to suggest that there was more to the charges against Spektor than "naked administering." He indicated that there was a group within the theater that was "in the practice of going around the collective, straight to the ministry" and was thus responsible for "the upheaval we have endured." Referring to *Rainstorm*, he claimed that this group had written a letter to the Ministry of Culture "without consulting the collective." Now the "same thing" was happening with Spektor. It is not clear how much Shlezinger knew about *Rainstorm*; he admitted only to having heard "rumors" about how the Vakhtangov Theater got stuck with the play. It is clear, however, that he overstated the number of the play's proponents.

In truth, Shlezinger's "group" comprised one person: the actor Mikhail Astangov (Ruzhnikov), the sole member of the artistic council to endorse *Rainstorm* in 1963, and the director of the play in 1964. Despite being outnumbered, Astangov's vote carried a great deal of weight. Astangov had studied with Fedor Shaliapin before Shaliapin went into emigration in the early 1920s. He also had a successful career at the Revolution and the Mossovet Theaters before coming to the Vakhtangov in 1945 with his wife, the actress Elena Adomaitis. As a *vakhtangovets*, Astangov was thrice the winner of the Stalin Prize (1948, 1950 and 1951), and he was named a "People's Artist of the Soviet Union" in 1955, the highest distinction for a Soviet cultural figure. Nonetheless, Astangov was one of

43. TsAODM, f. 3954, o. 1, d. 9, ll. 2, 4, 12–13.

the few actors at the theater who did not study with Vakhtangov or at the Shchukin School and was always pegged by his colleagues as an outsider. This perception was reinforced by Astangov's reserved demeanor and the relatively small circle of friends that he kept.[44]

Astangov confessed his role in *Rainstorm* soon after Shlezinger fingered the nonexistent group of conspirators. He said that he agreed to look at *Rainstorm* as a personal favor to Voitekhov, who had been a friend since 1938. He asked Furtseva and Nikolai Egorychev, the powerful secretary of the Moscow Party Committee, for help finding a stage in Moscow after the Pushkin Theater in Leningrad cancelled the play. Furtseva, apparently misinterpreting his request, asked what his colleagues thought of the play, and whether he would be willing to move to the Malyi Theater if they rejected it. Astangov then endorsed *Rainstorm* at a meeting on theater repertoire that the Central Committee's Ideological Commission sponsored in November 1963. He claimed after the fact that he spoke only in a personal capacity, but his caveat must have eluded Furtseva. "I am saying this so that you'll see that there was no force or compulsion from the ministry. Blame me, because if it weren't for me, none of this would have happened."[45] This was clearly not the sort of confession the theater wanted to hear. By placing the blame on himself, Astangov effaced the guilt of his patron, Furtseva. He also suggested the whole debacle was the product of a few misunderstandings. Simonov, who had known Astangov since their days in Shaliapin's studio, was outraged by what he considered half-truths.

> Everything is your fault. Everything depended on you: you suggested the play; you sponsored it; and in reality, the Ministry of Culture was not culpable, because the initiative came from Mikhail Fedorovich [Astangov], even at a wide forum like the ideological [commission] meeting. . . . As the theater's artistic director, I demand answers from you. Do you understand?[46]

44. TsAODM, f. 3954, o. 1, d. 9, l. 14; and Etush, *I ia tam byl*, 100, 104–6.
45. TsAODM, f. 3954, o. 1, d. 9, ll. 37–42. The stenographic record of the Ideological Commission meeting was published in abridged form in *Ideologicheskie komissii TsK KPSS, 1958–1964: Dokumenty*, ed. E. S. Afanas'eva, V. Iu. Afiani, L. A. Velichanskaia, Z. K. Vodop'ianova, and E. V. Kochubei (Moscow, 1998), 293–381. Astangov's speech was not included.
46. TsAODM, f. 3954, o. 1, d. 9, l. 65.

Astangov never had an opportunity to give a fuller account. A month after his clash with Simonov, he died unexpectedly of peritonitis.

The case involving Spektor pertained to similar questions of outside meddling. The theater's employees met with the party organization on March 11, 1965 to discuss Spektor's stewardship of the theater. According to one actor, not since 1914 had the entire theater gathered for an event. The focus of discussion was a meeting at the Ministry of Culture, in late 1964, where the sisters Galina and Larisa Pashkova, Andrei Abrikosov, and Liudmila Tselikovskaia reputedly asked Furtseva to fire Spektor, because Iuliia Borisova, Spektor's wife, had an unfair advantage in the competition for salary and roles. Their concerns were not unique. "Borisova is a very gifted actress," one critic admitted, "but if she weren't Spektor's wife she wouldn't have achieved such heights. Even [Boris] Shchukin did not occupy such a privileged position in the theater as Borisova, and he was the most talented actor of our time." Abrikosov and Tselikovskaia also complained that Spektor had an unusual amount of influence over artistic affairs. Nonetheless, Spektor's critics faced several significant obstacles in their campaign to remove him. Spektor was widely considered a competent administrator, and some people resisted calls to fire him simply because they thought it would be impossible to hire anyone as skilled. Moreover, Spektor was a graduate of the Shchukin School, and despite his administrative posting, was no dilettante in artistic affairs. Finally, Spektor was a member of the party and had spent twenty-nine years at the Vakhtangov Theater. His wife was a delegate to the Supreme Soviet and a "People's Artist of the RSFSR." In short, Spektor could not be taken lightly, which may explain why his adversaries tried to enlist Furtseva's help.[47]

The chief obstacle faced by Spektor's opponents had nothing to do with Spektor himself. Rather, it was the sense that their meeting at the Ministry of Culture in late 1964 was inappropriate because it pertained to theater-wide affairs and had not been cleared by the artistic council and the party organization beforehand. To mitigate this perception, Tselikovskaia claimed that she was "summoned" to the ministry, a choice of verbs that drew several requests for clarification. Similarly, Abrikosov insisted that no Soviet citizen was "prohibited from going where he wants," and asserted his "right" to visit Furtseva or any other political figure. Abrikosov's principled stand offended colleagues who thought he was trying to mask his own unprincipled behavior. Referring to the

47. TsAODM, f. 3954, o. 1, d. 9, ll. 27, 79, 153.

period following Khrushchev's dismissal, Mikhail Ul'ianov claimed that Abrikosov had manipulated a "particular moment to knock off another person," which was "not good, nor honest." The one thing everyone agreed on was that the theater's "collective" was in poor shape. Spektor's friends wondered about the purpose of a politically empowered "collective," which was, after all, one of the chief achievements of the thaw, when it was so easily subverted by disgruntled individuals. Nikolai Timofeev, an actor and the secretary of the theater's party organization, said he was "highly distressed" that Abrikosov, Tselikovskaia, and the Pashkova sisters had failed to bring their concerns to the artistic council and the party organization first. For his part, Abrikosov claimed that he had been afraid of the response: "I knew that if I spoke in the collective, you would say to me: 'Why are you saying this? Are you the chief director? The administrative director?'"[48]

Furtseva did not fire Spektor. Instead, she offered to promote him to deputy director of Goskontsert, the government's ticket and booking agency. When Spektor declined the offer, Furtseva called Simonov and Timofeev into her office to assure them that Spektor was being transferred, not fired, and to stress that "he should not decline the higher post that has been offered to him." Despite Furtseva's pressure, Spektor refused to leave the Vakhtangov Theater; he even got Aleksei Popov, the RSFSR Minister of Culture, to support his position. After Furtseva met with Spektor a second time to ask him to reconsider, she dropped her request altogether, leaving Spektor's fate to the "collective." Of the ten persons in the theater's party bureau who later sat in judgment of Spektor, only one voted to dismiss him from the post of administrative director.[49]

On the surface, the Vakhtangov Theater outmaneuvered Furtseva twice in late 1964 and early 1965. There is little doubt, however, that the controversies surrounding *Rainstorm* and Spektor were highly dispiriting, even for the victors. Nikolai Timofeev admitted in a report to the party organization that Tselikovskaia and Abrikosov's visit with Furtseva in late 1964 produced a "nervous and unhealthy atmosphere in the theater," especially since it came on the heels of a similar meeting between Astangov and Furtseva. The problem was not simply Furtseva's meddling, but the realization that she did so at the request of persons within the theater. "Not everyone in the theater is equal," one party

48. TsAODM, f. 3954, o. 1, d. 9, ll. 27–28, 59–60, 76, 88.
49. TsAODM, f. 3954, o. 1, d. 9, ll. 151–52, 155.

member noted. "The sun does not shine on all." This was not a new problem. One of Boris Zakhava's old friends pointed out that Zakhava and Orochko were fired under similar circumstances in 1959. It was an imperfect comparison, since Zakhava initiated the contact with ministerial officials that led to his dismissal. But the broader point was undeniable: despite a decade of reform, and the optimism engendered by the revival of *Princess Turandot*, subjectivism was not the sole affliction of Stalin, Khrushchev, and Furtseva. "To settle a score by going to the Minister," Mikhail Ul'ianov noted at the party meeting devoted to Spektor's alleged sins, "is not a 1964 position or a 1965 position. . . . I am not accusing you of anything, [I want to say] only that this was never our [position] through all this history, which, by the way, dear Andrei L'vovich [Abrikosov], is what got you in hot water. . . . Do you understand what you have done?"[50]

Even though Astangov and Abrikosov violated the theater's tacit code governing interaction with political leaders, patronage was so embedded in the history of the theater that no one bothered to ask whether it was possible to condemn one sort of interaction, like Astangov's promotion of *Rainstorm,* and permit another, like Etush's request for a larger apartment. In fact, the opposite was true. Vakhtangov actors defended the "right" to petition political leaders for assistance at the same time that they condemned Astangov and Abrikosov for doing so. "Our Soviet system forbids no one from appealing to any level of authority," Nikolai Timofeev argued, "and we do not have the right to incriminate in this regard. A revolution occurred in the name of this, and hundreds of thousands of people perished." The difference between exercising a fundamental Soviet right and circumventing the will of the collective lay in the nature of the matter at hand. As Astangov discovered, however, the line separating personal and collective issues was often hazy and perilous.[51]

The controversies at the Vakhtangov Theater straddled the divide between the Khrushchev and Brezhnev eras. For *Rainstorm* the context was especially significant. If Khrushchev had remained in power, it is likely that Furtseva would have continued to defend the play, even after the disastrous rehearsal at the end of October. Khrushchev's dismissal not only forced Furtseva to withdraw her support, but made it possible for Vakhtangov employees to criticize her openly. At the party meeting in March 1965, Vladimir Shlezinger referred to Aleksei Rumiantsev's

---

50. TsAODM, f. 3954, o. 1, d. 9, ll. 59–60.
51. TsAODM, f. 3954, o. 1, d. 9, l. 28.

famous article in *Pravda*, where he argued that both Khrushchev and Stalin had a penchant for "subjectivism and arbitrariness," and indicated that the new Kremlin leadership would do a better job of honoring the expertise and autonomy of the intelligentsia.[52] Rumiantsev's first assertion came as no surprise to anyone at the Vakhtangov Theater. His second assertion had yet to be proven, and that was the crux of the problem. Suffice it to say that Furtseva's meddling suggested that habits honed by Stalinism were hard to unlearn. Simonov promised that *Turandot* would transform the theater's "underlying atmosphere" for the better. Timofeev, in contrast, warned that meddling from above had done the opposite. What little optimism remained at the Vakhtangov Theater after *Rainstorm* disappeared when the Ministry of Culture retracted the repertory autonomy that had existed since 1956. Beginning in 1967, all new productions had to be cleared by the ministry before any work could begin. No matter how the new legislation was spun, actors and administrators realized that it legitimized the sort of interference that had caused so many problems two years earlier. Intrusive *"chinovniki"* were the theater's "misfortune," the actor Nikolai Plotnikov said in 1967. "How can it be that I understand [the theater] worse than people who sit around [at the ministry]. I think artists understand these affairs better than they do."[53]

In this atmosphere of dejection, the irony of the theater's predicament apparently went unnoticed. A play whose message was bitterly anti-Stalinist had become nothing less than proof of the tenaciousness of Stalinism. It is not hard to imagine Voitekhov withdrawing the play from the Vakhtangov Theater had he realized the controversy it would cause. Evidently, his insight into the theater's inner workings was as flawed as his prose. Nor did it matter that the revival of *Turandot* was a critical success, so much, in fact, that the play and the theater became even more inseparable. Like actors who are forever typecast into their first acclaimed roles, the Vakhtangov Theater was never able to live down the success of *Turandot*. Even in the late 1990s, a kitschy bronze statue of the princess appeared outside the theater, apparently without any forewarning. "We had no idea why it was built and who did it," said Mikhail Ul'ianov, who played Brighella in 1963, and who later became the theater's artistic director. "But that golden lady has no relation to the princess."[54] Perhaps old-timers like Ruben Simonov realized that the nostalgia that drove the

52. A. Rumiantsev, "Partiia i intelligentsia," *Pravda*, February 21, 1965, 2.
53. TsAODM, f. 3954, o. 1, d. 10, l. 82ob.
54. Mikhail Ul'ianov, "'Tut vsegda bylo uiutno . . . ,'" *Arbatskie vesti* 6 (March 2001): 3.

revival of *Turandot* was as cruel as it was seductive. For them, the play was merely a vehicle for something more important—the innocence, egalitarian spirit, and youthful inventiveness of Evgenii Vakhtangov's studio. But just as it is impossible to turn back the clock, these things could not be revived. What is certain is that theirs was not the only case of thwarted nostalgia in the Arbat during the thaw. A few blocks north of the Vakhtangov Theater, nine shiny glass and concrete skyscrapers were constructed in the 1960s, a project so modern and Western-looking that it seemed out of place in a city that still retained much of its nineteenth-century appearance. Few people realized that Novyi Arbat, as the project was called, also sought to recapture something from the 1920s. It too was unsuccessful, albeit for entirely different reasons.

CHAPTER FOUR

Remembering the Avant-garde

In the early 1960s, bulldozers and wrecking cranes cleared a vast, kilometer-long corridor in the densely built alleys between Arbat Square in the east and the Moscow River in the west. By 1968, nine shiny glass and concrete skyscrapers, each more than twenty stories tall, lined the void that had been carved out of the Arbat neighborhood. The four towers on the south side were designed to look like open books that had been propped upright; they sat atop a two-story gallery of stores and offices that ran nearly the entire length of the corridor. The more conventional towers on the north side resembled five pairs of vertical rectangles that were offset but conjoined along part of one side. They shared space with a new movie theater, a post office, Moscow's largest bookstore, and even a few pre-revolutionary buildings that had been spared demolition. Between the towers, a new radial street linked the center of Moscow to Kutuzovskii Avenue, famous for its concentration of ornate Stalin-era buildings, and to the elite dacha communities west of the city. By the standards of Moscow's medieval layout, the street was immense. It accommodated six lanes of traffic, two of which were reserved for the black Volgas and ZIL limousines that ferried important persons to and from the Kremlin and other points in central Moscow. In commemoration of Mikhail Kalinin, the old Bolshevik and Soviet head of state who died in 1946, the new street was named Kalininskii Avenue. But Muscovites were more apt to call it Novyi (New) Arbat, the name that urban planners attached to it in the 1930s when they first began to discuss proposals for its construction.

Novyi Arbat reinforced the sense of irreversible change in the Arbat. During the Stalin period, the Arbat had been spared the sweeping reconstruction projects that transformed the layout of Gorky (Tverskaia) Street, Marx Avenue (Hunter's Row), and other places. Consequently, a map of the Arbat in 1917 largely resembled a map of the Arbat in 1960. Spatial continuity made it easy for residents to believe that they were walking in the footsteps of earlier generations of writers and artists; in a literal sense, they were. This is what the essayist Oleg Volkov had in mind when he lamented the Arbat's imperiled architecture and streetscape in 1968: "The quiet residence on the Arbat lane whispers, '[the writer Nikolai] Gogol's penetrating gaze once lay upon me.'"[1] Novyi Arbat, however, necessitated the destruction of huge swaths of the neighborhood. It isolated the areas near Malaia and Bol'shaia Molchanovka Streets and Vorovskii (Povarskaia) Street, essential parts of *priarbat'e*, from the heart of the neighborhood. And on a scale that was unprecedented in post-Stalinist Moscow, it introduced into the Arbat a type of architecture that many persons thought inappropriate, foreign, and destructive to what made the neighborhood unique. From the safe vantage point of the 1990s, Okudzhava penned a sarcastic ditty for the architects who were the Arbat's "destroyers": "Let the Arbat look foreign," he sang, "so we can win an award."[2]

Yet there was more to the Novyi Arbat project than the construction of skyscrapers of questionable taste in the middle of a nineteenth-century neighborhood. This and the following chapter show how Novyi Arbat and the buildings that were demolished to accommodate it became contested "sites of memory," where different people discerned different and often contradictory understandings of the past. This chapter begins with the historical meanings ascribed to the towers themselves, whose designs generated a great deal of enthusiasm at the Moscow Section of the Union of Architects (MOSA). Like the actors at the Vakhtangov Theater who tried to recover the cultural dynamism of the 1920s by restaging *Princess Turandot*, architects and architectural historians at MOSA saw in the modern shapes of Novyi Arbat a chance to rehabilitate the constructivist architecture of the early-Soviet period. The obstacles they faced were formidable. During the 1920s, constructivist theorists like Moisei Ginzburg argued that the clean lines and conspicuous lack of ornamentation in their buildings revealed the social meaning and transformative power of socialist architecture. Their imaginative designs

1. Oleg Volkov, *Vse v otvete: publitsistika* (Moscow, 1986), 420.
2. Bulat Okudzhava, "Pesenka razrushitelei Arbata," in *Arbatskii arkhiv*, vyp. 1, ed. S. O. Shmidt (Moscow, 1997), 134.

and lively theoretical debates came to an end in 1931, however, when Lazar Kaganovich, then head of the Moscow Party Committee, denounced constructivism as formalist nonsense. The most accomplished architect of the early-Soviet period, Konstantin Melnikov, was forced into early retirement. His famous double-cylinder residence on Krivoarbatskii Lane, a block south of the Arbat, became a monument to the unrealized potential of the avant-garde.[3] Many constructivist architects of lesser stature were forced to take up work in the neoclassical and gothic aesthetics of Stalinism to avoid professional banishment, official harassment, and arrest.[4]

During the early 1960s, nonetheless, MOSA architects managed to rescue constructivism from the trash heap of Stalinism. Their collective memories of the constructivist past were mediated by the Cold War rivalry and Khrushchev's new party program, which was approved at the Twenty-second Party Congress in 1961. They underscored the egalitarian spirit and the worldwide acclaim that constructivism enjoyed in the 1920s. They saw their own tasks as similar to those of the early-Soviet avant-garde. And they took advantage of the unique position of architecture in the culture and politics of the thaw to wage a campaign for rehabilitation. Even though the standards that governed literature, music, and the arts loosened significantly in the 1950s and '60s, the party never challenged the validity of socialist realism. Consequently, many of the most important cultural products of the thaw came to light precisely because their proponents framed them as important contributions to the socialist-realist canon. For example, Aleksandr Tvardovskii, the editor of the journal *Novyi mir* (New World), claimed that Aleksandr Solzhenitsyn's landmark novella about the gulag, *One Day in the Life of Ivan Denisovich*, confirmed "the unchanging meaning of the tradition of truth in art" and countered "false innovationism of the formalist, modernist sort."[5] The same could have been said about any socialist-realist classic.

3. Vladimir Rezvin, "Chto budet s domom Mel'nikova?" *Arkhitektura i stroitel'stvo Moskvy* 10 (October 1998): 24–25; and Iu. Nikitin, "Konflikt v Krivoarbatskom," *Arkhitektura i stroitel'stvo Moskvy* 4 (April 1989): 30.
4. On constructivist architecture in the 1920s and '30s, see Hugh D. Hudson, *Blueprints and Blood: The Stalinization of Soviet Architecture, 1917–1937* (Princeton, N.J., 1994); idem, "'The Social Condenser of Our Epoch': The Association of Contemporary Architects and the Creation of a New Way of Life in Revolutionary Russia," *Jahrbücher für Geschichte Osteuropas* 34, no. 4 (1986): 557–78; and S. Frederick Starr, *Konstantin Melnikov: Solo Architect in Mass Society* (Princeton, N.J., 1977).
5. "'Literatura sotsialisticheskogo realizma vsegda shla ruka ob ruku s revoliutsii.' Interv'iu glavnogo redaktora *Novyi mir* A. T. Tvardovskogo korrespondentu iunited press interneishnl G. Shapiro," *Pravda*, May 12, 1963, 4, quoted in "Tvardovsky Reappears," in *Khrushchev and the Arts: The Politics of Soviet Culture, 1962–1964*, ed. Priscilla Johnson and Leopold Labedz (Cambridge, Mass., 1965), 212.

6. The rear (northern) side of Konstantin Melnikov's double-cylinder residence on
Krivoarbatskii Lane. Photograph by Andrey Shlyakhter.

Yet in architecture, the elaborate neoclassical and wedding-cake structures of Stalinism disappeared completely from drafting tables after 1953, as Khrushchev demanded cheaper construction from prefabricated concrete panels to alleviate housing shortages. Khrushchev was a kind of architect manqué, familiar with the latest construction technology and confident in the merits of the austere, modernist buildings he endorsed. During the 1950s and '60s, he intervened repeatedly in architectural affairs to revise blueprints and discipline architects who did not cut costs. Contrary to the proponents of constructivism at MOSA, he was not motivated by aesthetic concerns or abstruse theoretical debates about the power of architecture to reshape human consciousness. Instead, he emphasized the practicality of the new designs. The mass housing campaign that he oversaw improved the living conditions of millions of Soviet citizens. The total amount of housing built annually in Soviet cities jumped from 20.7 million square meters in 1950 to 57.5 million square meters in 1964. In Moscow, where the increase was even more dramatic, the per capita living-space allotment reached 8.2 square meters in 1966, exactly double what it had been twenty-six years earlier when the city's population was only two-thirds as large.[6]

Moscow's Architectural-Planning Administration (Main Architectural-Planning Administration after 1960) was one of the prime beneficiaries of these new priorities. Through much of the Khrushchev and Brezhnev periods, the administration was the domain of Mikhail Posokhin, one of the most accomplished architects of the late-Soviet period. Born in the Siberian city of Tomsk in 1910, Posokhin moved to Moscow at the height of Stalin's construction boom in the mid-1930s to work with Aleksei Shchusev, a former constructivist who had reinvented himself as a neoclassicist under Stalin. Posokhin's early structures, like the Moscow City Council (Mossovet) building, were archetypically Stalinist in their borrowing of classical elements. After 1953, however, Posokhin limited his historical and sentimental flourishes to the pastorals he painted for pleasure and dedicated himself to the modern forms that Khrushchev and Brezhnev preferred. Among the many high-profile buildings he saw to completion were the Olympic Sports Complex on the north side of Moscow, the Soviet embassy in Washington, D.C., the Ministry of Defense on Arbat Square, and the resort at Pitsunda on the Black Sea.

6. Timothy J. Colton, *Moscow: Governing the Socialist Metropolis* (Cambridge, Mass., 1995), 758, 796–97; and Gregory D. Andrusz, *Housing and Urban Development in the USSR* (Albany, N.Y., 1985), 21. The population of Moscow in 1965 was about 6.5 million people.

Posokhin's success during these years was the product of both luck (he experimented, apparently on a lark, in construction from prefabricated components prior to 1953), and his skill in navigating the architectural politics of the era. In 1960, he became Moscow's chief architect, and, in 1963, he was appointed chairman of the State Committee on Architectural Affairs, the highest architectural posting outside the Union of Architects, and one that eventually gained ministerial status. In 1962, on Khrushchev's insistence, Posokhin was awarded the Lenin Prize, the Soviet Union's highest honor, for his most famous and controversial structure, the Palace of Congresses in the Kremlin.[7]

Posokhin was also the lead architect for Novyi Arbat, the largest project undertaken in Moscow's crowded center after 1953. From the outset, Posokhin billed Novyi Arbat as a new type of project. It was proof that the Soviet Union had committed itself to an ambitious urban-planning agenda, and that it could build retail and office complexes every bit as magnificent as the Manhattan skyscrapers. Posokhin saw himself as a Soviet Robert Moses, the master builder of mid-century New York, curing urban social ills, like unsanitary living conditions, by replacing the cramped and chaotic alleys of old Arbat with wide streets and gleaming towers.[8] As one of his coauthors claimed, Novyi Arbat was only "a fragment of the new center."[9] But Novyi Arbat meant different things to different people. Similar to Vienna's Ringstrasse in the 1860s, that "iconographic index to the mind of ascendant Austrian liberalism," Novyi Arbat was the focal point for a great deal of "cultural self-projection."[10] While Posokhin emphasized the coherence of a planned city, many of his MOSA colleagues highlighted the similarities between the buildings lining the street and early-Soviet constructivism. Like their forefathers in the 1920s, Posokhin and his team designed buildings to reshape consciousness and alter the patterns of everyday life. Like their forefathers, they thought that excessive decoration obscured the political meaning and the transformative power of architecture. If Novyi Arbat was good architecture, could constructivism really be bad?

7. For additional biographical information, see N. A. Pekareva, *M. V. Posokhin: narodnyi arkhitektor SSSR* (Moscow, 1985); and M. V. Posokhin, *Dorogi zhizni: iz zapisok arkhitektora*, ed. M. M. Posokhin (Moscow, 1995).

8. On Moscow's catastrophic postwar living conditions, see Donald Filtzer, "Standard of Living versus Quality of Life: Struggling with the Urban Environment in Russia during the Early Years of Post-war Reconstruction," in *Late Stalinist Russia: Society between Reconstruction and Reinvention*, ed. Juliane Fürst (London, 2006), 81–102.

9. RGALI, f. 2466, o. 4, d. 110, l. 12.

10. Carl E. Schorske, *Fin-de-Siècle Vienna: Politics and Culture* (New York, 1981), 26–27.

Posokhin was undoubtedly surprised by the significance his fellow architects attributed to Novyi Arbat. Few could have anticipated that Khrushchev's denunciation of Stalinist architecture would kindle talk of rehabilitating constructivism. Even fewer were willing to act on that talk without a clear signal from above. Posokhin's response, and indeed that of most officials, was calculated silence. But it was not illogical that architects turned to the pre-Stalin period after so much of what followed had been discredited. As teachers at the Gnesin Institute and actors the Vakhtangov Theater were well aware, similar processes of re-imagining the past and remembering Stalin's victims were underway in other fields as well. MOSA architects argued that present-day realities had absolved constructivists of their alleged sins, and that contemporary Soviet architecture had become constructivist in essence, if not in name. Like good Marxists, they argued in public that the muse of history, Clio, was an unbiased judge of constructivism. They may have admitted in private, however, that she was a frustratingly slow deliberator.

ARCHITECTURAL CRISIS

Even though the construction of Novyi Arbat did not begin until the early 1960s, its roots were in the Stalin period. A new radial street west of the Kremlin was first envisioned in the 1935 master plan for the reconstruction of Moscow as a way to alleviate traffic congestion. Its construction was delayed first by war and then by reconstruction priorities elsewhere. Similarly, the buildings that lined Novyi Arbat originated in postwar efforts to maximize scarce resources though architectural design.[11] Nearly every bureaucracy and enterprise in Moscow controlled some segment of the city's housing stock, typically so managers could provide employees with housing. In order to reduce labor turnover, many managers pressed for greater investment in "mass housing," a catchphrase that included everything from dormitories to modest single-family apartments. In 1947, four architects at the Institute of Construction Techniques, an affiliate of the Academy of Architecture, responded to calls for cheaper housing by constructing a four-story

11. On the debate over the proper use of scarce construction resources, see E. Taranov, "Gorod kommunizma (idei liderov 50–60-kh godov i ikh voploshchenie)," in *Moskovskii arkhiv: istoriko-kraevedcheskii al'manakh*, vyp. 1, ed. E. I. Kavtaradze, V. F. Kozlov, T. N. Nikol'skaia, A. N. Shakhanov, and I. F. Iushin (Moscow, 1996), 372–74; and V. Iu. Afiani, "Ob izmenenii Genplana rekonstruktsii Moskvy. Zapiska MK KPSS i ispolkoma Mossoveta G. M. Malenkovu i N. S. Khrushchevu. 1953 g.," *Istoricheskii arkhiv* 5–6 (1997): 51–52.

residential building on Moscow's Sokolin Hill from prefabricated, reinforced concrete rather than traditional masonry. The building was an early example of what would become known as "large-panel" or "frame-panel" construction. During the following year, Mikhail Posokhin and his longtime collaborator, Ashot Mndoiants, designed a residential complex on Khoroshevskoe Highway for large-panel construction. These early buildings only vaguely resembled the mass housing of the Khrushchev era. Consistent with late-Stalinist architecture, their facades were ornate and apartment sizes large. Nonetheless, they marked the first significant attempt to cut residential construction costs since architects began work with "large-block" masonry a decade earlier.[12]

These attempts to reduce construction costs through architectural design failed to garner much political support during the late 1940s and early '50s. By arguing cost constraints, Aleksei Kosygin, then a deputy chairman of the Council of Ministers, and from 1948–52, a member of the Central Committee Presidium, managed to delay construction of the Palace of Soviets, a colossal white elephant that was planned for the site of the former Cathedral of Christ the Savior. (Blueprints foresaw a structure taller than the Empire State Building.) Yet Kosygin's success was a rare example of prudence in the postwar years. When officials in the Ministry of Finance tried to shave four million rubles off the budget for a lesser building in 1949, Stalin demanded that the funds be reinstated. It was unforgivable, he asserted, to "build in Moscow senseless, cheap things . . . the point is not four million, which someone has decided to save, but that we build a genuine monument of the epoch, so that future generations will feel in every home and every built structure the spirit of the epoch of communism."[13] Stalin also ordered architects to design only apartment buildings "worthy of Muscovites," a statement that was used to justify even the most egregious largesse. Posokhin abandoned his experiments in frame-panel construction to design the wedding-cake skyscraper on Vosstanie Square and a number of other ornate Stalinist buildings. Aleksandr Vlasov, Moscow's chief architect, explicitly rejected calls from fellow architects for less expensive, standardized construction. He cited Stalin's "special directive about the unacceptability" of such buildings.[14]

12. Pekareva, *M. V. Posokhin,* 43–44; and Andrew Elam Day, "Building Socialism: The Politics of the Soviet Cityscape in the Stalin Era," (Ph.D. diss., Columbia University, 1998), chap. 5.
13. TsAODM, f. 88, o. 21, d. 15, l. 113, quoted in Taranov, "Gorod kommunizma," 372–73.
14. Quoted in Taranov, "Gorod kommunizma," 374.

Khrushchev was more enthusiastic about the possibilities of large-panel construction. Critics often ridiculed his obsession with architectural and construction minutiae, but his interest was genuine. According to his memoir, it reflected his sense that Soviet workers suffered even worse housing conditions than their tsarist predecessors.

I got married in 1914, when I was twenty years old. Because I had a highly skilled job, I got an apartment right away. The apartment had a sitting room, kitchen, bedroom, and dining room. Years later, after the Revolution, it was painful for me to remember that as a worker under capitalism I'd had much better living conditions than my fellow workers now living under Soviet power.[15]

As party chief for Moscow's Krasnopresn'ia and Bauman districts and the city as a whole in the 1930s, Khrushchev participated in and oversaw a number of large-scale construction projects—the underground metro, Gorky Street, and the Moscow-Volga Canal, among others. Khrushchev was also on friendly terms with many of the most prominent architects of the era, in part because so many of them were involved in the postwar reconstruction of his own bailiwick, Kiev. After Khrushchev returned from Kiev in 1949 to succeed Georgii Popov as Moscow party chief, he criticized Vladimir Promyslov, a civil engineer who oversaw construction for the Moscow Party Committee, for ignoring the housing needs of ordinary Muscovites. He secured Stalin's approval for the construction of two factories that would produce reinforced concrete panels for construction, despite opposition from the State Construction Committee. And he managed to safeguard his sponsorship of prefabricated construction from skeptical Kremlin rivals like Beria and Kaganovich.[16] Very few of Khrushchev's plans were realized during the last years of Stalin's life, but he laid the foundation for a new approach to housing and architecture. When Stalin died, the changeover was swift.

During the spring and summer of 1953, astute observers of Soviet architecture understood that change was afoot. Speaking to residents of Moscow's Kalinin district, Khrushchev promised that the age of the

---

15. N. S. Khrushchev, *Khrushchev Remembers: The Last Testament*, trans. and ed. Strobe Talbott (Boston, 1974), 87.
16. Ibid., 93–98; William Taubman, *Khrushchev: The Man and His Era* (New York, 2003), 89–97, 226–27; and William K. Wolf, "Russia's Revolutionary Underground: The Construction of the Moscow Subway, 1931–1935," (Ph.D. diss., The Ohio State University, 1994).

interminably long housing queue would soon end. He later pledged an apartment to every family with a residential permit, regardless of work tenure. To accommodate these new commitments, economists raised budget allocations and construction targets, and architects reduced apartment sizes. During the summer of 1953, frame-panel construction projects were approved for the Izmailovo, Sokol'niki, and Ostankino regions of Moscow. One of the city's construction trusts increased production so that it could complete a new and soon to be ubiquitous 2,200 square-meter, five-story apartment building every thirty days.[17] In September, the leaders of Mossovet and the Moscow Party Committee jointly petitioned Malenkov and Khrushchev to revise the specifics of the 1952 master plan for the reconstruction of Moscow. They were keen to see more money funneled toward "mass housing projects" in the city's peripheral areas where construction costs were low. They also asked that building heights and designs be standardized, so an economy of scale might be achieved among construction agencies.[18]

Architects initially responded to these changes with confusion and skepticism. In the summer of 1953, in the aftermath of the semiannual conference of the Moscow Section of the Union of Architects, the secretary of the Union, Sergei Chernyshev, asked Khrushchev to clarify the party's position on architecture. Chernyshev complained that the conference proceedings had been marred by the speech of an obscure architect named K. Ivanov, who purportedly described the wedding-cake skyscraper on the Kotel'nicheskaia Embankment as a "monster with bumps like those on a bed." Ivanov also claimed that Soviet architecture was divided between "geniuses with the exclusive right to attack all places" and the "gray masses" who were kept silent. Ivanov's unexpected attack was made all the more bewildering by the party representative at the conference, who claimed that Aleksander Vlasov, Moscow's chief architect, showed an "incorrect attitude toward criticism." The party representative even recommended that MOSA members formally censure the work of their superiors for trying to stifle dissent. According to Chernyshev, the whole episode had "disoriented" architects at the conference, who had not expected any substantive debate, much less one that challenged a long-held orthodoxy. Chernyshev also feared that it complicated the "battle against the remnants of condemned architectural trends," especially constructivism.[19]

17. Taranov, "Gorod kommunizma," 375–77.
18. Afiani, "Ob izmenenii Genplana," 53–54.
19. RGANI, f. 5, o. 30, d. 40, ll. 64–65, 67.

After a five-month investigation, Moscow party officials apologized to Chernyshev for appearing to sanction an insurrection at MOSA. But they also affirmed that their representative at the conference had acted within his official capacities when he criticized Vlasov. They took no position on the substance of Ivanov's complaint, probably because Khrushchev felt similarly. In the aftermath of the conference, municipal officials took steps to dispel the confusion that was clearly mounting among architects. In February 1954, Mossovet issued an ambitious plan for standard-design construction from prefabricated parts (*tipovoe proektirovanie*) for the new construction season. The plan, which appears to have been the first of its kind in the capital, required architects to draft uniform designs for residential buildings, hospitals, maternity clinics, and other structures.[20] It was the first attempt to force *tipovoe proektirovanie* on a skeptical architectural profession. In May, city party leaders met with prominent architects to sell the line "supported by Khrushchev," and to emphasize that a mixed package of standard-design construction and individual planning was not an alternative. According to the historian E. Taranov, the meeting marked the final defeat of Stalinist planning in the capital. Despite scattered opposition from a handful of architects who hoped to preserve the 1952 master plan, Mossovet began to funnel "all resources" toward the construction of standard-design, concrete-panel buildings.[21]

Khrushchev used the All-Union Convention of Construction Workers in December 1954 to seal his victory and to apply Moscow's new construction standards to the rest of the Soviet Union. In his massive keynote address, Khrushchev pinned blame for Moscow's housing crisis on architects who cared "to build only buildings of an individual character . . . monuments to themselves." He singled out Arkadii Mordvinov, the president of the Academy of Architecture and the primary author of the Hotel Ukraine skyscraper, as one of the chief purveyors of Stalinist extravagance. Mordvinov and his colleagues "have forgotten about the most important issue—about the cost per square meter of space—they have become carried away with the unnecessary decoration of the facade, and allowed many excesses." Grigorii Zakharov, one of the designers of the ornate Kurskaia metro station, also fared poorly. Khrushchev claimed that Zakharov cared more about "pretty silhouettes" than

20. "O plane tipovogo proektirovaniia na 1954 god," *Biulleten' ispolkoma Moskovskogo gorodskogo soveta* [hereafter BIM] 4, 298 (February 1954): 13–15.
21. Taranov, "Gorod kommunizma," 377–78.

the apartments desperately needed by the residents of the capital.[22] Khrushchev also addressed the issue that Chernyshev had raised in his letter a year and a half earlier. He noted that some architects were trying to justify the extravagance of their designs by referring to the battle against constructivism. "What is constructivism?" Khrushchev asked from the podium.

In part, this is how the *Great Soviet Encyclopedia* defines this trend: "Constructivism . . . subordinates the artistic work to the 'appearance of construction' (from this comes the name constructivism), and to naked *tekhnologizm*. Answering the demands of functionality, of construction 'expediency' and 'rationality,' constructivists prefer in practice the aesthetics of form in isolation from content. A consequence of this is the anti-artistic, cheerless 'box style' that is characteristic of recent bourgeois architecture."[23]

Khrushchev warned architects that austere facades and sparsely decorated interiors were not, by themselves, indicative of constructivism. He disingenuously asserted that architects who thought otherwise were themselves guilty of constructivism, since they were emphasizing extravagant décor (form) rather than sufficient living space (content).

In the months following the convention, standard design construction from prefabricated parts—*tipovoe proektirovanie*—became the official architectural dogma of the Soviet Union. According to figures compiled by the RSFSR Construction Bank, more than 80 percent of all housing built in the RSFSR in 1959 was *tipovoe proektirovanie* (for a total of 15.5 million square meters of living space), up from less than 1 percent in 1951, and 3 percent in 1953.[24] Vladimir Promyslov, whom Khrushchev had attacked after returning from Kiev, was given the odious task of

22. The full title of this gathering was the All-Union Convention of Construction Workers, Architects, and Employees of Construction-Material, Road-Construction, and Machine-Construction Industries, and of Design and Scientific-Research Organizations. For a synopsis, see Colton, *Moscow*, 370–71.

23. N. S. Khrushchev, "O shirokom vnedrenii industrial'nykh metodov, uluchenii kachestva i snizhenii stoimosti stroitel'stva," *Pravda*, December 28, 1954, 4. The definition that Khrushchev cited is from vol. 22 of the *Great Soviet Encyclopedia* (1953).

24. Tsentral'nyi munitsipal'nyi arkhiv Moskvy [hereafter TsMAM], f. 534, o. 1, d. 424, l. 189. For a more detailed analysis of the shift to prefabricated construction, see Blair A. Ruble, "From *khrushcheby* to *korobki*," in *Russian Housing in the Modern Age: Design and Social History*, ed. William Craft Brumfield and Blair A. Ruble (Cambridge, 1993), 235–44.

supervising the implementation of *tipovoe proektirovanie* as chief of Glavmosstroi, the newly consolidated Main Administration for Residential and Civil Construction in Moscow.[25] The Central Committee lent an official patina to the whole affair in November 1955, when it too denounced the architectural "excess" of the Stalin period, and endorsed the reforms proposed by Khrushchev.[26]

Mikhail Posokhin remembered these years in an uncritical light. *Tipovoe proektirovanie*, he wrote in his memoir, was "the single possible alternative in the existing circumstances."[27] Yet many others questioned the headlong rush toward standard design. The new construction was unappealing at best, and efforts to cut costs often verged on the comical. Bathroom tiles were glued to building facades to make them waterproof. Less expensive wooden toilet seats replaced their plastic counterparts. Hotels were outfitted with bunk beds to increase their capacity. And building heights were limited to five stories so the elevators and trash chutes legally mandated in taller structures could be eliminated.[28]

Khrushchev was the first to admit that *tipovoe proektirovanie* limited the "flexibility" of architects, who naturally wanted "every building to have a distinctive appearance."[29] But he was determined to quell resistance. At Moscow's Architectural-Planning Administration, he pushed aside his onetime ally, Aleksandr Vlasov, as well as Zakharov, Chernyshev, Boris Iofan, Leonid Poliakov, and Dmitrii Chechulin, all prominent architects, in favor of a new leadership more sympathetic to *tipovoe proektirovanie*.[30] For Vlasov and Chechulin, the demotion was hardly catastrophic. Vlasov continued to enjoy a comfortable retainer in the Union of Architects administration. Chechulin saw two of his most famous designs—the Rossiia Hotel, supposedly the largest in Europe, and the White House, the seat of the RSFSR government—to completion during the coming decades. But for the others, the change in leadership spelled the effective ends of their creative careers, as they were pushed into obscure back-office positions to draft the technical documentation for more favored architects.

25. V. F. Promyslov, "Za vnedrenie tipovykh proektov, likvidatsiiu izlishestv, snizhenie stoimosti stroitel'stva," *Gorodskoe khoziaistvo Moskvy* 2 (February 1955): 1–5.
26. *Kommunisticheskaia partiia Sovetskogo Soiuza v rezoliutsiiakh i resheniiakh s'ezdov, konferentsii i plenumov TsK*, vol. 8 (Moscow, 1986), 532–36.
27. Posokhin, *Dorogi zhizni*, 57.
28. TsMAM, f. 150, o. 1, d. 2067, ll. 217–18; and Colton, *Moscow*, 371–72.
29. Khrushchev, *The Last Testament*, 98.
30. Pekareva, *Posokhin*, 44–50; and Colton, *Moscow*, 370–71.

Those who benefited from the change, like Iosif Loveiko, Moscow's new chief architect, and Posokhin, one his deputies, were quick to adapt to the new construction priorities. One of Loveiko's first acts was to slice 230 million rubles from the cost estimates for 800 residential and civil construction projects. Even buildings close to completion were altered to lower costs. Posokhin, who was also one of the principal architects at Mosproekt, one of two design studios subordinate to the Architectural-Planning Administration, immersed himself once again in design work for several large-panel residential buildings.[31] Yet the nature of Loveiko and Posokhin's victory was uncertain, if only because the prerogatives of the organization they inherited were no longer absolute, and architecture itself was in flux. A Mossovet decree in 1951 made the Architectural-Planning Administration the chief guarantor of architectural and construction quality in Moscow. In theory, its Architectural-Construction Control Inspectorate oversaw all residential and civil construction projects in Moscow with budgets of more than 300,000 rubles. It could fine or file criminal charges against construction agencies and clients that ran projects of poor quality, or projects that violated the "rules and norms of construction."[32] Similarly, the administration's Architectural-Construction Council (later called the Urban-Planning Council) was supposed to review the aesthetic merits of all projects before the beginning of construction. The council could pass projects on to higher authorities for final approval, or order architects to revise and resubmit.[33]

In reality, however, the administration's prerogatives fell victim to the privileging of construction targets. In the fall of 1954, Mossovet petitioned the Council of Ministers for permission to make the Architectural-Planning Administration subordinate to Glavmosstroi, the capital's chief construction agency. Fearing that "the transfer to Glavmosstroi of functions foreign to it" would violate their traditional watchdog functions, several of the administration's architects managed to halt the reshuffling.[34] But in a climate where any overt opposition to the accelerated

31. Colton, *Moscow*, 370–71.
32. "Polozhenie ob Inspektsii gosudarstvennogo arkhitekturno-stroitel'nogo kontrol'ia Arkhitekturno-planirovochnogo upravleniia gor. Moskvy," *BIM* 2, 272 (January 1953): 10–12; and William Taubman, *Governing Soviet Cities: Bureaucratic Politics and Urban Development in the USSR* (New York, 1973), 104–7.
33. See, for instance, the discussions about the construction of a ministerial office building on Smolensk Square in 1946. TsMAM, f. 534, o. 1, d. 86, ll. 25–250b; and d. 89, ll. 157–63.
34. TsMAM, f. 496, o. 1, d. 221, l. 28; and RGANI, f. 5, o. 30, d. 85, ll. 27, 30–33.

construction tempos was professionally risky, it was impossible to thwart entirely the erosion of the architects' influence. By the late 1950s, the Architectural-Construction Council summarily waved thousands of standard design projects through for final approval at the Mossovet Executive Committee. Even high profile projects merited only perfunctory discussions. This was in stark contrast to the activities of the council of a decade earlier, when discussions tended to be long and technical, and blueprints were frequently rejected for minor reasons.[35] The Architectural-Construction Control Inspectorate was similarly emasculated; it had simply become impolitic for it to fine or file criminal charges against construction agencies that sanctioned poor work.[36] The implications were clear. Under Stalin, architecture had been one of the most celebrated fields of artistic endeavor. Under Khrushchev, it had become the unfortunate handmaiden to the construction industry.[37]

In the mid-1950s, however, a number of outside observers began to question the Architectural-Planning Administration's complicity in uninspiring design. In a letter to Khrushchev in June 1957, Aleksandr Vlasov—understandably a critic of *tipovoe proektirovanie*, given that he had been fired two years earlier—argued that the struggle against architectural "excess" had become little more than a justification for shoddy construction techniques. He advocated a policy of "author surveillance" that would allow individual architects to monitor the quality of their own projects.[38] Additional criticism came from the ranks of the Moscow Section of the Union of Architects. As early as 1954, MOSA members censured the Architectural-Planning Administration for its careless attitude toward quality. "I do not understand how it is possible to build this project," said one critic, referring to a project on the Garden Circle, but speaking also about the broader changes in Soviet architecture. "What was the council thinking about when it gave its approval? . . . What are we doing? There is an Academy [of Architecture], an Architectural

---

35. See, for instance, the lengthy discussions in the council in 1946 on the construction of a residential building on Tchaikovsky Street (part of the Garden Circle). TsMAM, f. 534, o. 1, d. 89, ll. 177–79, 279–80, 343–54.

36. RGANI, f. 5, o. 30, d. 19, l. 29; and RGALI, f. 674, o. 3, d. 1838, ll. 34–35.

37. This development was also evident in a variety of bureaucratic reshufflings at high levels in the party and state that subordinated architectural officials to their construction counterparts. See RGANI, f. 5, o. 30, d. 40, ll. 11, 29–30.

38. RGANI, f. 5, o. 30, d. 215, ll. 115–16. On architects' unhappiness with prefabricated construction, see Ruble, "From *khrushcheby* to *korobki*," 254–56.

[-Construction] Council, a Union . . . and they don't even bother to review what they're building."[39]

Critics also condemned the mind-numbing monotony of new construction, as thousands of identical, five-story apartment buildings appeared in Moscow's peripheral areas.[40] At the Eighth Conference of Moscow Architects in May 1961, Vitalii Lagutenko, an architect who had previously collaborated with Posokhin on the Khoroshevskoe Highway experiment in prefabricated construction, and who had trained with Shchusev, bluntly asserted that *tipovoe proektirovanie* was an aesthetic failure: "At the present time, this is not what we are waiting for. We are waiting for something better than this."[41]

Novyi Arbat proved to be the solution to the uniformity and poor quality that plagued Soviet architecture during the late 1950s, the "something better" that Lagutenko craved. The skyscrapers that were designed for the street were among the first examples of a new design and construction method called *tipizatsiia*. Like a child's Lego set, *tipizatsiia* allowed architects to achieve genuine diversity of form, but it did not violate Khrushchev's stipulation that the construction components be prefabricated. Instead of reproducing a single design thousands of times over, architects worked with prefabricated concrete panels to create unique structures. For Posokhin and other officials at the Architectural-Planning Administration, Novyi Arbat vindicated their decade-long struggle to create an architectural style that was suitable for the post-Stalin period. For many others, it promised something even greater.

Novyi Arbat and the "New Life"

When architects began to work in earnest on Novyi Arbat in 1959, they envisioned only a connector street, less than nine meters wide, between Serebrianyi Lane and Bol'shaia Molchanovka Street. Its total cost would be less than 220,000 rubles.[42] By the mid-1960s, Novyi Arbat had become the largest undertaking in Moscow in the post-Stalin period. It consisted

39. RGALI, f. 2466, o. 1, d. 366, l. 28.
40. A. Korobov, P. Reviakin, V. Tydman, and N. Chetunova, "Kak dal'she stroit' Moskvu," *Moskva* 3 (March 1962): 151–52.
41. RGALI, f. 2466, o. 2, d. 80, ll. 3–4.
42. TsMAM, f. 655, o. 1. d. 113, ll. 1–8, and first two unnumbered pages after l. 99.

of four separate projects: the street, the Council of Economic Cooperation (Comecon) building at the entrance to the street along the river, the skyscrapers that resembled open books on the south side of the street, and the residential towers and October Theater on the north side. Together, they were a powerful symbol of the renaissance in Soviet architecture after decades of Stalinist classicism and post-Stalinist austerity. They were also the focus of an unexpected campaign to rehabilitate constructivism.

Novyi Arbat was not always a high priority. The only extant copy of the 1959 plan lacks the signatures necessary to make it a decree, and the nine buildings scheduled for demolition that year were still standing three years later when Mossovet approved a proposal for a larger thoroughfare. This second plan foresaw the demolition of more than a hundred buildings within a corridor forty-six meters wide, and the resettlement of 3,147 people. The chairman of Mossovet gave Glavmosstroi the impossible task of having the street open for traffic in time for the forty-fifth anniversary of the October Revolution, November 7, 1962, the first of many missed deadlines.[43] Posokhin began design work on the residential and administrative complex planned for the north and south sides of the street during the summer of 1961, but was halted by an unexpected obstacle. Permission to work outside the strict cost restraints of *tipovoe proektirovanie* could only be granted by the RSFSR Council of Ministers, which was initially unconvinced of the necessity of the project.[44] In February 1962, the chief of Mosproekt asked Posokhin to stop all design work until the Council of Ministers could issue the appropriate decree, a delay that lasted more than a year. Work progressed in a more timely fashion on the Council of Economic Cooperation (Comecon) building near the river, which in view of the future tenant's international stature enjoyed the patronage of Dmitrii Ustinov, a deputy chairman of the Council of Ministers. Yet the rest of the project continued to stagnate. In May 1963, the Mossovet Executive Committee ordered that the street be open for traffic by October 1, 1963, almost a year later than the initial deadline. It refused to set a deadline for the residential and administrative complex, acknowledging instead that it was a three- or four-year project.[45]

43. TsMAM, f. 534, o. 1, d. 474, l. 175; and f. 150, o. 1, d. 2773, ll. 423–35.
44. TsMAM, f. 534, o. 1, d. 478, l. 13; f. 655, o. 1, d. 132, l. 50; and f. 773, o. 1, d. 38, l. 6.
45. TsMAM, f. 534, o. 1, d. 478, l. 34; d. 479, l. 67; and f. 773, o. 1, d. 23, ll. 47–48.

Khrushchev finally dispelled the lethargy surrounding Novyi Arbat by visiting the worksite with Posokhin and several city officials in May 1963. Khrushchev had discussed Novyi Arbat with architects on one previous occasion, May 26, 1962, but offered little in the way of input.[46] He was less circumspect the second time. He ordered architects to incorporate a greater number of "hotel-type buildings" with small, single-family, furnished apartments. These buildings would be used as long-term residential hotels for persons who were not permanent residents of the capital, presumably party and governmental elites from the provinces.[47] During the following week, Posokhin's architects dutifully jettisoned much of the earlier design work to accommodate Khrushchev. On May 21, the Mossovet Presidium, a small group within the Executive Committee, drafted a new schedule of construction deadlines. Three days later, Posokhin presented sketches of the redesigned Novyi Arbat complex to the Mossovet Executive Committee. Plans for the south side of the street were largely unchanged—they comprised four residential skyscrapers that resembled open books, connected by a gallery of stores and restaurants. On the north side, Posokhin inserted five residential hotels alongside a previously planned movie theater and a low-rise office building. The dimensions of the newly proposed complex were immense. The width of the entire thoroughfare, street and sidewalks, was revised upwards to seventy-eight meters. Because of the slow pace of planning and construction, the Mossovet Executive Committee gave Posokhin 200,000 rubles to expedite the drafting of technical documentation. The Architectural-Planning Administration also reassigned fifty of its own architects to the project, causing one official to suggest that all other projects in the city be put on temporary hold.[48]

Khrushchev's interference in the Novyi Arbat planning underscored the growing importance of the project. Long regarded by city leaders as an unrealizable boondoggle, Novyi Arbat gained the support of the

46. Untitled announcement, *Stroitel'stvo i arkhitektura Moskvy* 6 (1962): 1. On Khrushchev's positive evaluation of another modernist project, the concrete and glass Palace of Pioneers, see "Vysokaia missiia iskusstva," *Izvestiia*, December 4, 1962, 1; and Priscilla Johnson, "The Politics of Soviet Culture, 1962–1964," in *Khrushchev and the Arts*, 7–9. The *Izvestiia* article appeared on the same day that the newspaper published an account of Khrushchev's denunciation of modern art at the Manège exhibit hall. See "Vozvyshat' cheloveka, zvat' na podvig," *Izvestiia*, December 4, 1962, 1.
47. "N. S. Khrushchev osmotrel raiony novogo stroitel'stva i rekonstruktsii Moskvy," *Stroitel'stvo i arkhitektura Moskvy* 6 (1963): 1.
48. TsMAM, f. 150, o. 1, d. 2891, l. 22; f. 655, o. 1, d. 148, ll. 76–78; f. 773, o. 1, d. 23, ll. 64–65, 75–76, 78–87; and TsAODM, f. 2890, o. 1, d. 3, ll. 74–75.

7. Nikita Khrushchev reviewing a mock-up of Novyi Arbat on May 26, 1962. To Khrushchev's left is Petr Demichev, chief of the Moscow Party Committee. Behind Khrushchev is Frol Kozlov, a member of the Central Committee Presidium. From *Arkhitektura i stroitel'stvo Moskvy*, no. 6 (1962).

party's first secretary in May 1963. In the official lingo of the Architectural-Planning Administration, it was "task no. 1." During the summer of 1963, Khrushchev once again met with Posokhin's design team to review progress and offer advice.[49] Other federal authorities followed his lead. The Ministry of Foreign Trade facilitated the import of electrical goods, elevators, plumbing supplies, air conditioners, and kitchen appliances. The State Aviation Committee signed off on the production of aluminum and laminate facade panels, which had to be specially manufactured in airplane factories. Federal involvement in labor issues,

49. "Vstrecha v Moskovskom sovete," *Stroitel'stvo i arkhitektura Moskvy* 8 (1963): 1.

procurement problems, and construction schedules was so common that city officials feared their own prerogatives were under fire.[50]

The federal role in Novyi Arbat was indicative of the heightened political significance of architecture in the early 1960s. The idea that architecture was simply an auxiliary to the construction industry, where cost per square meter of built space was the paramount indicator of success, began to fade in the early 1960s. Although opportunities were initially limited to a few high-profile projects, architects began to re-ascribe aesthetic value to their work and to grapple overtly with issues that were characteristic of the cultural front. This development stemmed from the crisis caused by *tipovoe proektirovanie* in the late 1950s, and to two events that were peculiar to the late-Khrushchev period: rising Cold War tensions and the new party program.

In the fall of 1960, Khrushchev spent nearly a month in New York working with the Soviet delegation to the United Nations. Unlike his first trip to the United States twelve months earlier, which came at a relatively peaceful moment in superpower relations, Khrushchev's second trip was marred by the shooting down of Gary Powers' U2 spy plane near Sverdlovsk on May 1, and the cancellation of a summit meeting in Paris with Dwight Eisenhower scheduled for two weeks later. On September 30, Khrushchev famously showed his disgruntlement by banging his shoe on a desk at the United Nations to protest the speech of a Western delegate. During the usual fanfare following his return to Moscow on October 14, Khrushchev transposed these Cold War rivalries onto Moscow's landscape. He praised the quality of life in Moscow and indicated that the city now compared favorably with those in the United States.[51] Before the end of the year, Khrushchev's comments had served as a pretext for the expansion of Moscow's municipal boundaries.[52] In the spring of 1961, they elicited a debate over the differences between Soviet and Western architecture at the Moscow Section of the Union of Architects. For many architects, Khrushchev's observations underscored the central dilemma in the relationship between Soviet and Western architecture. Given the fact that perceptions of modernity and technological progress were constantly associated with the West—so much, in fact, that the West served as a yardstick for Soviet development—how were Soviet

50. Rossiiskii gosudarstvennyi arkhiv ekonomiki [hereafter RGAE], f. 5, o. 1, d. 73, ll. 5, 8, 53–54; TsMAM, f. 534, o. 1, d. 554, l. 132; f. 773, o. 1, d. 23, ll. 47–48; and d. 38, ll. 6–8, 96–97.
51. TsAODM, f. 1249, o. 1, d. 30, l. 9.
52. RGALI, f. 2466, o. 2, d. 67, ll. 6–49; and Colton, *Moscow*, 475–80.

architects to distinguish their work qualitatively? To put it another way, what characteristics made Soviet architecture "Soviet"?

In May 1961, the Eighth Conference of Moscow Architects convened to discuss the issues provoked by Khrushchev's comments. Posokhin, one of the keynote speakers, maintained that the fundamental characteristic of Soviet architecture was a state monopoly on development. He contrasted the experience of Moscow with three Western cities in "critical condition." Los Angeles was an "unlimited plane" of decentralized construction. In Paris, entrenched property rights made it impossible for successors to Baron Georges-Eugène Haussmann, Napoleon III's visionary urban planner, from building anything more ambitious than small apartment and office buildings in the city's densely settled center. London suffered from conflicts with suburban municipalities that prevented the development of "satellite cities."[53] Significantly, the distinction that Posokhin offered hinged only on the planning process and not on any peculiarities manifested in built structures. A subsequent speaker said much the same, namely, that Moscow was an "all-union laboratory for advanced experiments." Its experience was thus "worthy of recognition as an international urban-planning method."[54]

A handful of architects tried to identify more essential distinctions between Soviet and Western architecture. One MOSA official dismissed Western architecture as a "commodity" that had to be "fashionable."[55] Others poked fun at the "American way of life" and the way it affected urban development. "There exists a peculiar understanding about travel by automobile," one MOSA member remarked, "which is considered and advertised, like American Coca-Cola, as something that is impossible to do without."[56] The Central Committee meeting in June 1963 encouraged these more essential distinctions. Party leaders used the meeting to reinforce their campaign against the reform-minded intelligentsia and "bourgeois ideology" (a euphemism for Western culture) that had begun at the modern art exhibit at the Manège the previous December.[57] At a meeting of the Mosproekt-2 party organization during the following month, one architect urged his colleagues to put down their foreign journals, and to concentrate instead on designing structures

53. RGALI, f. 2466, o. 2, d. 80, ll. 11–12.
54. RGALI, f. 2466, o. 2, d. 81, l. 14.
55. RGALI, f. 2466, o. 2, d. 141, l. 23.
56. RGALI, f. 2466, o. 2, d. 67, l. 70.
57. *Kommunisticheskaia partiia Sovetskogo Soiuza v rezoliutsiiakh i resheniiakh s'ezdov, konferentsii i plenumov TsK*, vol. 10 (Moscow, 1986), 352–67.

that are "new and our own." Another architect demanded that Moscow architects destroy their "feckless attitude toward foreign models."[58] Later in 1963, city party leaders met with members of the Moscow Section of the Union of Architects to discuss "incidents of uncritical imitation, and the borrowing of fashionable methods of bourgeois architecture." In January 1964, much of the discussion at the Ninth Conference of Moscow Architects was devoted to similar issues.[59]

Soviet architects realized that the Cold War demanded they build differently than their Western counterparts, but few knew how to do so. The answer to their dilemma came in Khrushchev's new party program. Party leaders released the program in draft form in July 1961 to gauge its public reception. Delegates to the Twenty-second Party Congress confirmed it in October. Like its 1919 predecessor, which Lenin authored, Khrushchev personally presided over the three-year codification process. The program boldly asserted that the Soviet people stood on the cusp of communism. It predicted that the transition to a "communist society," and to the edenic "new life" (*novyi byt*) that it entailed, would be complete "in the main" by 1980, an assertion so sanguine that the program immediately became the object of private ridicule. The program also reflected Khrushchev's sense that the Soviet Union was no longer a "dictatorship of the proletariat," since the exploiting classes had been completely eradicated. Instead, the Soviet Union had become an "all-peoples' state," where class struggle could no longer be used as a justification for repression.[60]

In the months following the Twenty-second Party Congress, Moscow architects began to weigh the repercussions of the new party program. Few wanted to admit that the ubiquitous five-story apartment building—popularly referred to as the *khrushchoba* (a neologism created by combining Khrushchev and *trushchoba*, the word for slum) was consonant with the earthly paradise of communism. Most agreed that the

---

58. TsAODM, f. 2890, o. 1, d. 3, ll. 16, 62.
59. RGALI, f. 2466, o. 2, d. 214, l. 39.
60. *Programma i ustav KPSS* (Moscow, 1964), 203; *XXII s"ezd Kommunisticheskoi partii Sovetskogo Soiuza, 17–31 oktiabria 1961 goda. Stenograficheskii otchet*, vol. 1 (Moscow, 1962), 207–15; William J. Tompson, *Khrushchev: A Political Life* (New York, 1997), 239; Taubman, *Khrushchev*, 508–13; Roy Medvedev, *Khrushchev: A Biography*, trans. Brian Pearce (Garden City, N.Y., 1984), 199–202; Fedor Burlatsky, *Khrushchev and the First Russian Spring: The Era of Khrushchev through the Eyes of His Adviser* (London, 1991), 124–32; N. A. Barsukov, ed., "N. S. Khrushchev o proekte tret'ei programmy KPSS," *Voprosy istorii KPSS* 8 (August 1991): 3–8; and Erik Kulavig, *Dissent in the Years of Khrushchev: Nine Stories about Disobedient Russians* (New York, 2002), 74–83.

new life would require a new type of architecture. At the Central Committee plenum in November 1962, Khrushchev indicated that *tipizatsiia* fit the bill. He reminded architects that budget constraints demanded "simplicity of form and minimal variation of components," but he encouraged them to develop "reasonable, individual architectural-artistic nuances."[61] According to Boris Mezentsev, the keynote speaker at a MOSA meeting in July 1962, architects were supposed to use this new latitude to create buildings that were emblematic of the new life. In the convoluted language of Soviet architectural theory, he argued that the success of *tipizatsiia* could be gauged by the "organic link between the implementation of the social mandate . . . and the level of professional craftsmanship." Structures that successfully juggled social substance and artistic style comprised nothing less than the "perestroika of Soviet architecture."[62]

The discussion that followed Mezentsev's keynote address was marked by an unexpected turn of events. Several speakers drew parallels between *tipizatsiia* and the constructivist architecture of the 1920s. One claimed that the social mandate guiding the early *tipizatsiia* projects encompassed values opposite Stalin's elitist "palace method" of construction. Another thought *tipizatsiia* was proof Soviet architecture had finally freed itself from the "yoke of the cult of personality," and that architects "had received the possibility to think freely and create freely." The situation reminded him of the 1920s and early '30s, when Soviet architecture "was praised even abroad."[63] This latter observation was not merely wishful thinking. As one foreign architect told his Soviet hosts when he visited in 1963, contemporary Soviet architecture "looked" different. "He wrote that he saw things here that he had seen nowhere else before."[64] Apparently, the visiting architect did not intend his observation to be understood as a backhanded compliment.

Similar discussions about the specific dimensions of *tipizatsiia* projects, and about the way they might best reflect the new life, continued at MOSA during the remainder of 1962. During the following year, municipal officials intervened to sharpen the debate. In March, Vladimir Promyslov summoned architects to Mossovet to criticize them for the persistence of "monotonous, monotone construction" in the city's peripheral

61. N. Kuleshov, "Garmoniia goroda," *Izvestiia*, March 29, 1963, 3.
62. RGALI, f. 2466, o. 2, d. 286, ll. 8, 11, 44–45.
63. RGALI, f. 2466, o. 2, d. 287, ll. 4, 55.
64. RGALI, f. 2466, o. 2, d. 215, l. 19.

neighborhoods.[65] At the beginning of June, the Moscow Party Committee invited a number of prominent architects to party headquarters to discuss the recent Kremlin meetings between the party leaders and creative intelligentsia, important events in the cultural retrenchment that followed the Manège debacle. The discussion, which was less confrontational than the earlier meeting at Mossovet, hinged on an issue that bore a striking resemblance to early notions of Soviet architecture: *tipizatsiia* had to be both emblematic of the new life, and a stimulus for its development.[66] G. A. Shemiakin, the newly appointed secretary of the Union of Architects, told the audience that architecture should serve as a "weapon . . . for the amelioration of the welfare of the working people, a weapon for their education." He argued that architecture was the only realm of artistic endeavor that reflected the "fundamental connection and interdependence of the education of the new man with the creation of the material-technical preconditions of communism and the formation of communist social relations." Another spoke of architecture "fundamentally reconstructing our existence."[67]

Soviet architecture had come full circle. When Kaganovich attacked constructivism in the early 1930s, he was annoyed by the endless debates among the avant-garde about the way architecture shaped consciousness. He declared that Soviet cities were "socialist" by their location alone, not by any characteristics inherent in built structures. The Stalinist classicism that followed was meant to evoke awe and pride, not reconstruct social relations. It was elitist and hierarchical rather than democratic and egalitarian.[68] Yet in the spring of 1963, Soviet architects resurrected one of the guiding principles of the avant-garde: architecture was a powerful weapon in the struggle to create the new man, free from bigotry, superstition, and injustice. At the Moscow Party Committee meeting, architects agreed that the new social mandate required an "all-embracing" (*kompleksnyi*) approach to urban design. In practice, this meant the planning of neighborhood projects like Novyi Arbat, a tactic

65. N. Kuleshov, "Garmoniia goroda," *Izvestiia,* March 29, 1963, 3.

66. For discussions of early-Soviet architecture, see Day, "Building Socialism," chap. 1; Hudson, *Blueprints and Blood,* 15–51; and Stephen V. Bittner, "Green Cities and Orderly Streets: Space and Culture in Moscow, 1928–1933," *Journal of Urban History* 25, no. 1 (November 1998): 22–56.

67. RGALI, f. 2466, o. 2, d. 240, ll. 5, 26–27.

68. Vladimir Papernyi, *Kul'tura dva* (Moscow, 1996), 100–143; and Greg Castillo, "Gorki Street and the Design of the Stalin Revolution," in *Streets: Critical Perspectives on Urban Space,* ed. Zeynep Celik, Diane G. Favro, and Richard Ingersoll (Berkeley and Los Angeles, 1994), 57–70.

that Khrushchev endorsed in November 1963.[69] According to one com-
mentator, these new "all-embracing" ensembles, "actively affecting the
observer, create in him new representations, new understandings about
that which is beautiful in the best sense of the word, and form in him
new aesthetic criteria, and cultivate in him good tastes."[70]

The reemergence after more than three decades of one of the guiding
principles of the architectural avant-garde was not without confusion.
Architects often struggled to find words describing their vision of the
new life and the role of architecture in its creation. At the same time that
Gleb Makarevich, one of the coauthors of Novyi Arbat, called on architects to engage in an "avant-garde battle" for designs that were new, his
colleague Ashot Mndoiants claimed that architects had "mastered the
methods of socialist realism."[71] Few, it seems, sensed the historical contradiction in their statements. Proponents of *tipizatsiia* also displayed a
penchant for hyperbole. Mndoiants argued that Soviet architects were
now "limited only by the materials produced by our industry," an assertion that underscored the newfound premium on creativity, but glossed
over the less glamorous fact that a substantial amount of material for
Novyi Arbat was being imported from abroad. Others worried that the
heightened ideological significance of architecture would provide party
officials with a pretext to intervene in affairs best left to specialists, hardly
a baseless concern.[72] Notwithstanding their apprehension and contradictory rhetoric, however, the desire of architects to build structures that
were qualitatively different from Stalinist and Western architecture was
genuine. Novyi Arbat was their first great experiment.

In spring of 1963, Mndoiants made the first detailed presentation of
the Novyi Arbat plans in the pages of Moscow's primary architectural
journal, *Stroitel'stvo i arkhitektura Moskvy* (Construction and Architecture
of Moscow). Even though Khrushchev would later force architects to
redesign the north side of the street, the influence of the new party program was plainly evident. Consistent with the notion that the new life
required an entirely different pattern of residential settlement, Mndoiants
revealed that Novyi Arbat was only the first phase in the complete
reconstruction of the area west of the Kremlin. In the coming decade,
virtually every building would be razed in the Arbat. The open land

69. RGALI, f. 2466, o. 2, d. 214, ll. 16–18; and d. 240, l. 24.
70. TsAODM, f. 1249, o. 1, d. 34, l. 36.
71. TsAODM, f. 2890, o. 1, d. 3, l. 39; and RGALI, f. 2466, o. 2, d. 214, l. 10.
72. RGALI, f. 2466, o. 2, d. 258, l. 99.

would be divided into two micro-districts, the Soviet version of the neighborhood, where social scientists would determine the ideal population and a whole array of service norms. In the meantime, Mndoiants promised that demolition would be limited to only those buildings within the Novyi Arbat corridor to minimize short-term resettlement costs, and to make the project more palatable to municipal officials.[73]

The new party program also impacted designs for the individual buildings slated for construction. Initial sketches included the four residential skyscrapers that resembled open books, as well as a hotel, a commercial complex, and an administrative building. The projected skyscrapers were designed to maximize "the proximity of residential quarters to the network of public services" like a tailor, a self-service laundry, a café, a meeting hall, a children's playroom, and a haberdashery, which would lead to "the liberation of the population, especially women, from the everyday work connected with the household." These public services would be located in "collective use" areas within the residential buildings and in the gallery of shops and restaurants. Architects designed this latter area to minimize the volume of closed service space, which would supposedly reduce the number of service personnel and thus make the buildings "profitable."[74]

Mndoiants presented more detailed plans for Novyi Arbat to MOSA members in January 1965. By this date, blueprints foresaw the construction of 95,000 square meters of living space, which would house nearly three times as many persons (10,500) as had been displaced by the buildings.[75] Although this figure was misleading (it did not account for the considerably larger number of persons displaced by the street itself), it underscored the fact that Novyi Arbat had become a "fundamentally residential" project in light of the new party program. After Khrushchev's ouster, architects abandoned the hotel rooms planned for the towers on the north side of the street in favor of conventional one-, two-, and three-bedroom apartments. By Soviet standards, they were large. The three-bedroom model, designed for four persons, contained forty-nine square meters of "living space," an official measure that did not include kitchens, bathrooms, and halls. One architect feared that the inflated apartment sizes were "not economical for the government," and thus

73. A. Mndoiants, "Novyi Arbat," *Stroitel'stvo i arkhitektura Moskvy* 4 (April 1963): 15–21.
74. "Novyi Arbat," *Gorodskoe khoziaistvo Moskvy* 1 (January 1962): 23; and Mndoiants, "Novyi Arbat," 16–18.
75. RGALI, f. 2466, o. 4, d. 24, l. 4.

8. The view from the northern side of Novyi Arbat, looking east toward the Kremlin.

not representative of the type of housing suitable for a "communist society." Others saw the large apartments as a sign of good things to come.[76]

After Mndoiants' presentation, MOSA architects underscored what they thought to be the broader significance of Novyi Arbat. Iurii Shever-diaev, the lead architect for the new glass and steel Rossiia Cinema on Pushkin Square, claimed the project would finally place Moscow among the ranks of the world's leading architectural cities. He argued that Novyi Arbat reaffirmed the "experience of foreign countries": eclecticism was not inconsonant with beauty.[77] One of the last speakers to take the podium was Viacheslav Oltarzhevskii, a former Art Nouveau architect who had spent ten years living and working in New York in the 1920s and '30s. Oltarzhevskii wondered how well Novyi Arbat would weather the critical eye of history. Would it be "as fresh, as new, and as

76. RGALI, f. 2466, o. 4, d. 24, ll. 47–48, 89.
77. RGALI, f. 2466, o. 4, d. 24, ll. 23–26.

genuinely progressive after a similar period of time, as what our fathers built in the 1920s and 1930s?"[78]

Oltarzhevskii's question spoke to the legacy of the architectural experiments of the pre-Stalin period, as well as to the relationship between *tipizatsiia* and constructivism. During the previous year, MOSA architects debated these issues after the journal *Sovremennaia arkhitektura* (Contemporary Architecture) published a controversial account of early Soviet architecture, and after one architectural historian challenged the Stalinist line on constructivism. Instead of regurgitating the usual denunciations of constructivist formalism, many MOSA architects openly embraced the similarities between the Novyi Arbat towers and early-Soviet constructivism. Oltarzhevskii voiced an opinion shared by many: constructivism was the Soviet Union's greatest contribution to the international architectural canon. It was the only instance where Soviet architects pushed their practice well beyond that of their Western counterparts. Novyi Arbat was proof that Soviet architects had returned to the trail that constructivists had blazed.

REHABILITATING CONSTRUCTIVISM

Sovremennaia arkhitektura was the Russian edition of the French journal *L'architecture d'aujourd'hui*. It was translated, edited, and distributed by the Scientific Research Institute for the Theory, History, and Future Problems of Soviet Architecture (NII TIPPSA). In the spring of 1964, the journal's French editors devoted a double issue to the history of architecture during the preceding century. Articles included a survey of Le Corbusier's work in Europe and India, an account on Bauhaus and de Stijl architecture in Germany and Holland, and a history of skyscraper development in the United States. Only one article in the issue was controversial, a survey of Soviet architecture during the so-called "heroic period," the years 1918–30. The author was Georges (Gheorghios) Candilis, a Parisian architect of Greek descent who had been born in 1913 in Baku, then part of the Russian empire, and later emigrated to Greece and France. Editors decided to exclude Candilis's text from the journal, although not the accompanying photographs, and to attach instead a brief statement describing the author's "tendentious evaluation" of Soviet architecture.

78. RGALI, f. 2466, o. 4, d. 24, ll. 93–94.

Apparently, Candilis is simply unfamiliar with what he carelessly judges. The Soviet architects of that period, whom, it would seem, he is extolling . . . are simply unknown to him: in the long list of names of twentieth-century architects, he identifies them impersonally as the "Russian architects of the years 1920–27." At the same time, Candilis stresses the foreign architects, who, in his opinion, actively influenced the formation . . . of Soviet architecture (Le Corbusier, [Erich] Mendelsohn, Ernst May, and, in his words "many others"). Among those who inspired and led our architecture during those years, he names a number of artists, as well as [the poet Vladimir] Mayakovsky.[79]

The anonymous editors were disgruntled that Candilis had failed to mention the Vesnin and Golosov brothers, Moisei Ginzburg, Aleksei Shchusev, and Ivan Leonidov, all giants in early-Soviet architecture. Even though the architecture of the "heroic period" had been labeled as formalist in the 1930s, editors did not challenge Candilis's positive evaluation. Instead, they warned readers not to underestimate the Soviet contribution to constructivism. The architectural experiments of the pre-Stalin period were products of the October Revolution, they argued, and organically Soviet phenomena.

Debate over the legacy of early Soviet architecture continued later that spring, when the MOSA architectural-theory section convened to discuss a paper by the young architectural historian Selim Khan-Magomedov, "On Some of the Problems of Constructivism."[80] The ostensible purpose of the meeting was to discuss Khan-Magomedov's paper in light of his earlier work on the architect Moisei Ginzburg, famous for the communal housing facility he designed for the Commissariat of Finance in 1929, and two recent theoretical tracts by other scholars, "The Theoretical Fundamentals of Soviet Architecture" and "The Trend of Soviet Architecture." These latter works caused considerable consternation at the architectural-theory section three days earlier, on May 18, 1964.

79. "Ot redaktsii," response to G. Candilis [Zh. Kandilis], "1918–1930. Geroicheskii period v arkhitekture SSSR," *Sovremennaia arkhitektura* 3–4 (1964): 35.
80. Khan-Magomedov would later distinguish himself in both the Soviet Union and the West for his voluminous work on the Soviet architectural avant-garde. See, for instance, S. O. Khan-Magomedov, *Pioneers of Soviet Architecture: The Search for New Solutions in the 1920s and 1930s*, trans. Alexander Lieven, ed. Catherine Cooke (New York, 1987); idem, *Arkhitektura sovetskogo avangarda* (Moscow, 1996); idem, *Alexander Vesnin and Russian Constructivism* (New York, 1986); and idem, *Pervye vypuski molodykh storonnikov arkhitekturnogo avangarda: MPI-MIGI (1920–1924)* (Moscow, 1997).

K. I. Trapeznikov, an architect attached to the MOSA administration, thought that the works underestimated the achievements of early Soviet architecture, and that their authors needed to clarify their positions on the 1920s and constructivism in particular. Another critic claimed that "The Fundamentals of Theory" text did not fairly evaluate the work of Aleksandr, Viktor, and Leonid Vesnin, central figures in early Soviet constructivism, and was characteristic of a broader literature on constructivism that attached to it a "very superficial, incorrect evaluation . . . as an especially formalistic trend."[81]

Khan-Magomedov's paper was not transcribed into the stenographic record of the meeting on May 21, but it is clear from the subsequent discussion that he challenged much of the official line on constructivism. After listening to Khan-Magomedov's presentation, one architect called for a complete reevaluation of the genre. Never had Soviet architecture achieved the same "social meaning," he thought. Many speakers underscored the similarities between the architecture of the new life and the constructivist experiments of the early-Soviet period. "This is not simply a question of historical fairness . . . [the constructivists] grasped the correct path upon which we have been trying to embark." Another architect argued that constructivist architects had made possible the huge volume of residential construction of the Khrushchev period by experimenting with prefabricated components. By the end of the meeting, MOSA members had tallied a long list of constructivist accomplishments, from the idea of the *sotsgorod* (short for "socialist city") and micro-district, to the privileging of the "social aspect" of architecture.[82]

Similar to the Candilis incident, several MOSA architects cited patriotism as a reason to reevaluate constructivism. It was "in the interests of history," one member argued, "and important for us . . . and our youth" to insist that constructivism "belongs to us." He then quoted Mayakovsky, who wrote several essays on modern art while in Paris in 1925. "Where does the new art originate? In Soviet Russia, which has constructivism."[83] Others reiterated the NI TIPPSA position that constructivism had its origins solely in the October Revolution and was thus uniquely Soviet. Some tried to draw a distinction between Soviet and Western constructivism to eradicate any sense of foreign influence or innovation.[84]

81. RGALI, f. 2466, o. 2, d. 361, ll. 12, 24; and d. 362, l. 10.
82. RGALI, f. 2466, o. 2, d. 362, l. 10; and d. 363, ll. 4–5, 13.
83. RGALI, f. 2466, o. 2, d. 362, ll. 11, 13.
84. RGALI, f. 2466, o. 2, d. 363, ll. 10, 31.

This sympathetic view of constructivism was not entirely uncontroversial. At least one MOSA member objected to the emerging consensus that it was time to reevaluate constructivism. P. A. Volodin, who had made a name for himself in Sverdlovsk during the Stalin period, argued that the Soviet Union had already "rejected" constructivism. He labeled much of the day's discussion "complete nonsense." He criticized the assembled architects for forgetting the extent of class struggle in the late 1920s and early '30s. Constructivism was not simply a casualty of Stalin's dictatorship, as its proponents now claimed, but a relic of old Russia, made obsolete by the Soviet Union's rapid development and the struggle to overcome wreckers and saboteurs.[85] Volodin's remarks provoked a storm of protest. One MOSA member retorted that recent architectural achievements would have been impossible had architects continued to design the ornate structures of Stalinism that Volodin was known to prefer. Another member asked Volodin whether it was better to denounce constructivism foolishly, like their predecessors had done before 1953, or to evaluate it calmly and judiciously.[86] A handful of MOSA members offered more serious responses. One architect argued that the crucial difference between the "heroic" and contemporary periods was the absence of internal class conflict in the latter, an observation consistent with the new party program. He hoped this distinction would allow architects to avoid the mistakes made three decades earlier, when "the intensification of class struggle . . . gradually carried over into the creative disagreements of architecture."[87] The implication, reiterated by other speakers, was that constructivism owed its demise to class conflict gone awry. Other architects criticized the defunct All-Union Association of Proletarian Architects (VOPRA), once the chief institutional antagonist of constructivist architecture, for the "groundlessness" of its campaign. It was absurd, they argued, for VOPRA to call constructivism "an expression of imperialist ideology."[88]

By the end of the second day's proceedings on May 29, participants wondered what the wider repercussions of their discussions would be. Because the MOSA administration had been reluctant to authorize the meetings at the outset, several architects worried that officials outside the theory section would look unfavorably upon the events.[89] Even

85. RGALI, f. 2466, o. 2, d. 362, ll. 38–39.
86. RGALI, f. 2466, o. 2, d. 362, ll. 38–39.
87. RGALI, f. 2466, o. 2, d. 362, l. 22.
88. RGALI, f. 2466, o. 2, d. 363, ll. 67, 70.
89. RGALI, f. 2466, o. 2, d. 363, l. 76.

though Shemiakin had assured them that this was not the case, MOSA members were unable to reach a consensus on the chief question they had raised. Should constructivism be "rehabilitated"? They splintered among a group that was hesitant to make a bold move, a group that was uncertain, and a group that thought rehabilitation was long overdue. The first two groups rallied around what appeared to have been the ostensible purpose of the meeting. The point was not to rehabilitate constructivism, one architect declared, but to see what it offered contemporary architecture. Another participant, a dialectician to the end, called the period following the Twentieth Party Congress the "synthesis," which followed the "thesis," 1917–31, and the "antithesis," 1931–56. Architects were now duty-bound to appropriate that which was "most valuable" from all preceding periods, regardless of whether it was constructivist or Stalinist.[90] But the final group was unwilling to follow the path of least resistance. Georgii Gradov, an early critic of Stalinist architecture, wondered why the MOSA administration had waited nearly ten years after Stalin's denunciation to reevaluate constructivism: "Because we are living in fear and danger?" Gradov argued that the issue of rehabilitation had become a moot point. Given the many similarities between *tipizatsiia* and the experiments of the 1920s, contemporary Soviet architecture had become constructivist. Gradov claimed that Khrushchev rehabilitated constructivism ten years earlier, at the All-Union Convention of Construction Workers, when he attacked Stalinist architects for excessive ornamentation and insufficient attention to living-space. In what could only be considered a case of poetic justice, Khrushchev had shown that Stalinist architects were the real formalists.[91]

Shemiakin's assurance about the political ramifications of the meetings proved true. No response from higher officials, either negative or positive, was forthcoming. Nevertheless, in the wake of Khrushchev's dismissal, official policy toward architecture began to shift, and the question of rehabilitation was never definitively answered at levels higher than MOSA's architectural-theory section. The change in political leadership spelled the beginning of the end of the new-life campaign and the utopian promise of *tipizatsiia*. These developments were neither sudden nor well-articulated, but they had a marked effect on architecture. They first became apparent in May 1965, when the Tenth Conference of Moscow Architects convened. The keynote address was a mostly apolitical

90. RGALI, f. 2466, o. 2, d. 363, l. 14.
91. RGALI, f. 2466, o. 2, d. 363, l. 91.

treatise on the quality of architecture, a far cry from the Ninth Conference seventeen months earlier, which had been devoted to the new life.[92] During the subsequent discussion, several MOSA members linked persistent quality problems with Khrushchev's denunciation of Stalinist "excess" in 1954. V. N. Simbirtsev, an architect affiliated with the Scientific Research Institute for Urban Planning, called on architects to return their profession to where it had been before the All-Union Convention of Construction Workers. "Unfortunately, several years ago, our attitude toward architecture changed. We ceased to consider architecture an art, fearing that if we talk about architecture as art, it makes less significant the question of construction."[93]

As the utopianism of the new party program faded, so too did the attractiveness of the architecture it inspired. In 1969, construction workers removed the last scaffolding from Natan Osterman's House of the New Life in Moscow's Novye Cheremushki region, which had been designed for a national competition on collective housing in 1964. With its extensive network of communal services and kitchen-less apartments, Osterman's complex captured much of the radical optimism of the new party program. In the more staid atmosphere of the early-Brezhnev period, however, it proved unpopular among architectural pundits and municipal officials, who thought that Osterman was trying to homogenize everyday existence, and who rightly feared that residents would prefer a more traditional style of housing. After several institutional tenants refused to support the project, the twin towers were deeded to Moscow State University and turned into dormitories for foreign students.[94]

Novyi Arbat also lost much of its luster in the late 1960s. While the street had never been popular among some architects, in the late 1960s even those friendly with Posokhin had begun to question his penchant for "giganticism." "Undoubtedly, the [Novyi Arbat] structures are interesting," Iosif Loveiko told Posokhin at the end of 1967, "but we can in no way think that there will be many Arbats."[95] Citing the project's considerable cost overruns, one MOSA member implored Posokhin to plan smaller and more varied projects in other locales. G. N. L'vov was skeptical that Posokhin had succeeded in creating buildings that would be desired

92. On the Ninth Conference, see RGALI, f. 2466, o. 2, d. 214, ll. 10–40.
93. RGALI, f. 2466, o. 4, d. 10, l. 35.
94. Colton, *Moscow*, 532; and Victor Buchli, *An Archaeology of Socialism* (Oxford, 1999), 148–49.
95. RGALI, f. 2466, o. 4, d. 87, l. 33.

addresses. In the early 1980s, sociologists verified L'vov's doubts: most residents of the skyscrapers on the north side of the street were unhappy with their accommodations.[96] These cost-related concerns were aggravated by a final design change that symbolized the fate of the highly politicized architecture of the late-Khrushchev period. In 1967, at Aleksei Kosygin's orders, the towers on the south side of the street, once notable for their incorporation of the new life into their designs, were transformed into office space, and deeded to a number of federal ministries.[97] By the end of construction in 1968, the street that had once been emblematic of the renaissance in Soviet architecture and the social ideal that set it apart from Western architecture, had become known as "our Broadway." After more than half a decade of construction, only 80,000 square meters of living space were made available for resettlement along the street. The project's "all-embracing" approach to urban renewal spawned only one imitation, the austere Novokirovskii Avenue (Academician Sakharov Avenue) on the city's near north side.[98] *Tipizatsiia* survived its critics to remain the default genre for those architects fortunate enough to design structures outside of the strict cost regimen of *tipovoe proektirovanie*. But shorn of its ideological trappings, it never became as dominant or as consequential as its proponents once envisioned.

As the ideological upheaval of the Khrushchev years gave way to the official stability of Brezhnev, MOSA members abandoned their efforts to rehabilitate constructivism. Khan-Magomedov continued to praise the avant-garde in his work, but few architects argued that constructivism had much to contribute to contemporary debates. Insofar as there was any acknowledged difference between Soviet and Western architecture after 1964, it was the state monopoly on planning that Posokhin had identified in May 1961. The more essential distinctions spawned by the new life were mostly forgotten or gently ridiculed. In truth, the official line on constructivism was never clear after 1964. When presented with an opportunity to denounce constructivism at the completion of Osterman's building in 1969, cultural authorities kept their silence, perhaps fearing that they would reignite a debate that had already exhausted itself. They were happy to entertain the patriotic nostalgia surrounding

96. RGALI, f. 2466, o. 4, d. 110, ll. 32, 79; and T. Grossman, "Khorosho li zhit' na Kalininskom prospekte?" *Stroitel'stvo i arkhitektura Moskvy* 10 (October 1981): 10–11.
97. TsMAM, f. 534, o. 1, d. 614, l. 38.
98. RGALI, f. 2466, o. 4, d. 87, l. 38.

constructivism (hence Khan-Magomedov's continued publication), but were unwilling to spend additional money on costly buildings that few people wanted to inhabit. Like Khrushchev in the 1950s, the Brezhnev government was utilitarian at its core: cost per square meter of living space mattered a lot more than reshaping consciousness. Even though the Brezhnev government retained the Spartan aesthetics of the Khrushchev years, its disaffection for the rhetoric of the new life suggests that its understanding of architecture was similar to Kaganovich's formulation in the early 1930s: Soviet architecture was socialist by location rather than essence. According to this view, architecture did not make the man.

Much of the interest in constructivism can be explained by the fact that so many architects saw it as the antipode of Stalinism. But it was hard for architects to fission their collective memories from biases shaped by the present. Similar to the actors at the Vakhtangov Theater, several architects treated constructivism as a surrogate for the NEP period, when it was possible to "think freely and create freely." For them, rehabilitating constructivism meant restoring the perceived tolerance and pluralism of NEP. But their memories of early-Soviet history elided much that was unflattering to constructivists. While it is true that constructivism flourished during the relatively permissive NEP, its acme was the Cultural Revolution (1928–31), when proletarian militants applied the rhetoric of class warfare to the cultural sphere. It was hardly a period notable for its tolerance. Moreover, because constructivists proposed the creation of an entirely new setting for human life, their interests actually coincided with the leading faction in the party during the late 1920s, the Stalinists, who were keen to underscore the limited imagination and reactionary doubts of Nikolai Bukharin's right opposition and other advocates of NEP.[99] Constructivism may have been more entwined in Stalinism than its latter-day proponents cared to admit. As James Wertsch reminds us, because collective remembering is mediated through present-day political and cultural resources that are not "neutral cognitive instruments," it tends to privilege clarity and political utility over accuracy.[100]

99. S. Frederick Starr, "Visionary Town Planning during the Cultural Revolution," in *Cultural Revolution in Russia, 1928–1931*, ed. Sheila Fitzpatrick (Bloomington, Ind., 1978), 209; and Sheila Fitzpatrick, *The Cultural Front: Power and Culture in Revolutionary Russia* (Ithaca, N.Y., 1992), 119–125.
100. James V. Wertsch, *Voices of Collective Remembering* (Cambridge, 2002), 7, 9.

To be sure, most architects kept their distance from potentially troublesome topics like artistic autonomy, political freedom, and NEP. Instead, they were "recycling material and symbolic elements of the past" in order to transform an architecture of the present that was uninspiring and monotonous, and an architectural profession that had been shorn of its cultural and political prestige.[101] They argued that constructivism raised important questions that were at the heart of the Soviet mission. What did it mean to build communism? What were communist social relations? What role did architecture play in these endeavors?[102] They tried to show that present-day realities had resulted in the de facto resurrection of constructivism. They demanded only its de jure rehabilitation to accord policy with life. And they savored the fact that constructivism had a meaning that transcended the bounds of their profession. Their reticence on issues broader than these may have reflected fears that their efforts were precarious to begin with. When they first broached the issue of rehabilitation in 1963–64, Khrushchev was reining in cultural figures in other fields. Not only were architects untouched by this development, but they were seemingly held to a different standard altogether.[103] Their blueprints were modern. Their intentions were avant-garde. And their buildings were groundbreaking. The thaw, as they may have realized, was a fickle thing.

Novyi Arbat stood as proof that no single person or group had a monopoly over the meanings that were embedded in the Arbat's rapidly changing streetscape. In the vast construction site north of Arbat Street, Posokhin saw an opportunity to redeem a decade of mostly uninspired architecture. Khrushchev saw remnants of an old Russia that were inconsonant with the stature of the new. Latter-day constructivists saw an opportunity to rehabilitate their avant-garde predecessors. And, as the next chapter will show, many historical preservation activists saw an utter catastrophe.

---

101. Madeleine Yue Dong, *Republican Beijing: The City and Its Histories* (Berkeley and Los Angeles, 2003), 3.
102. The thaw encouraged Soviet journalists to ask similar questions about the social and political role of their craft. See Thomas C. Wolfe, *Governing Soviet Journalism: The Press and the Socialist Person after Stalin* (Bloomington, Ind., 2005), 33–70.
103. On this paradox, see Alain Besançon, "Soviet Painting: Tradition and Experiment," *Survey* 46 (January 1963): 86.

Preserving the Past, Empowering the Public

One of the most beloved casualties of the Novyi Arbat demolition was Sobach'e Square, a small triangle created by the intersection of three lanes a few blocks north of Arbat Street. Before its destruction, Sobach'e Square was the site of a nineteenth-century fountain commemorating the "Lord's Dogs," a reference to the tsar's kennel that once stood on the spot. The fountain sat in a small park, fenced with wrought-iron, which had been built for the Sixth International Festival of Youth and Students in 1957. The one and two-story buildings that surrounded the square were some of the best examples in Moscow of the neoclassical, empire style that had been popular in the decades following the fire of 1812. Like so many places in the Arbat, Sobach'e Square had longstanding ties with the intelligentsia. After returning from exile at his mother's estate in northern Russia in 1826, Alexander Pushkin lived on the square at the house of his friend, the humorist and book collector Sergei Sobolevskii. In the 1830s and '40s, many of Russia's most influential minds—social-ists, Westernizers, and Slavophiles—gathered at the house of Aleksei Khomiakov, one of the founders of Slavophilism. Khomiakov, the West-ernizer Petr Chaadaev, and the writer Ivan Turgenev sometimes visited another neighbor, Mikhail Orlov, a general who had been implicated in the Decembrist revolt in 1825. After Orlov's brother, a friend of Tsar Nicholas, appealed for mercy, Orlov was sentenced to a life of idleness and police surveillance on Sobach'e Square. Leo Tolstoy's friend V. P. Perfil'ev, supposedly the model for Stiva Oblonskii in *Anna Karenina*, also lived nearby. In their novels *Tarantass* and *Smoke,* Vladimir Sollogub and Ivan Turgenev wrote about Sobach'e Square's aristocratic refinement. Conversely, the poet Vladimir Mayakovsky ridiculed a "little scum" who lived on the square named "Petr Burzhuichikov," or Peter Petite-Bourgeoisie.[1] Whatever values were attached to it, Sobach'e Square objectified the centrality of the Arbat in the history of the Russian intelligentsia. According to a 1917 guidebook, it was a place where "the old look of bygone Moscow was preserved, and where its spirit wafted."[2]

The buildings that surrounded Sobach'e Square comprised only a small percentage of the 150 structures that were razed to accommodate Novyi Arbat, but critics thought that their fate epitomized what was odious about the project.[3] Novyi Arbat threatened the intimate, historic, and unplanned spaces that were increasingly rare in central Moscow. It replaced the quirky, narrow, and heterogeneous lanes that reflected traffic patterns at the time of Ivan the Terrible with a massive empty space lined by skyscrapers, what Jane Jacobs, the great critic of American urban renewal, would have called a "Great Blight of Dullness."[4] And Novyi Arbat necessitated the resettlement of thousands of lifelong residents to new developments on the periphery of Moscow. When Novyi Arbat was built atop Sobach'e Square, residents of the neighborhood lost something far more precious than old buildings and a fountain. Novyi Arbat "demolished not only the buildings and green spaces," Sigurd Shmidt wrote, "but also the peculiarity of the 'Arbat' way of life, which led to the destruction of the way of thinking characteristic of '*arbattsy*,' and their manner of interaction."[5]

Despite rumors that Novyi Arbat was Khrushchev's pet project, Shmidt held Mikhail Posokhin and his architects wholly responsible for the

---

1. S. O. Shmidt, "Arbat v istorii i kul'ture Rossii," in *Arbatskii arkhiv,* vyp. 1, ed. S. O. Shmidt (Moscow, 1997), 81–84; Oleg Volkov, *Kazhdyi kamen' v nei zhivoi: iz istorii Moskovskikh ulits* (Moscow, 1985), 163–73; S. K. Romaniuk, *Moskva. Utraty* (Moscow, 1992), 182–86; and Nikolai Malinin, "Sobach'e ploshchadka (mysli i tsitaty)," *Arkhitektura i stroitel'stvo Moskvy* 11 (November 1989): 25–26.
2. N. A. Geinike, N. S. Elagin, E. A. Efimov, and I. I. Shitts, *Po Moskve: progulki po Moskve i eia khudozhestvennym i prosvetitel'nym uchrezhdeniiam* (Moscow, 1917; reprint, Moscow, 1991), 342n1.
3. On the number of buildings demolished, see TsMAM, f. 150, o. 1, d. 2773, ll. 423–33; and f. 773, o. 1, d. 23, ll. 75–87.
4. Jane Jacobs, *The Death and Life of Great American Cities* (New York, 1961), 144.
5. Shmidt, "Arbat v istorii i kulture Rossii," 116. For a photographic record of the destruction, see Vladimir Potresov, *Arbat nashego detstva: fotografii Aleksandra Potresova (1902–1972)* (Moscow, 2006).

destruction of Sobach'e Square and adjacent areas during the 1960s. Novyi Arbat's designers were without any "feelings of historical responsibility and aesthetic order." They cynically manipulated "government leaders' lack of culture," and "ruthlessly and forcibly" imposed a "vertical jaw," a popular epithet for the street, on an unwilling public.[6] Shmidt's anger grew out of a debate that was at the heart of the contradictory meanings that Khrushchev, Posokhin, and the proponents of constructivism attached to Novyi Arbat in the previous chapter: Who rightfully determines the value of past culture? Under Stalin, the answer was straightforward. The party, with the assistance of loyal experts in the arts, created a canon of pre-revolutionary and early Soviet classics that served the interests of the new socialist society. Peter Tchaikovsky, the realist painter Il'ia Repin, and the young Maxim Gorky, then a committed Marxist, were in the canon; Igor Stravinsky, the abstract painter Kasimir Malevich, and the middle-aged Gorky, who had become ambivalent about Soviet power, were not. In 1953, however, this arrangement crumbled. Emboldened by the rapidly changing political climate, cultural figures of all sorts began to challenge the party's role as the "intellectual center" of Soviet society.[7] Many proposed alternate yardsticks for evaluating the past. The architects who designed Novyi Arbat and who rallied around constructivism argued that professional expertise should be paramount in assessments of past culture.[8] Faced with the demolition of a large swath of the Arbat, a handful of preservation activists proposed something more radical: the public should be the decisive authority.

The political elevation of the Soviet public (*obshchestvennost'*) was an important component of the thaw. In order to lessen the hyper-centralization of Stalinism, Khrushchev tried to harness the talents of Soviet citizens in a myriad of "public self-administration" organizations and

6. Sigurd Shmidt, "Bulat Okudzhava i 'arbatstvo'," in *Tvorchestvo Bulata Okudzhavy v kontekste kul'tury XX veka. Materialy Pervoi mezhdunarodnoi nauchnoi konferentsii, posviashchennoi 75-letiiu so dnia rozhdeniia Bulata Okudzhavy, 19–21 noiabria 1999 g., Peredelkino* (Moscow, 2001), 18.
7. Karl Eimermacher [Aimermakher], "Partiinoe upravlenie kul'turoi i formy ee samoorganizatsii (1953–1964/67)," in *Ideologicheskie komissii TsK KPSS, 1958–1964. Dokumenty*, ed. E. S. Afanes'eva, V. I. Afiani, L. A. Velichanskaia, Z. K. Vodop'ianova, and E. V. Kochubei (Moscow, 1998), 7.
8. Their arguments were akin to those made by architects in postwar Sevastopol, who wanted more local experts involved in the reconstruction process. See Karl D. Qualls, "Local-Outsider Negotiations in Postwar Sevastopol's Reconstruction, 1944–53," in *Provincial Landscapes: Local Dimensions of Soviet Power*, ed. Donald J. Raleigh (Pittsburgh, 2001), 276–98.

other newly empowered local institutions. In theory, these organizations would take control of local affairs during the transition to communism, and expedite the dissolution of the state that Marx forecast in *The Communist Manifesto*.[9] In reality, efforts to create self-sufficient citizen-activists out of a population cowed by Stalinism sometimes had unintended consequences. Preservationists seized on the rhetoric of an empowered public to challenge the construction of Novyi Arbat and the prerogatives of Posokhin's Architectural-Planning Administration (Main Architectural-Planning Administration after 1960), which supervised nearly all architectural and construction affairs in the capital. They envisioned the public not as a mobilized arm of the state, but as a counterweight to unscrupulous officials and misguided policies. They proposed the formation of a public organization dedicated to architectural preservation that would resemble the voluntary societies of tsarist Russia: it would exist at the will of the state, but be independent in its daily activities.[10] Preservationists hoped that a preservation organization would provide a forum where Muscovites could speak freely about projects like Novyi Arbat. The Architectural-Planning Administration always claimed that it had the support of the public; skeptical preservationists challenged the administration to prove that it was true.

Opponents of Novyi Arbat demanded greater public input in the urban-planning process because of their own political weakness. Only a few dozen persons in Moscow could rightly call themselves preservation activists. Some had been members of the group Old Moscow, which had been forcibly disbanded in 1930. Some were employed by the impotent agencies that supervised preservation and restoration in Moscow. And a few were prominent artists, writers, and scholars brave enough to lend their support. Because many of the preservationists were architects by training, they gathered at the Moscow Section of the Union of Archi-

9. See, for instance, L. G. Churchward, "Continuity and Change in Local Soviet Government," *Soviet Studies* 9 (January 1958): 256–85; Theodore H. Friedgut, *Political Participation in the USSR* (Princeton, N.J., 1979), 156–62; Jeffrey W. Hahn, *Soviet Grassroots: Citizen Participation in Local Soviet Government* (Princeton, N.J., 1988), 68–70; George W. Breslauer, *Khrushchev and Brezhnev as Leaders: Building Authority in Soviet Politics* (London, 1982), 42; and V. V. Zhuravlev, ed., *XX s"ezd KPSS i ego istoricheskie real'nosti* (Moscow, 1991), 229–38. Oleg Kharkhordin offers a dissenting view to the existing literature on the empowerment of the public by arguing that public organizations represented new, more invasive forms of social control. See *The Collective and the Individual in Russia: A Study of Practices* (Berkeley and Los Angeles, 1999), 297–303.
10. Joseph Bradley, "Subjects into Citizens: Societies, Civil Society, and Autocracy in Tsarist Russia," *American Historical Review* 107, no. 4 (October 2002): 1094–123.

tects, which represented the professional interests of the three thousand architects working in Moscow and maintained the creative orthodoxy required by the party. The "extreme institutionalization" of Soviet architecture, itself a product of its regimentation under Stalin, turned MOSA into a community of shared expertise and culture that became a surrogate for an autonomous public sphere after 1953.[11] Consequently, by the early 1960s MOSA had become a relatively freewheeling arena for the discussion of architectural issues. In many instances, even nonmembers interested in preservation were invited to participate. Preservationists initially argued that MOSA was the best representative of Moscow's "architectural public opinion." They asked that officials at the Architectural-Planning Administration honor MOSA's views in issues regarding preservation. Faced with the demolition of a large swath of the Arbat in the early 1960s, however, preservationists demanded the consideration of the broader public, one that included all Muscovites. Extreme circumstances, they decided, called for extreme measures.

Preservationists confronted an agency with extensive ties to the party leadership. Mikhail Posokhin was on friendly terms with Khrushchev and was indebted to him for the purge of Stalinist architects in 1954–55. After preservationists questioned the wisdom of the modernist Palace of Congresses in the Kremlin, a controversial structure known as the "punk among nobles," Khrushchev strayed from the soporific commentaries on grain yields at a Central Committee meeting in 1961 to fire back. "You know and understand the importance of this monument of antiquity," Khrushchev raged at preservationists.

You, and only you, can evaluate this historical monument. You are the one who understands and can assess the importance of the fact that such-and-such a famous person strolled in this spot; you can tell us that this is where he sat and thought up his projects, and this is the place where, in a fit of anger, he spat on the ground. I am not exaggerating, comrades. These kinds of outrages exist.[12]

11. Roger D. Markwick, *Rewriting History in Soviet Russia: The Politics of Revisionist Historiography, 1956–1974* (New York, 2001), 28; Marc Rakovski [György Bence and János Kis], *Toward an East European Marxism* (London, 1978), 48; and Douglas R. Weiner, *A Little Corner of Freedom: Russian Nature Protection from Stalin to Gorbachev* (Berkeley and Los Angeles, 1999), 9.
12. *Plenum Tsentral'nogo komiteta Kommunisticheskoi partii Sovetskogo Soiuza, 10–18 ianvaria 1961 g. Stenograficheskii otchet* (Moscow, 1961), 602, quoted in Weiner, *A Little Corner of Freedom*, 295–96.

Contrary to Khrushchev's charge of pretentiousness, however, it was the preservationists, not the urban planners, who marshaled the rhetoric of an empowered public to their side. They did so because they lacked the resources of urban planners, and because urban planners were unresponsive to requests to honor the opinion of the architectural public. Preservationists argued that the meanings and values Soviet citizens attached to the past—their collective memories—had priority over those of urban planners, latter-day constructivists, and even Khrushchev himself. The implications of their campaign were potentially momentous, and not only for the Arbat.

POSTWAR PRESERVATION

The preservation movement that developed in response to Novyi Arbat drew on Khrushchev's rhetoric of an empowered public, yet it operated within an institutional and historical framework that was shaped in important ways by Stalinism. During the Cultural Revolution, avant-garde architects and militant atheists saw oppression and obscurantism in the churches, palaces, and alleys of old Russia. They were obliged by a state that was initially determined to stamp out the architectural remnants of the past and increasingly eager to glorify Stalin with new buildings. In Moscow alone, dozens of significant structures were razed during the 1920s and '30s. Among the casualties was the largest church in Moscow, the Cathedral of Christ the Savior, which was built to commemorate Napoleon's defeat in 1812. It was destroyed in 1931 to clear ground for the Palace of Soviets, a building of mythical proportions that was abandoned after more than two decades on the drafting table. Other victims included the walls surrounding Kitai Gorod, the financial and commercial district north of Red Square; the Sukharev Tower, a seventeenth-century military fortification on the Garden Circle; and building ensembles like Manège and Pushkin Squares.[13] During the late

13. The literature on architectural demolition and reconstruction under Stalin is large. For a representative sample, see Andrew Gentes, "The Life, Death and Resurrection of the Cathedral of Christ the Saviour, Moscow," *History Workshop Journal* 46 (1998): 63–95; Vladimir Papernyi, "Moscow in the 1930s and the Emergence of a New City," in *The Culture of the Stalin Period,* ed. Hans Gunther (New York, 1990), 229–39; Greg Castillo, "Gorki Street and the Design of the Stalin Revolution," in *Streets: Critical Perspectives on Urban Space,* ed. Zeynep Celik, Diane G. Favro, and Richard Ingersoll (Berkeley and Los Angeles, 1994), 57–70; Lazar Kaganovich, *The Socialist Reconstruction of Moscow and Other Cities in the USSR* (Moscow, 1931), 39; and S. Frederick Starr, "Visionary Town Planning during the Cultural Revolution," in *Cultural Revolution in Russia, 1928–1931,* ed. Sheila Fitzpatrick (Bloomington, Ind., 1978), 207–40.

1930s and '40s, the rate of demolition slowed as official tastes veered toward tradition and the cultural losses of the German occupation became clear. The late-Stalinist state was not always amenable to the concerns of preservationists, but neither was it the hostile regime of the Cultural Revolution.[14]

In October 1948, the Council of Ministers created an elaborate oversight mechanism for architectural and historical monuments that endured through the Khrushchev and early-Brezhnev periods. The Council of Ministers ordered the federal Committees on Architectural and Artistic Affairs to assume control of the technical minutiae of preservation. It made local soviets responsible for the everyday maintenance and restoration of monuments and for protecting the integrity of the preservation zones that surrounded them. It also ordered republic officials to compile "preservation registries" in consultation with experts from the Academy of Sciences. These registries divided monuments among three functional categories and codified a hierarchy of historical and architectural value. Inclusion on the registries was not an ironclad guarantee against demolition or decay, but it did provide some level of protection. Later legislation required local authorities to draw up blueprints and make extensive photographic records of any monument threatened with alteration or destruction. Removal from the registry was possible only with the approval of republic or federal officials.[15]

A similar RSFSR resolution in May 1947 made the Moscow City Council (Mossovet) responsible for the upkeep of all monuments in the capital. Mossovet then deferred most preservation concerns to the various bureaucracies, ministries, enterprises, and organizations that

14. On preservation efforts before 1953, see Elena Ovsiannikova, "Staraia Moskva i 'Staraia Moskva,'" *Arkhitektura i stroitel'stvo Moskvy* 9 (September 1988): 94–97; Timothy J. Colton, *Moscow: Governing the Socialist Metropolis* (Cambridge, Mass., 1995), 39, 111–12, 229–33; B. F. Kozlov, "Istochniki ob otnoshenii k istoricheskim pamiatnikam v RSFSR v 1917–1930 gg. (po materialam moskovskikh arkhivov i muzeev)," in *Voprosy okhrany i ispol'zovaniia pamiatnikov istorii i kul'tury*, ed. M. A. Poliakova and E. A. Shulepova (Moscow, 1990), 40–54; the collection of articles in *Petr Baranovskii. Trudy, vospominaniia sovremennikov*, ed. Iu. A. Bychkov, O. P. Baranovskaia, V. A. Desiatnikov, A. M. Pomerantsev (Moscow, 1996); and Iu. A. Bychkov, *Zhitie Petra Baranovskogo* (Moscow, 1991). On later preservation efforts, see R. A. French, "Conserving the Past in Soviet Cities," Kennan Institute for Advanced Russian Studies, Woodrow Wilson International Center for Scholars, Occasional Paper no. 235 (Washington, D.C., 1990); and John Patrick Farrell, "If These Stones Could Only Speak: Historical and Cultural Preservation in a Soviet Context, 1955–1966" (Ph.D. diss., University of California, Davis, 2004).
15. *Sobranie postanovlenii i rasporiazhenii Soveta ministrov SSSR*, 1948, no. 6 (Moscow, 1938–1949), 136–44; Iuridicheskaia komissiia pri Sovete Ministrov RSFSR, *Sistematicheskoe sobranie zakonov RSFSR, ukazov Prezidiuma Verkhovnogo Soveta RSFSR i reshenii pravitel'stva RSFSR* (Moscow, 1968), 12:606–13; and TsAODM, f. 4, o. 80, d. 10, ll. 1–4.

had monuments "on the balance sheet," an accounting expression that was used to indicate the possession of durable assets. Another Mossovet decree in September 1949 required that leasing fees collected from monuments be used solely for their restoration and upkeep, as well as for maintaining the supposedly inviolable "preservation zones" that surrounded them. The municipal branch of the State Architectural Preservation Inspectorate, an enthusiastic but understaffed agency of six employees, supervised preservation efforts on Mossovet's behalf.[16]

By 1955, there were 911 structures in Moscow under the protection of the registries; 850 were located outside the Kremlin walls. Nearly a third of all monuments were used as residential buildings; the remaining two-thirds were schools, museums, medical clinics, printing shops, churches, and so on. This wide range of uses elicited an equally wide range of opinions about what constituted reasonable preservation efforts. Monuments belonging to municipal agencies, roughly half the total, tended to be in worse shape than those with institutional or ministerial owners. Between 1946 and 1954, 242 monuments underwent restoration work in Moscow; only 60 of these were under municipal control. Of the 121 million rubles spent to fund this work, only 19.1 million came from municipal sources.[17] There were several reasons for this difference. In some cases, municipal authorities leased monuments to ministries and bureaucracies in need of office or residential space. Leases for these buildings usually included a "preservation contract" that obligated tenants to finance all necessary restoration work on their own and abide by the spirit of the 1948 Council of Ministers decree and other relevant legislation. According to the head of the Moscow branch of the federal Preservation Inspectorate, Boris Kuznetsov, some tenants simply refused to sign the contract, citing the difficulty of obtaining financing for the restoration of buildings that were not on their own balance sheets. Moreover, the Moscow Finance Administration, the official bookkeeper for the city, frequently ignored the Mossovet decree that required municipal agencies to set aside all rent from monuments for restoration and upkeep. Much of this money was allocated instead to the renovation of the municipal housing fund. Subsequent attempts to require the Architectural-Planning Administration to draw from a "special account" in order to fund renovation work came to a halt when it became clear that possession

16. RGALI, f. 2466, o. 1, d. 399, ll. 4–5, 26.
17. RGALI, f. 2466, o. 1, d. 399, l. 6.

of the monuments would have to be transferred to the administration's balance sheet in order to abide by federal accounting standards. Moscow's Housing Administration and local soviets were also complicit in the neglect, since they preferred to spend the funds allocated for renovation on buildings that were not on the preservation registries, because this tended to be less expensive. Several local soviets even tried to transfer possession of their monuments to other organizations rather than spend money on their upkeep.[18]

This unfriendly attitude toward preservation reflected political imperatives at the local level. Municipal authorities were under tremendous pressure to ameliorate the housing crisis in Moscow. Restoration work on monuments was more time-consuming and expensive than the construction and renovation of conventional buildings. During the 1950s, Kuznetsov pressed for the establishment of a construction agency that would deal solely with architectural and historical monuments, hoping that an economy of scale would staunch the flight of capital away from restoration work. He also proposed that the punitive functions of the Preservation Inspectorate be reinforced. A 1949 law gave prosecutors the right to file criminal charges against individuals who violated the preservation legislation, but even in egregious cases they rarely exercised it.[19] As a result, the gap between federal law and local reality persisted. While Kuznetsov recognized the good intentions of federal authorities, he feared that local organizations were insufficiently equipped to deal effectively with preservation issues. By the end of the 1950s, many other preservationists had come to a more drastic conclusion: some local authorities, particularly Moscow's urban planners, were unduly hostile to architectural and historical monuments.

Preservationists' suspicions were fueled by the growing ambitions of urban planners. In 1952, the Council of Ministers approved the second master plan for the reconstruction of Moscow, which outlined the extent and location of all construction in the capital for the remainder of the decade. Even though the most expensive aspects of Stalinist planning were under attack during the late 1940s and early '50s, the plan remained monumental and elitist in orientation. Nearly all construction was slated for densely built areas lining the radial streets and river

18. RGALI, f. 2466, o. 1, d. 399, ll. 21–22; TsMAM, f. 150, o. 1, d. 2772, ll. 394–403; and E. S. Afanas'eva, ed., "Ravnodushie k kul'turnomu naslediiu stolitsy. Pis'mo moskovskikh arkhitektorov N. S. Khrushevu. 1954 g.," Istoricheskii arkhiv 3 (1997): 100–104.
19. RGALI, f. 2466, o. 1, d. 399, ll. 23–25.

embankments.[20] Only days after Stalin's death, however, the chief of the city party committee, Nikolai Mikhailov, and the chairman of Mossovet, Mikhail Iasnov, asked Khrushchev and Georgii Malenkov, then the head of government, to open the 1952 plan for revision.[21] Their request stands as one of the precursors to Khrushchev's repudiation of Stalinist architecture in 1954. It also marked the end of expensive projects in Moscow's historic center, a development that helped slow the rate of demolition. In October 1954, K. I. Trapeznikov, an official at Moscow's Architectural-Planning Administration, tried to reassure members of MOSA's urban-planning and construction section that the end of Stalinist "excess" did not signify the demise of plans to rebuild the center of Moscow. He admitted, nonetheless, that there had been no discussion with the new Kremlin leaders about which projects would be undertaken in coming years. Ambitious urban planning, it seemed, had died alongside Stalin.[22]

Fortunately for Trapeznikov and others, rumors about the demise of urban planning in Moscow proved greatly exaggerated. In 1959 and 1962, MOSA members discussed separate proposals for the reconstruction of the area within the Garden Circle. Both proposals envisioned the sort of massive demolitions necessitated by Novyi Arbat, since they were based on the modernist principle of "functional zoning," which kept residential, commercial, administrative, and recreational areas separate. Ivan Zhol'tovskii, the author of the 1959 plan and an architect who had distinguished himself four decades earlier by drafting some of the first plans to rebuild Moscow along socialist lines, proposed that the area within the Garden Circle be reserved for federal institutions. Zhol'tovskii also called for the demolition of the ornate GUM building, which housed a shopping center, the Historical Museum on Red Square, and the lower trading rows in Kitai Gorod to accentuate the grandiosity of the Kremlin. The author of the 1962 proposal, N. N. Ullas, the chief of the Institute of the Master Plan, left the Kremlin district untouched, but proposed that the area between the Lenin Library and the Pushkin Museum, southwest of the Kremlin, be set aside for important cultural institutions. He also

20. Colton, *Moscow,* 352–54; and V. Iu. Afiani, "Ob izmenenii Genplana rekonstruktsii Moskvy. Zapiska MK KPSS i ispolkoma Mossoveta G. M. Malenkovu i N. S. Khrushchevu. 1953 g.," *Istoricheskii arkhiv* 5–6 (1997): 51–74.
21. E. Taranov, "Gorod kommunizma (idei liderov 50–60-kh godov i ikh voploshchenie)," in *Moskovskii arkhiv: istoriko-kraevedcheskii al'manakh,* vyp. 1, ed. E. I. Kavtaradze, V. F. Kozlov, T. N. Nikol'skaia, A. N. Shakhanov, and I. F. Iushin (Moscow, 1996), 374.
22. RGALI, f. 2466, o. 1, d. 370, ll. 6–7.

suggested that a new half-circle boulevard be built between Arbat Square in the west, Kuznetskii Bridge in the north, and Three-Bridges Square in the east, at the intersection of the Moscow and Yauza Rivers. Both authors assumed that residential areas in the center of Moscow needed "deconsolidation," a euphemism for the forced resettlement of residents to peripheral regions. Ullas proposed that the population of central Moscow be cut from 900,000 to 200,000 by tearing down "every ancient, worthless building." Zhol'tovskii had a more ambitious target of 150,000.[23]

Both proposals to rebuild the center of Moscow were lightning rods for controversy. During the discussion of Zhol'tovskii's proposal in 1959, the historian Petr Sytin, the author of several authoritative books on the history of Moscow, tried to compromise with urban planners. Sytin agreed that the GUM building, which had been built in the 1890s on the site of the upper trading rows, could be torn down if it were necessary to widen Red Square. But he demanded that the lower trading rows and the Historical Museum, which guarded the western entrance to Red Square, be preserved, and that planning work on the Rossiia Hotel cease.[24] Sytin's attempt at compromise was indicative of the bête noire that this latter structure had become among preservationists, and the bitter medicine some were willing to take to thwart the project. The proposed site for the hotel, in the Zariad'e district adjacent to Red Square and Kitai Gorod, was razed during the late 1940s to accommodate a wedding-cake skyscraper. Khrushchev abandoned these plans in 1954 amid concerns of excessive cost. Two years later, work again began at the site when the city's Urban-Planning Council approved Dmitrii Chechulin's designs for a structure so immense that several pre-Petrine churches and the sixteenth-century Palace of the English Court on the adjacent Razin Street would have to be demolished. With more than 3,000 rooms, the Rossiia would be the largest hotel in Europe and would loom behind St. Basil's Cathedral.[25]

Not everyone was willing to compromise, even to thwart the construction of the Rossiia Hotel. Several MOSA members bluntly vilified Zhol'tovskii and Ullas for proposing the demolition of architectural monuments. One architect claimed that they were Russia's "primordial enemies," and were complicit in the destruction of national treasures. Several others urged urban planners to spend more time reflecting on

23. RGALI, f. 2466, o. 2, d. 29, ll. 20–22, 25; and d. 258, ll. 11, 13–14, 19.
24. RGALI, f. 2466, o. 2, d. 29, ll. 77–81.
25. Colton, Moscow, 555–58; and Romaniuk, Moskva. Utraty, 70–72.

the history and tradition of Moscow before proposing any demolition.[26] Some architects questioned the fiscal soundness of demolition in the city's densely populated center. After Ullas claimed that the reconstruction of the area within the Garden Circle would only cost 620 million rubles to implement fully, preservationists pointed out that his calculation did not account for the value of destroyed infrastructure, or for the cost of replacement housing in peripheral areas, a figure that was much higher. Others challenged the logic behind Moscow's so-called red-line policy, often the litmus test for demolition, and attacked architects who fostered a "cult of the red line." During the 1930s, urban planners plotted red lines on the maps of radial streets to facilitate their widening; buildings that encroached on the red lines were scheduled for demolition. Even in the late 1950s, many urban planners assumed that all radial streets would be widened so they resembled Gorky Street, the elite commercial and residential corridor northwest of the Kremlin that was one of the most celebrated reconstruction projects of the 1930s.[27] "We are not fanatics," one MOSA member assured the architects in Zhol'tovskii's studio in 1959, "and we know that there will be victims in the reconstruction of Moscow. But we have already lost so much in Moscow that we must now take steps to insure that the number of victims will be as small as possible."[28]

MOSA activists also spent a great deal of time trying to ascertain the "indisputable . . . scientific basis" of architectural and historical monuments, since they commonly assumed that one of the chief problems plaguing preservation efforts was a lack of consensus about what constituted a monument. In March 1960, at the impetus of the Academy of Sciences and the Ministry of Culture, MOSA members discussed a report entitled "The Fundamental Principles for the Registration and Preservation of Cultural Monuments." The author, the architectural historian Nikolai Voronin, reiterated the standard materialist line that the national culture of every people was manifested in art, architecture, and music. But he also said something that proved more controversial: the value attributed to this output was historically contingent. A subsequent speaker put a more casual spin on it. Personal "taste" was the decisive factor in determining what constituted a monument.[29] Of

26. RGALI, f. 2466, o. 2, d. 30, l. 4; d. 258, l. 89; and d. 383, l. 42.
27. RGALI, f. 2466, o. 1, d. 399, l. 20; and d. 258, l. 55.
28. RGALI, f. 2466, o. 2, d. 30, l. 5.
29. RGALI, f. 2466, o. 4, d. 490, ll. 12–24, 51–53.

course, this raised an important question. Which person or organization should be the final arbiter of taste in issues regarding preservation?

At this early point, most preservationists were willing to defer to the organizations that had traditionally held sway in these affairs—the Council of Ministers and the Ministry of Culture (formerly the All-Union Committee on Artistic Affairs). Their reasoning was simple. Beginning in 1948, federal authorities had taken sizeable steps to protect architectural and historical monuments with the creation of preservation registries and buffer zones. Ensuring that these measures were implemented in the proper spirit at the local level had now become the most pressing issue. One preservationist argued that the chief problem plaguing preservation work in Moscow was ignorance at Mossovet about the plight of monuments. Similarly, Kuznetsov, head of the city's Preservation Inspectorate, blamed administrators at the Architectural-Planning Administration who all too often saw demolition as "the line of least resistance."[30]

Because preservationists saw local authorities as their primary adversaries, they repeatedly pressed party leaders to halt the decentralization of the preservation oversight and enforcement mechanism. In March 1956, Boris Mikhailov, head of the federal Preservation Inspectorate, petitioned Khrushchev to abandon proposed legislation that would delegate all authority vested in his organization to a network of local inspectorates, subordinate to district, city, and oblast soviets. Mikhailov claimed that local inspectorates were often run by persons with little regard for preservation. In those instances when they legitimately championed the interests of monuments, they were frequently thwarted by unsympathetic bosses in the soviets. Party organizations, the most significant power at the local level, typically ignored complaints about preservation altogether. Mikhailov warned that the federal Preservation Inspectorate was the only administrative agency capable "of raising and resolving questions on the preservation and support of cultural monuments in our country."[31] Later that month, Igor Grabar', a curator at the Tretiakov Gallery and once a friend of Anatolii Lunacharskii, the first Commissar of Enlightenment, warned Khrushchev that the new legislation meant the destruction of the unified system of preservation that was embodied by Lenin's 1918 decree that nationalized cultural treasures. Nikolai Voronin and Petr Baranovskii, who was chairman of the

---

30. RGALI, f. 2466, o. 2, d. 30, l. 6.
31. RGANI, f. 5, o. 36, d. 26, ll. 51–52.

preservation section in the Union of Architects, a former member of Old Moscow, and one of the Soviet Union's most accomplished architectural restorers, said much the same in a telegram to the Central Committee. At the end of the summer, the writer Ilya Ehrenburg and the artist Pavel Korin requested a personal meeting with Mikhail Suslov, the Central Committee's chief ideologue, to discuss the new legislation before its final approval at the Council of Ministers. The preservationists' persistence paid off: in December 1956, the Central Committee formally rejected the legislation, citing the input from Mikhailov and others.[32]

For preservationists, it was a modest victory. The federal Preservation Inspectorate could continue to meddle in local affairs, thus preserving a status quo that was not ideal, but perhaps better than the narrowly avoided alternative. At the same time, however, a handful of MOSA activists began to question their reliance on federal power, and pushed their organization, albeit carefully and haltingly at first, to assume a more active and formal position in the urban-planning process, and to become the final arbiter of "taste" in issues regarding historical and architectural preservation. Their efforts were fueled by two events in the spring of 1962. The first was the publication of a controversial article in the journal *Moskva* that disparaged virtually every aspect of urban planning in the capital. The second was the beginning of the Novyi Arbat demolition.

THE *MOSKVA* AFFAIR

The article "How Should Moscow Now Be Built?" was the most frank public assessment of Soviet urban planning in more than thirty years.[33] The authors—Petr Reviakin, a member of MOSA; A. A. Korobov, a member of the Moscow Section of the Union of Artists; Nataliia Chetunova, a member of the Moscow Section of the Union of Writers; and V. Tydman, an engineer active in preservation issues—made only a vague reference to Novyi Arbat, but the issues they raised would later be seized on by

32. RGANI, f. 5, o. 36, d. 26, ll. 54–56, 93–95.
33. A. Korobov, P. Reviakin, V. Tydman, and N. Chetunova, "Kak dal'she stroit' Moskvu," *Moskva* 3 (March 1962): 147–60. For a synopsis of the article, see Colton, *Moscow,* 419–21. For less tendentious evaluations of urban planning and historical preservation, see Vladimir Soloukhin, "Berech' proshloe—dumat' o budushchem," *Neva* 11 (1962): 195–203; and D. S. Likhachev, "Berech' pamiatniki proshlogo," *Neva* 3 (1963): 195–96.

those who opposed the street. The article purported to be a summary of a roundtable discussion between architects from the Institute of the Master Plan, an agency subordinate to the Architectural-Planning Administration, and representatives from the editorial board of the journal, which was affiliated with the Moscow Section of the Union of Writers. While its authors admitted beforehand that they "did not agree about everything" with the institute's architects, their goal was to provoke a "wide discussion" about urban planning in Moscow. The authors attacked a variety of shortcomings at the Architectural-Planning Administration: urban planners' neglect of industrial pollution and air quality in residential areas; the "unscientific" basis of planning; the poor condition of Moscow's parks, gardens, and boulevards; the monotony of its new peripheral neighborhoods; and the seemingly uncontrolled nature of its sprawl. But the two issues that proved most contentious concerned the state of architectural and historical preservation in the capital and the secrecy that still clouded much of the urban-planning process.[34]

The case that Reviakin and his coauthors built against the Architectural-Planning Administration's record on preservation was devoid of the pleasantries and qualifications that typically accompanied criticism of prominent officials in the Soviet press. They argued that the administration repeatedly violated the fundamental principle governing preservation in the Soviet Union: all cultural treasures belonged to the people; consequently, the people alone should make decisions regarding demolition and preservation. The authors drew a controversial parallel between the fate of Pskov and Petrodvorets, architectural treasures that were destroyed by the Germans during the war, and the "modernization" of Moscow, which in their opinion was proceeding with little regard for the will of Muscovites.[35] They claimed that urban planners had insulated themselves from the public's disdain by keeping their work secret.

It is no longer tolerable that the Master Plan of Moscow, which decisively affects every Muscovite, is "kept secret" from the inhabitants of the capital. We must put an end to a situation where Muscovites see only "accomplished facts," where the magical tenet "This Has Already Been Decided" is king.

34. Korobov et al., "Kak dal'she stroit' Moskvu," 147.
35. On the official response to this assertion, see RGALI, f. 2931, o. 1, d. 42, l. 15.

This was used to suppress all opinions about "settled" questions, to eliminate any criticism that would transgress upon the "personal" decision of Stalin or Moscow's "guardian," Kaganovich.[36]

Paradoxically, the impetus for "How Should Moscow Now Be Built?" came from Petr Demichev, chief of the Moscow Party Committee. In June 1961, Demichev met with the head of the *Moskva* editorial board, Evgenii Popovkin, to suggest that the journal allot more space to discussions about the future of Moscow.[37] Demichev's intervention served as official approbation for an article that had long been stalled in the netherworld of potentially incendiary journalism—a review of the Architectural-Planning Administration's stewardship over the capital. Four years earlier, in June 1957, the writer Efim Dorosh encouraged the *Moskva* editors to look into urban planning in the capital. It is not clear whether Dorosh had any relationship with the authors of the 1962 article, but his criticisms were similar: urban planners showed little regard for the capital's architectural and historical monuments; plans for Novyi Arbat gave the impression that the street would transverse an "empty space" rather than the historical heart of Moscow; and the Mossovet officials who oversaw planning and construction in the capital consistently ignored the "voices of the masses." "We are old Muscovites," Dorosh wrote, "and over the course of many years we have unsuccessfully tried to make Mossovet employees understand that . . . we have special spiritual needs, manifested in love for our city. . . . Unfortunately, Mossovet continues to sanction the destruction of our cultural treasures . . . despite the protests of the public."[38]

After the meeting with Demichev, the journal's editorial board decided on a "roundtable discussion," a format that had become popular in the years since Stalin's death, and that had previously been used to outline the opposition to the Rossiia Hotel project and to talk about preservation more broadly.[39] On September 30 and October 3, 1961, the

36. Colton, *Moscow,* 421, quoting Korobov et al., "Kak dal'she stroit' Moskvu," 150. Kaganovich evoked special ire among preservationists because he served as chief of the Moscow Party Committee in the early 1930s, when he oversaw the demolition of dozens of monuments. He was also Jewish, which did not endear him to the many Russian nationalists who were sympathetic to the preservation movement.
37. RGALI, f. 2931, o. 1, d. 42, l. 2.
38. RGALI, f. 2931, o. 1, d. 14, l. 24.
39. "Pamiatniki kul'tury—pod okhranu naroda!," *Literatura i zhizn',* April 13, 1960, 2; and N. Chetunova, "Zariad'e: chto tam budet?," *Moskva* 9 (September 1961): 200–203.

journal invited several prominent architects from the Institute of the Master Plan to discuss the future of urban planning in Moscow. The transcripts from these meetings served as the basis for the article.

Official reaction to the article came on May 10, 1962, when *Pravda* ran an unsigned rebuttal to the article inside a broader denunciation of architects who perpetuated Stalinist "excess in architecture and construction." A day later, officials from the Architectural-Planning Administration published an even more vitriolic denunciation in *Pravda*.[40] Timothy Colton suggests that Khrushchev personally signed off on these rebuttals, citing his complicity in the destruction of numerous historical monuments while chief of the Moscow Party Committee in the 1930s.[41] Although the records of the journal's editorial board are silent on this issue, they do provide a rough outline of the sequence of events that preceded the *Pravda* articles. On May 9, 1962, the Moscow Party Committee summoned Vasilii Kulemin, a member of the *Moskva* editorial board, and two colleagues from the journal's current-affairs department to discuss the implications of the article with officials from the Architectural-Planning Administration. "I expected that there would be an exchange of opinions," Kulemin later told his colleagues on the editorial board,

> where comrades would say what they thought was right and wrong. It was nothing of the sort. It was a complete tirade. They told us that the article was anti-Soviet; it was insufficiently vigilant; it was worthy of a white-guard pamphlet published in Paris; it was against the party and government.

With the exception of Mikhail Posokhin, nearly every prominent official at the Architectural-Planning Administration was present. Few minced words in their denunciations. One architect accused the authors of engaging in a "petit-bourgeois/kulak" campaign against the Soviet Union. Another claimed to have found a more evenhanded analysis of Soviet urban planning in a Vatican gift shop. Referring to the time he spent chaperoning Richard Nixon around Moscow during the American Economic Exhibit in 1959, the latter critic added that even staunch anticommunists "recognized our achievements in construction." Back at the journal's editorial offices, Kulemin reassured his colleagues that

40. "Eshche raz po povodu izlishestv v stroitel'stve i arkhitekture," *Pravda*, May 10, 1962, 2; and "Protiv vrednoi putanitsy v voprosakh gradostroitel'stva," *Pravda*, May 11, 1962, 4.
41. Colton, *Moscow*, 420.

much of this had just been for "show." But for those who shared responsibility for the article, it was an unnerving experience.[42]

The threat of punishment forced the journal's editors to reevaluate the process that led to the article's publication. The article purported to be an objective report from a roundtable discussion, but even the editors admitted that it was slanted in favor of preservationists. "We took the meaning [of their comments], and developed it," one editor admitted, clouding the line between viewpoint and verity. Another editor admitted that prior to publication he had ignored complaints from urban planners that a draft of the article did not fairly represent their views, an egregious breach of normal Soviet journalistic protocol.[43] In the end, the *Moskva* staff judiciously decided to reprint the second *Pravda* denunciation alongside an article by Mikhail Posokhin on the Architectural-Planning Administration's future plans for Moscow.[44] Judging by the public response, however, Posokhin enjoyed little support beyond the halls of the Moscow Party Committee. During the latter part of May, the editorial board at *Moskva* received dozens of letters congratulating it for publishing the article. One writer confessed that she believed every word, because urban planners had already spoiled much of her own neighborhood.[45] Many others were critical of *Pravda* for providing space for "mean-spirited" denunciations. *Pravda* editors failed to pay attention to the "rude, unworthy, and undemocratic tone" of the urban planners' rebuttal. Some thought the denunciations were reminiscent of the Stalin period. "And how did our architects react to the correct and highly necessary criticisms of construction in Moscow? . . . They used statements out of context, misrepresentations, and also a weapon from the arsenal . . . of the cult of personality—attacks on people who say things that are not pleasing to them."[46] Finally, nearly every writer took issue with the central point of the *Pravda* denunciations—that the type of criticism in the *Moskva* article was unhealthy and misleading. "You can no longer think the people are fools," one anonymous writer admonished *Pravda* in a letter that veered from urban planning to Shostakovich's Fourth Symphony, which the composer abandoned in 1936 during the controversy surrounding *Lady Macbeth of the Mtsenk District.* "It's time to throw Stalin in the grave."[47]

42. RGALI, f. 2931, o. 1, d. 42, ll. 11, 15–16.
43. RGALI, f. 2931, o. 1, d. 42, ll. 13–14.
44. RGALI, f. 2931, o. 1, d. 42, ll. 23, 28; and M. Posokhin, "Kontury nashego zavtra," *Moskva* 6 (1962): 169–71.
45. RGALI, f. 2931, o. 1, d. 42, l. 40.
46. RGALI, f. 2931, o. 1, d. 42, ll. 52, 56.
47. RGALI, f. 2931, o. 1, d. 42, ll. 54, 76.

MOSA members convened on June 11, 1962 to discuss the article and decide the fate of Petr Reviakin, a member of the organization for nearly three decades, and one of its most outspoken defenders of architectural and historical monuments. The meeting was closely supervised by K. I. Trapeznikov and a number of officials from the Architectural-Planning Administration. Support for Reviakin from preservationist quarters was mostly muted. Only Boris Kuznetsov, chief of the city's Preservation Inspectorate, showed sympathy by explicitly refusing to denounce him.[48] In his keynote address, Trapeznikov hewed closely to the *Pravda* denunciations. He acknowledged that the idea for a round-table on urban planning was not bad, but he insisted that MOSA members exercise special tact when speaking to the press. Trapeznikov also denied that the secrecy surrounding the city's master plan hindered public discussions about the state of planning and construction in Moscow. And he characterized the demand that all planning be conducted in the open as "naïve" and "demagogic." "One thing is for certain," he argued, "the demand for 'freedom of criticism' *without consideration of government interests is an unhealthy tendency.*"[49]

In the end, Reviakin fared reasonably well. He received only a "strict reprimand" from the MOSA board, despite the silence of preservationist allies. Although he admitted that the roundtable discussion had an "unprofessional, dilettantish character" about it, he suggested that this might have been remedied had professional journals sponsored the event instead of the popular *Moskva.* He refused to recant the criticisms that he and his coauthors had lodged against urban planners, and he insisted that the whole affair would have a positive impact on the state of planning in the capital.[50]

For Posokhin and his Novyi Arbat team, Reviakin's censure was timely. On July 19, 1962, N. N. Selivanov, chief of Moscow's Planning Commission and a member of the Urban-Planning Council that granted final approval to projects before construction, supervised the first formal presentation of the Novyi Arbat project to MOSA members. If Selivanov's patronage of Novyi Arbat conflicted with the independence that the Urban-Planning Council required, MOSA members were not brave enough to mention it. During the previous months, there had been occasional grumbling within the organization about the administration's disregard for MOSA input in the project, and members' reluctance to be

48. RGALI, f. 2466, o. 2, d. 141, l. 34.
49. RGALI, f. 2466, o. 2, d. 141, ll. 7–8, 10, 16. The emphasis is in the original document.
50. RGALI, f. 2466, o. 2, d. 141, ll. 42–44.

more outspoken. Novyi Arbat had not been sufficiently "thought through," one member warned, "the public and the union are standing on the side. . . . [We need] to discuss the actual problems and not be afraid of what the Moscow Party Committee and Mossovet will say."[51] During this first meeting, Selivanov kept a tight rein on the podium. Mostly compliant MOSA members discussed Novyi Arbat and a variety of other projects in the context of the Twenty-second Party Congress. Although preservationist sentiment was absent, a handful of architects summoned the courage to make oblique references to the *Moskva* affair. One MOSA member called on his colleagues to "battle with the chief architect [Posokhin], even though he has been vested with great power," to ensure that all construction projects enjoyed the support of architects. Another asked why Posokhin was not present at the discussion. Was it not another instance where "everything is decided, but nothing is discussed," another "relapse to the cult of personality"?[52]

During the early 1960s, issues concerning historical preservation and the role of the public in the urban planning process became increasingly entangled. Preservationists renewed calls for the creation of a voluntary preservation organization. In 1958, the Central Committee convened a special commission to create the framework for such an organization, only to have the corresponding legislation stall when it was submitted to the Council of Ministers.[53] MOSA lent its support to the idea in 1960, when its preservation section recommended that "volunteer" preservation organizations be attached to every district, city, and oblast soviet to check the prerogatives of executive committees.[54] Attendees at the Third Congress of Architects endorsed a similar resolution urging the government to expedite legislation on a preservation organization in 1961.[55] They envisioned an organization like the Georgian Society for the Preservation of Cultural Monuments, which had been formed in 1959 and quickly grew to 300,000 members in 3,900 local chapters. The Georgian Society provided assistance to authorities charged with the enforcement of preservation laws and voluntary labor for restoration projects. Similar preservation organizations existed at the union level in Azerbaijan and Latvia, and locally in the Ukrainian cities of Sevastopol, Odessa, and Zhytomyr. As John Farrell points out, the fact that Russia was denied its

51. RGALI, f. 2466, o. 2, d. 258, ll. 98–99.
52. RGALI, f. 2466, o. 2, d. 287, ll. 33, 44, 57.
53. RGANI, f. 5, o. 55, d. 49, l. 55.
54. RGALI, f. 2466, o. 4, d. 492, l. 26.
55. RGALI, f. 2466, o. 4, d. 10, l. 75.

own preservation organization, and that the Soviet government had seemingly endorsed a double standard for Russians and Georgians, only augmented preservationists' anger.[56]

The Novyi Arbat project was one of the chief reasons for the resurgence of calls for greater public input in the urban-planning process. When construction began in 1962, preservationists rallied around three buildings on Kompozitorskaia Street and Sobach'e Square, nos. 5, 7, and 12. Because they were associated with Aleksei Khomiakov and the great intellectual debates of the 1830s and '40s, the first two buildings enjoyed the protection of the preservation registry. The third building had been home to a young Vladimir Lenin before he went into exile in Siberia in the 1890s, usually a sufficient pedigree to thwart demolition. Preservationists claimed to have received a guarantee from Mossovet that the buildings would be raised, placed on rollers, and moved outside the demolition corridor, a procedure that architects had used in the 1930s in response to public opposition to the reconstruction of Gorky Street.[57] Yet in June 1962, the Mossovet Executive Committee, citing excessive costs, received permission from the Ministry of Culture to raze the two buildings under official protection.[58] Later that summer, a deputy chairman at Mossovet approved the demolition of the third building, leaving preservationists feeling betrayed. Petr Reviakin, Nikolai Voronin, Boris Mikhailov, and a number of other preservationists cited the case in a letter to Ekaterina Furtseva, the Minister of Culture, as evidence of the lack of popular input in the planning process, and of the necessity of a public organization to counterbalance the prerogatives of Mossovet and the Architectural-Planning Administration. The buildings were destroyed, they wrote, "despite the sharp protests of the Soviet public."[59]

How widespread were these protests? Anecdotal evidence confirms the presence of considerable apprehension among the public about the Novyi Arbat project. According to a Union of Architects report, the majority of unsigned letters that the Union received on the eve of its Third Congress in 1961 pertained to Novyi Arbat. Many included requests that construction be halted altogether.[60] Only a handful of these letters are

56. RGANI, f. 5, o. 55, d. 49, ll. 99–102; and Farrell, "If These Stones Could Only Speak," 240–41.
57. On public opposition to the demolition on Gorky Street, see Raisa Orlova, *Memoirs*, trans. Samuel Cioran (New York, 1983), 28.
58. GARF, f. A-259, o. 42, d. 9697, l. 74.
59. RGANI, f. 5, o. 55, d. 49, l. 56.
60. RGALI, f. 674, o. 3, d. 1841, l. 92.

extant, but they confirm the type of "sharp protests" that Reviakin, Voronin, and Mikhailov cited. One Muscovite chastised planners for thinking that Moscow's central districts needed "still more open spaces," and worried about the impact of Novyi Arbat on the capital's housing crisis. Another insisted that the Architectural-Planning Administration's dubious record to date, like its decision to locate the building for Patrice Lumumba University next to a crematorium, necessitated the creation of a public oversight council (*obshchestvennyi sovet*), less it ruin the Novyi Arbat project as well.[61]

In August 1963, Dmitrii Polikarpov, deputy director of the Central Committee's Ideological Department, rejected the notion of an independent, voluntary preservation organization. Even though Furtseva threw her support behind the idea—she thought it corresponded nicely with Khrushchev's emphasis on "self-administration"—Polikarpov concluded that the public could better be mobilized under the supervision of an existing institution. He recommended that the Central Committee formally jettison plans for the organization.[62] A similar development was underway at MOSA, where administrators were trying to restrict public input in the urban-planning process. Prior to the Ninth Conference of Moscow Architects in January 1964, the MOSA board ordered the keynote speaker to include an explanation of the appropriate role of the non-architectural public in urban-planning affairs.

> Popular opinion—based on adherence to party principles, professional experience, and skill—is a huge force, capable of exerting a decisive influence on the development of practical work . . . but the wide architectural public—truly apprehending the meaning and significance of the urban-planning and technological policies carried out by the party—exerts paramount influence on the realization of architectural work and the elimination of previous mistakes.[63]

This explanation was obviously restrictive. It recognized the potential utility of popular opinion, but called for its subordination to architects' expertise. It was an unambiguous rebuttal of the *Moskva* article.

Fortunately for preservationists, it was also temporary. In October 1964, the Central Committee removed Nikita Khrushchev as first secretary,

61. RGALI, f. 674, o. 4, d. 10, ll. 6–9, 142–43; and Volkov, *Kazhdyi kamen' v nei zhivoi*, 167.
62. RGANI, f. 5, o. 55, d. 49, ll. 69–94.
63. RGALI, f. 2466, o. 2, d. 215, l. 2.

citing, among other things, his growing cult of personality and indifference to criticism. The most significant manifestation of internal party democracy since the factional struggles of the 1920s provoked the most thorough and ardent debate yet over the public's role in urban planning and preservation. Once again, Novyi Arbat was at the center of it all.

After Khrushchev

On February 18, 1965, members of MOSA's architectural preservation section convened a joint meeting at the Shchusev Architectural Museum near Arbat Square with Mossovet's lackluster Commission for Architectural Preservation, the Moscow Section of the Union of Artists, and the federal Union of Writers in order to determine "general principles" for architectural and historical preservation. The meeting was chaired by Nikolai Evstratov, the chief architect at the Institute of the Master Plan. The keynote address was given by Nikolai Shchepetil'nikov, the head of the Architectural-Planning Administration's municipal affairs section and its public liaison. Although attendance was by invitation only, nearly every prominent MOSA preservationist was present. This meeting, and its sequel two weeks later, was the acme of the preservation movement in Moscow in the 1950s and 1960s. At no other time did preservationists so vigorously attack officials at the Architectural-Planning Administration and Mossovet. At no other time was there more optimism about the potential for reform.

The meeting got off to an inconspicuous start with Shchepetil'nikov's humdrum speech. He recited a list of mostly meaningless preservation statistics, and complained, disingenuously many thought, about the accounting restraints that prevented the administration from intervening on behalf of monuments that were not "on the books" of the municipal government. Midway through his speech, however, he mentioned something that was surely news to most in the audience: the Architectural-Planning Administration had recently received permission to remove nine structures from the preservation registry, a step that usually preceded demolition. Shchepetil'nikov insisted that this was simply an unfortunate and unavoidable product of the reconstruction of Moscow. The administration was not "waiting for the day when there will be less architectural monuments in Moscow, when it will have less worries."[64]

64. RGALI, f. 2466, o. 4, d. 25, l. 28.

Shchepetil'nikov's justification struck many in the audience as spurious. As soon as he stepped down from the podium, the auditorium erupted in protest. When Evstratov tried to answer a question submitted on paper about the status of a proposal to enlarge "preservation zones," a popular idea because they would protect entire swaths of the city rather than individual buildings, the stenographer recorded the following exchange.

> We in the Institute of the Master Plan tried to find these areas for preservation, but honestly speaking, we couldn't find them (laughter, noise in hall)
>
> (From the hall: You didn't look hard enough!)
>
> I understand why you're upset.
>
> (From the hall: This is outrageous!)
>
> The point is that . . . the Kropotkinskaia Street area [on the southern fringe of the Arbat neighborhood] . . . has to a significant extent been destroyed already.
>
> (From the hall: And that means that it's necessary to destroy every last bit of it?)[65]

The commotion laid bare the chasm that had opened between urban planners and Mossovet officials on one side, and preservationists on the other. Contrary to the situation following the *Moskva* controversy in 1962, no one felt obliged to voice polite support for Posokhin and his colleagues. One MOSA member claimed that urban planners and Mossovet officials were "insufficiently competent" to make any decisions regarding architectural and historical monuments in the capital. Another said that it was dishonest for the administration to cite accounting restraints as an impediment when the Urban-Planning Council, a subordinate organization, could veto any project that negatively impacted monuments.[66] Peter Reviakin, whose popularity was only enhanced by the official reprimand he had received in 1962, joked from the podium that there were two types of Mossovet decrees on preservation:

1. "On shortening the list of architectural monuments in Moscow."
2. "On the failure to carry out in the proper time frame 'On shortening the list. . . .'"

65. RGALI, f. 2466, o. 4, d. 25, l. 42.
66. RGALI, f. 2466, o. 4, d. 25, ll. 54, 73.

"And do you know what you call the [second] decree?" Reviakin asked a dismayed Evstratov and Shchepetil'nikov to considerable amusement, "On the amelioration of the affairs of architectural preservation!"[67]

Speakers presented a long list of demands. Several MOSA members wondered why urban planners were trying to replicate New York's skyline on Novyi Arbat. They called for legislation that would prohibit the construction of any building in the center more than six-stories tall. Another speaker called for the immediate formation of blanket preservation zones with public control over their boundaries and enforcement. Reviakin urged party officials to allow greater contacts with preservation groups in the West. A. A. Korobov, one of the coauthors of the *Moskva* article, demanded that criminal proceedings be initiated against the Mossovet official who had approved the destruction of the building on Kompozitorskaia Street where Lenin had lived. Numerous others rallied behind the voluntary preservation organization that the Central Committee had torpedoed two years earlier.[68]

Similar to the *Moskva* affair, many of these demands hinged on the public's role in urban planning. Referring to Khrushchev's dismissal four months earlier, Reviakin reassured MOSA members that the "weather" was finally changing.

> After many years of nihilism in relation to our architectural inheritance, a holiday has come. Now we may toss aside arguments about whether to preserve or tear down architectural monuments. Now we are obligated to concentrate on the fundamental principles of preservation. . . . The first principles of preservation are openness, accountability, and attention to the will of the public—meaning the scientific, artistic, and professional publics, and also the general public. These principles should lead to the abolition of . . . secrecy, unaccountability, and neglect of popular opinion.

Less than three years after similar comments nearly resulted in his expulsion from MOSA, Reviakin was widely applauded. Numerous persons approached the podium to reiterate what he had said. One speaker demanded that newspapers publish the text of Reviakin's speech.[69]

When the speeches went late into the evening, the audience managed to force MOSA administrators to schedule a second session for March 3.

67. RGALI, f. 2466, o. 4, d. 25, ll. 79–80.
68. RGALI, f. 2466, o. 4, d. 25, ll. 74–75, 82, 109, 137.
69. RGALI, f. 2466, o. 4, d. 25, ll. 76–77, 112, 134.

This was an extraordinary development, and one that was indicative of the strong feelings that architectural and historical preservation evoked. It was also clearly unpopular among the officials from the Architectural-Planning Administration who were present. One speaker even joked about the expressions of those sitting in the front rows where there was "not much enthusiasm." At the beginning of the second session, one of Posokhin's deputy directors made an overture to preservationists. He encouraged MOSA members to form a commission with the Unions of Writers and Artists to help the Architectural-Planning Administration review preservation issues in Moscow, the first time the administration had agreed to any sort of public infringement on its prerogatives.[70] Nevertheless, the second meeting turned out to be even more raucous than the first. A member of the Union of Artists told Posokhin's deputy that the Architectural-Planning Administration had perverted the "noble slogan" of the party for its own ends. "We will take care of the people, just as long as they do not bother us." He compared the "narrow-mindedness" of urban planners and their political patrons to Aleksei Arakcheev, an adviser to Alexander I in the early 1800s and the personification of the authoritarian proclivities of the tsarist government. Urban planners were "torn from the people (for whom they build), shut away in a special corner with the Arakcheev regime, long ago transformed into its assistant, building its own estate from the materials of ancient Moscow." Other speakers again attacked Novyi Arbat and promised a fight should similar projects be planned for other parts of Moscow. Even the prodigal son of Soviet architecture, the great constructivist Konstantin Melnikov, rose to the podium to speak in support of preservation. He claimed that it was the first time he had set foot in the meeting hall at the Shchusev Museum in forty years.[71]

V. Tydman, one of the coauthors of the *Moskva* article, explained why preservationists were willing "to speak so openly" in the spring of 1965. He cited a recent article in *Pravda* about the famous collection of eighteenth-century wooden churches on Kizhi Island in Karelia, near the Finnish border. In Tydman's mind, the article affirmed the centrality of inherited tradition in Soviet culture. Tydman also referred to a second *Pravda* article, which appeared to sanction preservationists' criticism of the Architectural-Planning Administration. When Soviet citizens

70. RGALI, f. 2466, o. 4, d. 26, ll. 19, 60.
71. RGALI, f. 2466, o. 4, d. 26, ll. 67, 78b, 92, 118–22.

review the plans and policies of their government, "they enhance them with their experience, ideas, and knowledge."[72] Finally, Tydman mentioned Khrushchev's dismissal at the October Central Committee plenum as reason to speak frankly. Like Stalin and Kaganovich, Khrushchev "looked at Moscow as if it were his own hereditary estate." Among Khrushchev's many mistakes was his "strong-armed" implementation of Moscow's master plan. Public criticism was the only way to prevent similar mistakes in the future.[73]

Like the meeting two weeks earlier, the podium stayed crowded late into the evening. Once again preservationists tried to force an extension. By this time, however, tempers among MOSA officials and urban planners were high. When Petr Baranovskii, chief of the preservation section of the Union of Architects, drifted beyond the five-minute time slot for his speech, Selivanov's warning nearly led to fisticuffs on the podium.[74] After MOSA officials refused to convene an additional session, preservationists rallied around the drafting of a summary resolution. Again, MOSA officials refused to yield. Selivanov declared that MOSA administrators alone had the right to draft the summary resolution, since the February 18 and March 3 discussions had been meetings (*zasedaniia*) of MOSA's administrative board, not general assemblies (*sobraniia*) of its membership. Exclusion by technicality rankled an already hostile audience, and for several minutes the meeting degenerated into bedlam.[75] To the surprise of everyone, however, Selivanov wearily read a list of board-approved candidates to draft the summary resolution that included several prominent preservationists. He also agreed to consider any additions to the list.[76] At the outset, MOSA officials expected that a discussion of the "general principles" of preservation would take a few hours. After two long sessions, there were still many people waiting for their turn to speak.

Selivanov's concessions proved to be meaningless. In the weeks following the March 3 meeting, MOSA administrators refused to sanction the drafting of any summary resolution, regardless of the composition of the editorial committee. Although administrators did not attempt

72. L. Pochivalov, "Na ostrove sokrovishch," *Pravda*, February 11, 1965, 4; and L. Karpinskii, "Kritika i samokritika—mogushee oruzhie partii," *Pravda*, February 14, 1965, 2.
73. RGALI, f. 2466, o. 4, d. 25, ll. 103–104, 107.
74. RGALI, f. 2466, o. 4, d. 26, l. 130.
75. RGALI, f. 2466, o. 4, d. 26, ll. 136–37.
76. RGALI, f. 2466, o. 4, d. 26, ll. 137–38.

to punish outspoken preservationists, they decided to let the whole episode pass without acknowledgment. When the Tenth Conference of Moscow Architects convened two months later, the frustration among preservationists was palpable. Nikolai Vinogradov, chief of the MOSA section for elderly and retired architects, condemned the board for its failure to act after the March 3 meeting, and demanded that it "battle" against projects like Novyi Arbat that were "contrary to opinions expressed in public discussions." He also called for a temporary halt to construction on Novyi Arbat, insisting that the proposed designs be subjected first to a thorough public review.[77] Vinogradov's comments proved to be one of the last statements at MOSA about the link between preservation and the role of the public in urban planning. Still reeling from the February and March meetings and sensitive to the changing political climate of the early-Brezhnev years, MOSA officials resorted to more exclusive invitation policies and stricter discussion requirements to prevent a recurrence. The activists from the Unions of Artists and Writers who had been participants in preservation events at MOSA during the early 1960s were not present after the March meeting. MOSA preservationists who persisted with their agenda during meetings were advised to "speak more closely to the theme," lest they be shunned altogether from future discussions.[78]

The dwindling space for preservationist criticism at MOSA reflected other developments as well. In 1966, the voluntary preservation organization that MOSA activists had long sought, the All-Russian Society for the Preservation of Historical and Cultural Monuments, was established amid considerable fanfare. Even though its prerogatives were narrowly defined, the society helped formalize the public's role in preservation. Official approbation of its mission also lent it a gravity that was absent at MOSA and deprived MOSA members of their central role in the movement. This had important repercussions. By the late 1960s, historical preservation was more closely associated with an officially sanctioned brand of Russian cultural nationalism than with the types of public-input issues that had been predominant during the Khrushchev period.[79]

77. RGALI, f. 2466, o. 4, d. 10, ll. 74–75, 77.
78. RGALI, f. 2466, o. 4, d. 63, l. 88.
79. Dirk Kretzschmar [Krechmar], *Politika i kul'tura pri Brezhneve, Andropove i Chernenko, 1970–1985 gg.*, trans. M. G. Ratgauz (Moscow, 1997), 34–47; John B. Dunlop, *The Faces of Contemporary Russian Nationalism* (Princeton, N.J., 1983), 63–92; and Yitzhak M. Brudny, *Reinventing Russia: Russian Nationalism and the Soviet State, 1953–1991* (Cambridge, Mass., 1998), 67–70, 138–42.

In the newly ascendant nationalist discourse, Novyi Arbat ceased to be odious because it trumped the will of the public, however that public was defined. Instead, preservationists emphasized the parallels between Novyi Arbat and a crude variety of Western architecture. "The threat," one architect warned in January 1966, "is that Moscow will look too much like some kind of American city." This sort of criticism was not entirely new, but it did become more common in the months following the March meeting. In May 1965, MOSA architects overwhelmingly rejected plans to build several "American-size" skyscrapers, sixty to seventy stories tall, within the Garden Circle. They cited the skyscrapers' incompatibility with Moscow's "traditional silhouette." Likewise, a competition for proposals to reconstruct Moscow's center in 1966 evoked several nationalist condemnations. One architect warned that those who wished to rebuild the center were the same people who would burn the writings of Tolstoy.[80]

Like the founding of the All-Russian Society, changes at the Architectural-Planning Administration in the late 1960s impacted the preservation movement in Moscow. Many urban planners retained their faith that Moscow would one day be rebuilt along "socialist" lines, an endeavor that would require "not 40 or 50 percent demolition, but 100 percent."[81] In 1968, the essayist Oleg Volkov encountered an architect who promised the eventual destruction of the Hotel Prague on Arbat Square, so the slight bend in Novyi Arbat, its only imperfection, could be straightened.[82] Yet even the most determined urban planners admitted that this day lay in the distant future. For the time being, financial constraints and political imperatives dictated a more limited approach. In the late 1960s and '70s, only three Moscow churches were razed, a figure that reflected the fact that so many churches had already been destroyed, but also the growing pragmatism governing projects in the center of the city.[83] There were other, less ambivalent reasons for preservationists to be happy. In 1965, the Politburo ordered Dmitrii Chechulin to redesign the western approach to the Rossiia Hotel to preserve the pre-Petrine structures on Razin Street. In 1967, Posokhin urged urban planners to pay greater attention to Moscow's housing shortage, an implicit acknowledgment that large-scale demolition in the crowded center was

---

80. RGALI, f. 2466, o. 4, d. 63, ll. 80–81, 88; d. 281, l. 149; and f. 674, d. 207, ll. 95–96.
81. RGALI, f. 674, o. 5, d. 21, l. 20.
82. Oleg Volkov, *Vse v otvete: publitsistika* (Moscow, 1986), 427.
83. Colton, *Moscow*, 555.

too costly to be sustainable, and that a greater volume of construction would be designated for the city's undeveloped peripheral regions. In addition, Posokhin underscored the importance of continuity in the capital's architecture, claiming that the most beautiful cities were those with a clear line of historical "progression."[84] Other architects emphasized that the new master plan, ratified after much delay in 1971, was "not dogma," but a set of guiding principles that offered considerable flexibility in the evaluation of specific construction issues. After viewing the plan, one MOSA member admitted his relief that the reconstruction of Moscow would not mean that "the city will be leveled, and built anew."[85]

In 1968, the construction of Novyi Arbat finally came to an end. With a few exceptions, the street looked very much like the mock-ups that Posokhin and his team of architects had assembled several years earlier: a broad, tree-lined boulevard, surrounded by office buildings on the south, and residential towers on the north. It is easy, therefore, to dismiss the impact that preservationists had on the project. Timothy Colton writes that the sixteenth-century Church of Simeon Stolpnik, located at the intersection of Novyi Arbat and Vorovskii (Povarskaia) Street, was saved at the last minute by protest. In 1967, L. I. Antropov, an architect who had honed his restoration skills with Petr Baranovskii, supposedly sat in the bucket of a land mover that was poised to demolish the building, risking his own life to save the church.[86] Of samizdat provenance, this story nicely illustrates the extreme measures that many preservationists were willing to take on behalf of threatened monuments. There is no mention of the protest among the records of MOSA or the Architectural-Planning Administration, but, if it occurred, it was probably unnecessary, since urban planners had agreed early on to spare the church. In fact, Simeon Stolpnik was the widely flaunted poster child of the Architectural-Planning Administration's preservation-friendly designs. "One might get the impression," said Boris Tkhor, one of the Novyi Arbat coauthors, "that the construction in the old center of large, modern ensembles is detrimental to architectural and historical monuments. . . . The example of [Novyi Arbat] proves the exact opposite."[87]

84. RGALI, f. 674, o. 5, d. 21, ll. 6, 12.
85. RGALI, f. 674, o. 4, d. 207, ll. 6, 20.
86. Colton, *Moscow*, 558.
87. RGALI, f. 2466, o. 4, d. 110, l. 14. A later critic referred to the juxtaposition of Simeon Stolpnik and the Novyi Arbat highrises as "vandalism by construction." See S. S. Averintsev, "Ne utratit' vkus k podlinnosti," *Ogonek* 32 (1986): 11.

While MOSA activists failed to thwart the Novyi Arbat project, they succeeded in changing the terms of the preservation debate in Moscow. As late as 1960, the preservation movement comprised a handful of activists who spent a great deal of time appealing to Kremlin leaders to discipline unscrupulous local officials and halt the decentralization of the oversight mechanism for monuments. Theirs was a behavior honed by two decades of Stalinism. The shift to the public-input strand of preservation represented something new. Instead of making urban planners accountable to the Kremlin and the laws it enacted on behalf of architectural monuments, preservationists sought to make them subordinate to the people they supposedly served. On the eve of the Ninth Conference of Moscow Architects in 1964, MOSA officials insisted that the will of the public was subordinate to professional expertise. After the insurrection of 1965 and the formation of the All-Russian Society in 1966, similar assertions were impossible. The Architectural-Planning Administration frequently claimed that it acted in the interests of the public. By the late 1960s, it was obliged to show that the public agreed.

MOSA preservationists also set an important precedent in Soviet cultural politics. By arguing that the public was the rightful arbiter of the past, preservationists went well beyond most challenges to the party's prerogatives in the cultural sphere during the 1950s and '60s. Preservationists did not want to usurp the party's role as the "intellectual center" in Soviet society. They sought something more radical: to destroy the "intellectual center" altogether. MOSA activists were careful to limit their demands to the field of preservation, but the implications were potentially momentous. For the party, the emergence of the public as an arbiter of past culture represented the destruction of one of the pillars of Stalinist culture—control over the past. To be sure, similar developments were underway in other fields, where cultural figures demanded greater autonomy over an array of different issues. In the realm of architectural and historical preservation, however, activists did not want authority to devolve partly or fully to themselves; instead, they hoped it would pass them by entirely. Many cultural figures outside the preservation movement—even those with the most progressive credentials—would have been horrified to see the same principle applied to their own fields. Preservationists may have come to a similar conclusion in the 1980s, when urban planners transformed Arbat Street into a pedestrian mall. The project was widely opposed by the neighborhood's literati, who presciently feared that it would turn their home into an unrecognizable and unlivable amusement park, but embraced by a Moscow public long deprived of commercial and leisure diversions.[88] Fifteen years after the completion of Novyi Arbat, preservationists discovered that an empowered public could also inflict harm.[89]

In truth, MOSA preservationists never bothered to ask the most important question: if Muscovites were given the authority, would they really choose to halt the construction of Novyi Arbat? The evidence, though entirely circumstantial, is ambiguous on this score. On the one hand, the All-Russian Society for the Preservation of Historical and Cultural Monuments enjoyed tremendous popular support after its formation in 1966. By the late 1970s, it counted more than 600,000 members in chapters across the RSFSR. In the Arbat, Sigurd Shmidt was an example of the public's newfound role in preservation. Along with Okudzhava, he attended a variety of "roundtables" on the "tragedy" of Novyi Arbat, and was active in a local chapter of the All-Russian Society.[90] On the other hand, there were many people who were reluctant to get involved, perhaps feeling that the existing powers were intractable. The stage and film director Boris Bushmelev, a longtime resident of the Arbat, said that resistance to Novyi Arbat was an "impossible" endeavor.[91] Some people were also frustrated with preservationists' focus on individual monuments rather than the neighborhood as a whole. Nor is it clear that Novyi Arbat was universally thought of as the disaster that preservationists claimed it to be. Undoubtedly, many Muscovites were proud of Novyi Arbat, perhaps for the reasons examined in the previous chapter, but more likely because they naively associated the street with modernity, progress, and the skyscrapers of New York and Chicago. Moreover, for

88. On the controversies surrounding the pedestrian mall, see "Arbat. 16 rakursov odnoi ulitsy," *Arkhitektura SSSR* 4 (April 1986): 33–47; N. Miroslavskaia, E. Piatina, and S. Piatin, "Kakim byt' Arbatu," *Stroitel'stvo i arkhitektura Moskvy* 3 (March 1982): 8–9; T. Liutivinskaia, "'Skazki' starogo Arbata," *Stroitel'stvo i arkhitektura Moskvy* 4 (April 1986): 20; Andrei Ganeshin, "Uroki Arbata," *Arkhitektura i stroitel'stvo Moskvy* 2 (February 1988): 7–8; and N. M. Moleva, "Ulitsa dlia peshekhodov," in *Moskva 2000: Kakoi ei byt'*, ed. L. V. Vavakina (Moscow, 1990), 143–44.

89. V. Vinogradov, "Istoricheskaia Moskva i regeneratsiia obshchestvennogo soznaniia," *Arkhitektura i stroitel'stvo Moskvy* 6 (June 1987): 11; and S. O. Shmidt, "Pamiatniki v sisteme razvitiia nauki i obshchestvennogo soznaniia," in *Muzeevedenie: muzei mira*, ed. E. E. Kuz'mina (Moscow, 1991), 98–109. On attempts to incorporate public opinion into the urban-planning process during the glasnost period, see El'gen Grigor'ev, "Vozmozhno li demokratizirovat' upravlenie proektirovaniem v Moskve," *Arkhitektura i stroitel'stvo Moskvy* 2 (February 1990), 2–4.

90. Colton, *Moscow*, 407; Shmidt, "Bulat Okudzhava i 'arbatstvo,'" 18.

91. Boris Gennadievich Bushmelev, interview by author, April 10, 1998; Bulat Okudzhava, "Net zadvorok u Arbata," in *Arbatskii arkhiv*, 141.

several thousand people, the construction of the street accelerated a process that had been underway since the mid-1950s: resettlement from communal apartments in the Arbat to single-family apartments on the city's periphery. Undoubtedly, more than a few people thought of Novyi Arbat as a godsend, since it allowed them to cut to the front of the housing queue. Even Okudzhava, the neighborhood's mythologizer *par excellence*, became an "Arbat émigré" by moving out of the neighborhood, and was sensitive to charges that he idealized a way of life that was uncomfortable for many.[92] It may be the case that the characteristic response to Novyi Arbat was not the "sharp protests" that preservationists cited, but ambivalence. Arbat residents were sad to see bulldozers raze large swaths of the neighborhood, but excited for the day when they too could move to a single-family apartment.

The previous chapter showed how the collective memories of the architects who lobbied for the rehabilitation of constructivism were mediated by Khrushchev's new party program and heightened Cold War tensions. This chapter has argued that the retrospective gaze of preservation activists posed important and potentially de-stabilizing questions about the party's role as the principal arbiter of past culture. The final chapter will turn the tables on the thaw and show how an era that bred so much nostalgia for the pre-Stalin years, itself became an object of nostalgia.

92. Bulat Okudzhava, "Menia vospityval Arbatskii dvor," interview by Mikhail Pozdniaev (1988), in *Arbatskii arkhiv*, 148–49.

Dissidence and the End of the Thaw

For more than a century, the building at 25a Vorovskii (Povarskaia) Street has been associated with a tragedy. Designed in the 1820s by the Ticinese architect Domenico Ghilardi, a protégé of the Russian master Matvei Kazakov, the building is a relic of the wealth that congregated in *priarbat'e* after the Napoleonic Wars. Consistent with the tastes of the empire school, it is distinguished by three classical arches that cap the windows above the entranceway. The vaulted areas within the arches are decorated with *alto-relievo* wreaths and supported by Doric columns. Ghilardi's initial client was Sergei Gagarin, an aristocrat whose father was an adviser to Catherine the Great, and whose distant ancestors were princes in early Rus. Financial difficulties forced Gagarin to sell his ornate home before completion. It passed among several different owners before 1875 when the chief officer of the State Horse-Breeding Administration, Leonid Gortung, moved in with his wife, Mariia, Alexander Pushkin's oldest daughter and reputedly the model for Anna Karenina. Contrary to Tolstoy's novel, however, it was the male Gortung who scandalized high society by committing suicide in a Moscow courtroom after being convicted of embezzlement in 1877, an act that was widely understood as a condemnation of judicial arbitrariness. Tolstoy later memorialized Gortung by modeling Fedor Protasov, the protagonist in the play *The Living Corpse*, on him.[1]

---

1. L. N. Iokar and Z. K. Pokrovskaia, *"Dom literatury" na Povarskoi 25a* (Moscow, 1997), 40–44, 104.

In the years following the revolution, the building on Vorovskii Street witnessed ordeals of a different sort. It successively housed an academy for Red Army commanders, the Institute of Red Professors, and the International Lenin School, where foreign communists studied the art of revolution. In 1932, upon the fortieth anniversary of Maxim Gorky's "creative activity," the party transferred no. 25a to a new establishment devoted to literary criticism and the training of young writers from the peasantry and working class. At the end of the decade, the Gorky Literature Institute, the school for aspiring writers, moved several blocks away. The Academy of Sciences annexed the remaining departments and renamed them the Gorky Institute of World Literature, or IMLI, its commonly used acronym. Despite the arrest of its first director in 1940, the institute quickly became one of the Soviet Union's most prestigious centers for literary analysis, a rival to the famous Pushkin House (the Academy's Institute of Russian Literature) in Leningrad.

The building on Vorovskii Street was also the epicenter of the so-called Sinyavsky and Daniel affair. Andrei Sinyavsky, an accomplished literary critic and scholar, came to the Institute of World Literature in 1952, the year he defended his dissertation on Gorky's unfinished masterpiece, *The Life of Klim Samgin*, at Moscow State University. Iulii Daniel, an itinerant translator and veteran who had been wounded in the war, had friends among the institute's scholars and graduate students. In September 1965, Sinyavsky and Daniel were arrested by the KGB. After five months of pretrial detention, they were sentenced by a Moscow court to seven and five years hard labor, respectively, and five and three years internal exile for violating article 70 of the criminal code, which forbade the "dissemination . . . of slanderous inventions defamatory to the Soviet political and social system." They were convicted solely on the content of several satirical and allegorical novellas, short stories, and an essay that they had smuggled abroad through a visiting Frenchwoman and had published under the pseudonyms Abram Tertz and Nikolai Arzhak. Their trial marked a sharp departure from the party's earlier reaction to the unauthorized publication abroad of Boris Pasternak's *Doctor Zhivago* and Evgenii Yevtushenko's *A Precocious Autobiography*. Both Pasternak and Yevtushenko had been roundly criticized in the press, but neither had been threatened with imprisonment. At the Twenty-third Party Congress in April 1966, the writer Mikhail Sholokhov underscored the party's new line by criticizing the supposed leniency of

9. Statue of Maxim Gorky outside the Institute of World Literature. Photograph by Andrey Shlyakhter.

Sinyavsky and Daniel's sentences. He suggested that in better years they would have been shot.[2]

The events surrounding the arrest and trial of Sinyavsky and Daniel provoked a great deal of anxiety and agitation among the Soviet intelligentsia. On December 5, 1965, Constitution Day, a crowd of protesters gathered on Pushkin Square to demand an open trial for the accused, an action so daring that it was almost inconceivable.[3] According to Vladimir Semichastnyi, the head of the KGB, there was nothing "formally" criminal about the protest; nonetheless, it was symptomatic of the "nihilism, rebelliousness, and apolitical atmosphere" of the intelligentsia.[4] In the months that followed, hundreds of artists, writers, scholars, and scientists wrote letters to prominent political leaders and publications voicing their disgruntlement. KGB sources reported that many artists and writers were interpreting Sholokhov's speech as the beginning of a new "obscurantist line of the party, aimed at limiting the freedom of [artistic] creation" and rehabilitating Stalin.[5] Beyond the prying eyes of the KGB, assessments of the political climate were even gloomier. The writer Aleksandr Solzhenitsyn recalled rumors that the KGB was planning to arrest a "thousand intellectuals" in Moscow. The poet Igor Volgin remembered Sinyavsky and Daniel's trial as a "warning" to the intelligentsia that "shattered the last illusions of the 1960s. . . . leaving confusion, doubt, and bitterness in the soul."[6] After four more persons were arrested

2. *XXIII s"ezd Kommunisticheskoi partii Sovetskogo Soiuza, 29 marta—8 aprelia 1966 goda. Stenograficheskii otchet* (Moscow, 1966), 1:354–62; Max Hayward, ed. and trans., *On Trial: The Soviet State versus "Abram Tertz" and "Nikolai Arzhak,"* rev. and enl. ed. (Westport, Conn., 1980), 1–35; Abraham Rothberg, *The Heirs of Stalin: Dissidence and the Soviet Regime, 1953–1970* (Ithaca, N.Y., 1972), 151–67; and Wolfram [Vol'fram] Eggeling, *Politika in kul'tura pri Khrushcheve i Brezhneve. 1953–1970 gg.* (Moscow, 1999), 184–87.
3. A. Iu. Daniel, A. B. Roginskii, and Nikolai Kostenko, *Piatoe dekabria 1965 goda v vospominaniiakh uchastnikov sobytii, materialakh samizdata, dokumentakh partiinykh i komsomol'skikh organizatsii i v zapiskakh Komiteta gosudarstvennoi bezopasnosti v TsK KPSS* (Moscow, 1995); and Ludmilla Alexeyeva and Paul Goldberg, *The Thaw Generation: Coming of Age in the Post-Stalin Era* (Pittsburgh, 1993), 119–24. The Constitution Day protest on Pushkin Square became an annual event. On the 1967 reprise, see V. A. Kozlov and S. V. Mironenko, *Kramola: Inakomyslie v SSSR pri Khrushcheve i Brezhneve 1953–1982 gg.* (Moscow, 2005), 381–84.
4. RGANI, f. 5, o. 30, d. 462, l. 250.
5. RGANI, f. 5, o. 30, d. 486, ll. 72–75.
6. Aleksandr I. Solzhenitsyn, *The Oak and the Calf: Sketches of Literary Life in the Soviet Union*, trans. Harry Willetts (New York, 1975), 99; and Igor' Volgin, "Na ploshchadi Maiakovskogo materializovalos' vremia," interview by Liudmila Polikovskaia, in Liudmila Polikovskaia, *My predchuvstvie . . . predtecha . . . : ploshchad' Maiakovskogo, 1958–1965* (Moscow, 1997), 45–46. For similar reactions to the trial of Sinyavsky and Daniel, see Raisa Orlova and Lev Kopelev, *My zhili v Moskve, 1956–1980* (Moscow, 1990), 206; Andrei Sakharov, *Vospominaniia*, (Moscow, 1996), 1:369; Alexeyeva and Goldberg, *The Thaw Generation*, 119–29; and Gennadii Evgrafov and Mikhail Karpov, eds., "Po statei 70-oi: iz istorii sovremennosti," *Ogonek* no. 19 (May 1989): 20–24.

in 1967 for compiling and distributing the *White Book*, an anthology of press clippings and documents on Sinyavsky and Daniel, few would deny that Khrushchev's successors had embarked on a very different course. The dissident trials were accompanied by a vitriolic propaganda campaign that was reminiscent of the Doctors' Plot. They hinged on a Manichaean vision of the world that was a relic of Stalinism. And they condemned persons to prison for crimes of art and conscience. Beginning in the fall of 1965, party leaders revoked the autonomy that had been on loan to the intelligentsia since 1953. And when they did so, many Soviet citizens thought the thaw had come to an end.[7]

This much is well known. What is less evident, perhaps, is the incongruity between the intelligentsia's oft-stated fears about a return to Stalinism, and their actions, which were wholly inconsonant with Stalinism. By making the Brezhnev era seem more repressive than what preceded it, the trial of Sinyavsky and Daniel brought to the fore longstanding notions about the adversarial relationship between the state and the intelligentsia that had been muted during the previous decade because of waning repression. Like former Arbat residents Alexander Herzen, who was arrested in 1834 and exiled to Viatka, in northeastern Russia, for participating in a political discussion group, and Alexander Pushkin, who was exiled in 1820 to southern Russia for writing irreverent political poems, Sinyavsky and Daniel suffered the dire consequences of speaking truth to power.[8] In this context, it is not illogical that the trial seemed to mark a critical turning point in Soviet history, and helped transform the rapidly fading thaw into an object of nostalgia. Beneath this nostalgia, however, there was a good deal of continuity between the recent past and present. Events outside the institute suggested that the imprint of the thaw on Soviet society was in many ways indelible. And within the institute, where the backlash against the thaw could have been severe, Sinyavsky's friends and coworkers rallied to preserve many of the hard-won freedoms of the previous

7. On the Sinyavsky and Daniel trial as the final chapter of the thaw, see Dirk Kretzschmar [Krechmar], *Politika i kul'tura pri Brezhneve, Andropove i Chernenko, 1970–1985 gg.*, trans. M. G. Ratgauz (Moscow, 1997), 35; Paul Josephson, *New Atlantis Revisited: Akademgorodok, the Siberian City of Science* (Princeton, N.J., 1997), 263–304; T. M. Goriaeva, ed., "Glavlit i literaturu v period 'literaturno-politcheskogo brozhdeniia v Sovetskom soiuze,'" *Voprosy literatury* 5 (September-October 1998): 277; and John Garrard and Carol Garrard, *Inside the Soviet Writers' Union* (New York, 1990), 241.
8. On the tendency of the intelligentsia to cast itself as an opposition, see L. Gudkov and B. Dubin, *Intelligentsiia: zametki o literaturno-politicheskikh illiuziiakh* (Moscow and Kharkov, Ukr., 1995), 83.

decade. As the old building on Vorovskii Street might have attested, one tragic event can easily overshadow a more complex and varied history.

IMPERFECT REFORM

The one thing that Sinyavsky's friends and enemies at the Institute of World Literature could agree on was that the thaw, at least as it played out in their professional lives, had disappointing results. In the years following Stalin's death, Sinyavsky and his colleagues took up topics that had long been taboo. They began to interact with their counterparts in Western Europe and North America. And they successfully lobbied for greater academic freedom, which they understood chiefly as the right to choose and evaluate research agendas, "to certify scientific knowledge," independently of higher authorities.[9] According to one eyewitness to the institute's transformation, "people began to think, compare, criticize, and draw conclusions that were long in coming."[10] At the time of Sinyavsky's arrest, however, many of the institute's scholars considered these reforms incomplete, or worse, flawed in important ways. Administrators agreed, but for different reasons. They argued that excessive scholarly autonomy, careless contact with foreigners, and dangerous reevaluations of the Stalinist past had facilitated Sinyavsky's transgressions. De-Stalinization, in their view, had gone too far.

Reform at the institute began in December 1953, when one of the institute's deputy directors, Arfo Petrosian, challenged the meddling of administrators in scholarly affairs. Petrosian was a graduate of the Institute of Red Professors and had worked in the Central Committee and the Committee on Artistic Affairs (the precursor to the Ministry of Culture) before coming to the Institute of World Literature in 1952. According to an unauthorized history of the institute that Elena Evnina, a specialist in French literature, penned for samizdat in the 1970s, Petrosian merited little attention as a scholar. She was nominally a folklore specialist, but distinguished herself mainly by being outspoken during party meetings. When Ivan Anisimov took over the institute in 1952, in the midst of Stalin's anti-Semitic campaign against "cosmopolitans," he tried to prevent Petrosian from "throwing bombs" at him by inviting her into the

9. Alexander Vucinich, *Empire of Knowledge: The Academy of Sciences of the USSR (1917–1970)* (Berkeley and Los Angeles, 1984), 257.
10. N. Ianevich [E. M. Evnina], "Institut mirovoi literatury v 1930-e—1970-e gody," *Pamiat': istoricheskii sbornik* vyp. 5 (samizdat, 1981; Paris, 1982), 116.

administration. Anisimov had good reasons to fear for his security. The institute's first director, Ivan Luppol, was arrested in 1940; another director, Vladimir Shishmarev, was fired in the late 1940s after the institute approved Mikhail Bakhtin's "Freudian" dissertation on François Rabelais. Even after his appointment, many IMLI scholars privately vilified Anisimov as "Vanka-Cain," a reference to his denunciations of friends and colleagues during the 1930s.

Petrosian accepted Anisimov's invitation, but refused to keep quiet. She argued that Anisimov too often intervened in disputes better left to specialists. She thought that his penchant for "resolving issues single-handedly" resulted in "elements of arbitrariness" and "subjective attitudes" that diminished the quality of the institute's scholarship. She claimed that three sector heads (the equivalent of department chairs) had resigned to protest a situation where research sectors had "no responsibilities and no rights."[11] And she drew on resentments that had been building for years. One of Anisimov's first acts as director was to appoint Viktor Nikolaev, a "well-known scoundrel," to a position in the institute's foreign section, where he oversaw international contacts. After being denied admission to the institute's graduate program, Nikolaev orchestrated the attack on Shishmarev and Bakhtin from a post in the Central Committee, not a résumé that endeared him to his new colleagues.[12] In 1953, another administrator circumvented the party organization, the traditional forum for scholarly debate, to denounce scholars in the Soviet literature sector for needlessly "rehashing" their work. The implication was that the sector was incapable of finishing its work without outside supervision.[13]

Petrosian framed reform in terms of academic freedom, but there were other concerns as well. In January 1954, Nina Dikushina, a specialist on the poetry of the Silver Age (1890-1920), claimed that administrators frowned on the "wide openness" essential to scholarship, and propagated instead the "rotten formula . . . do not wash one's dirty linens in public."[14] Many scholars were also angered by the inferior role of the party organization in the institute's affairs. They drew on official rhetoric about the empowerment of the party, an important component of the

11. TsAODM, f. 2472, o. 1, d. 13, ll. 4–6.
12. Ianevich [Evnina], "Institut mirovoi literatury," 97–101, 113; Svetlana Alliluyeva, *Only One Year,* trans. Paul Chavchavadze (New York, 1969), 178; and Abram Tertz [Andrei Sinyavsky], *Goodnight!* trans. Richard Lourie (New York, 1989), 111.
13. TsAODM, f. 2472, o. 1, d. 13, ll. 5–6.
14. TsAODM, f. 2472, o 1, d. 13, ll. 12–13.

early de-Stalinization reforms that was associated with Beria's downfall and the end of terror. They criticized administrators who thought that "communists should not have opinions," and that the party organization did not have the "right to voice its opinion about the work of individual comrades." They condemned the administration's recent decision to fire a scholar despite a positive evaluation from the party organization, which graded the scholar as a "qualified worker and conscientious communist." And they wondered why their protests to the administration always seemed to fall on deaf ears. When Petrosian tried to intervene on behalf of the party member who was fired by the administration, she was blocked by an administrator who thought "time will pass, and the uproar will subside."[15]

Proponents of reform found additional support in June 1954 when the Central Committee's Science and Culture Department summoned Anisimov to discuss ways to improve the quality of the institute's scholarship, a sign that higher authorities were not happy with the status quo.[16] After the Twentieth Party Congress, reformers added demands for a flatter administrative hierarchy and a more collegial atmosphere. They argued that Stalin's abuses were facilitated by "iron discipline and a highly centralized government" that were contrary to the "nature of socialism." Khrushchev's revelations demanded that party leaders "widen Soviet democracy, unleash local initiative, and decentralize decisively governmental administration." This meant the end of unthinking deference to administrators, and the development of "the path of wide discussion, the exchange of opinions, and convincing argumentation." As one of the institute's chastened administrators admitted in the days following the Twentieth Party Congress, "Over the last ten days, we have grown five times wiser. Now we have to work in an absolutely different manner."[17]

This was easier said than done. Party officials and administrators spent much of 1956 and 1957 discussing the specific contours of reform. They again trained their sights on the sectors, which suffered from personnel shortages, humdrum research agendas, and the want of autonomy that Petrosian challenged two years earlier. In October 1956, Anisimov requested permission from the Central Committee and the Academy of Sciences to split the foreign literature sector into separate study groups for Western Europe and North America, the Far East, and the countries of

15. TsAODM, f. 2472, o 1, d. 13, ll. 12–13.
16. TsAODM, f. 2472, o 1, d. 15, l. 58.
17. TsAODM, f. 2472, o 1, d. 17, ll. 22–23, 73, 77.

the "socialist camp." At the same time, the institute's party bureau petitioned the vice-president of the academy for the right to determine research agendas, hire and fire scholars, evaluate graduate student applications, and send scholars on research and professional trips abroad without securing outside approval.[18] Party members also criticized a review process for scholarly work that did little to foster innovative research and writing. In the wake of the Twentieth Party Congress, Petrosian attributed the dearth of good work to the paranoia of Stalinism. She noted that Viktor Zhirmunskii's landmark monograph on the Kirghiz epos *Manas*—a product of the institute's two-year sojourn in Tashkent during the war— was pulled from press when the author was accused of cosmopolitanism. Even in the absence of Stalinist paranoia, however, scholars complained about the institute's overly rigorous editorial process, where books and articles were subjected to review at five different stages, and contrarily, about contractual requirements that encouraged them to sacrifice the quality of their published work for quantity.[19]

In March 1958, the director of the academy's Literature and Language Section, Viktor Vinogradov, warned that there was still too much talk about the reorganization of literary study, and not enough concrete action. Vinogradov convened a "special commission" to compile a seven-year research agenda, the literary version of Khrushchev's unorthodox seven-year plan for economic development.[20] The exact dimensions of Vinogradov's initiative became clear in February 1959, when the academy abolished outright the institute's sectors and ordered that research be distributed among "new, more flexible" working groups and sections. These groups had the freedom to determine the specific content of their research, but they had to conform to broad themes that the Literature and Language Section dictated. In theory, this new organizational structure would encourage scholars to work on transnational topics like "the fundamental stages of the development of realism in world literature," and "the genesis and development of the method of socialist realism."[21] In reality, the transnational focus was mostly nominal. But it did provide scholars with greater autonomy from an

18. TsAODM, f. 2472, o 1, d. 18, ll. 17, 20.
19. K. Zelinskii, "Institut i nauka," *Literaturnaia gazeta*, December 20, 1955, 1; and TsAODM, f. 2472, o. 1, d. 17, ll. 27–28, 30, 57.
20. "Obshchee sobranie Otdeleniia literatury i iazyka AN SSSR," *Izvestiia akademii nauk SSSR. Otdelenie literatury i iazykov* [hereafter *IAN SSSR. OLIa*] XVII, vyp. 4 (July–August 1958): 378–79.
21. TsAODM, f. 2472, o 1, d. 20, ll. 71, 108; and "Otchet Otdeleniia literatury i iazyka ob itogakh nauchnoi i nauchno-organizatsionnoi deiatel'nosti za 1958," *IAN SSSR. OLIa* XVIII, vyp. 2 (March–April 1959): 165–69.

administration that had previously determined research agendas. Another round of reshuffling came in July 1962, when the academy granted the institute's sections the sole right to determine and evaluate research, regardless of the academy's priorities. Reflecting on the organizational reforms at the end of 1962, the secretary of the institute's party organization claimed that "perestroika" had "opened the possibility for . . . creative initiative and independence" within the sections. The administration no longer regulated scholarly work "on a case by case basis." Instead, each section appointed a secretary from among its party members, thus ensuring that "control comes from within."[22]

This positive spin masked a number of new and enduring problems. Well into the 1960s, administrators complained about the growth of "mutual protection circles" within the sections, about "democracy" becoming "anarchy," and about scholars who treated the institute as if it were a "voluntary society of admirers of fine literature" instead of an Academy of Sciences affiliate.[23] For their part, scholars discovered that their evolving autonomy was far from absolute. De-Stalinization promoted individual initiative and independence, but it also created a climate that fostered—and often required—the intervention of administrators and higher officials, simply because so many of the core assumptions of the Stalin era were in flux. This first became evident after the Twentieth Party Congress when scholars began to focus their attention on the research opportunities it afforded. During the spring and summer of 1956, the poetry and drama of the NEP period, much of which fell into disfavor after the official embrace of socialist realism in the 1930s, were placed on the agenda of the Soviet literature sector. In July, Nina Dikushina petitioned the administration for permission to edit and publish the works of Anatolii Lunacharskii, the first Commissar of Enlightenment and the architect of many of the relatively tolerant cultural policies of the 1920s, and Georgii Plekhanov, the father of Russian Marxism and an important Menshevik who left Russia after the Bolsheviks came to power. Both Lunacharskii and Plekhanov had managed to avoid official condemnation in death, but their legacies remained clouded. Despite these endeavors, however, many of the institute's scholars were reluctant to undertake potentially impolitic research without clear authorization from above, a habit that Dikushina called the "inertia" of old ways. Scholars recognized that they had to distance

22. TsAODM, f. 2472, o 1, d. 22, ll., 36, 38. On the empowerment of party members at cultural institutions, see *Kommunisticheskaia partiia Sovetskogo Soiuza v rezoliutsiiakh i resheniiakh s"ezdov, konferentsii i plenumov TsK* (Moscow, 1986), 10:237–43.
23. TsAODM, f. 2472, o. 1, d. 25, ll. 192–93.

themselves from the type of petty deference that had been characteristic of the Stalin period, "when they waited for a newspaper to tell them what to do," but they still complained about the party's reticence about literary issues.[24]

Conversely, as the institute's scholars became more daring in their choice of research topics in the late 1950s, they were often stymied by administrators who were opposed to the scope of their inquiries. In late 1956, Dikushina asked that the administration cease hindering efforts to incorporate new topics into the institute's research agenda. In 1957, the party broke its silence on literary issues when Khrushchev denounced Vladimir Dudintsev's novel about bureaucratic arbitrariness, *Not by Bread Alone,* an act that was widely interpreted as an attempt to rein in public discussions of Stalinism. In the aftermath, one IMLI administrator cautioned scholars to moderate the "celebratory tones" they used when discussing Fyodor Dostoevsky, a writer who had been blacklisted by nineteenth-century social democrats for depicting the revolutionary movement as corrupt and immoral. Khrushchev's denunciation of Stalin, he warned, did not change the "composition of the classical canon."[25]

Officials from outside the institute also intervened frequently, usually to address publication issues. In 1958, the Central Committee ordered the institute to rewrite an introduction to a revamped anthology of the poetry of Sergei Esenin, one of the most popular writers of the 1920s, especially among young people. The revision was supposed to better explain the poet's "strengths and weaknesses," since so many of his poems already in circulation were "imbued with decadent, religious moods."[26] During the following year, the Central Committee got involved in two disputes regarding the legacy of the Futurist poet Vladimir Mayakovsky. The first involved the publication of volume 65 of the almanac *Literaturnoe nasledstvo* (Literary Inheritance), entitled "New Material on Mayakovsky." It comprised 125 letters and telegrams that Mayakovsky sent to his lover Lili Brik in the 1910s and '20s, as well as a number of speeches that had never been published in full. Only days after it appeared in bookstores at the end 1958, Mayakovsky's sister

24. TsAODM, f. 2472, o 1, d. 17, ll. 21, 28, 72–73, 77, 135.

25. TsAODM, f. 2472, o 1, d. 17, l. 77; and d. 18, l. 75. On the Soviet reception of Dostoevsky's work, see Vladimir Shlapentokh, *Soviet Intellectuals and Political Power: The Post-Stalin Era* (Princeton, N.J., 1990), 94.

26. *Ideologicheskie komissii TsK KPSS, 1958–1964: Dokumenty,* ed. E. S. Afanas'eva, V. Iu. Afiani, L. A. Velichanskaia, Z. K. Vodop'ianova, and E. V. Kochubei (Moscow, 1998), 61. The resulting five-volume set was published as S. A. Esenin, *Sobranie sochinenii,* ed. G. I. Vladykin (Moscow, 1961–62).

complained to Mikhail Suslov, the party's chief ideologue, that there was little of scholarly value in the almanac. In March 1959, the Central Committee's Culture and Agitprop Departments reported that the almanac had been edited in a thoughtless manner. In one of Mayakovsky's previously published speeches, editors restored the rejoinder from the audience, "Lenin has sent us to hell." In another, they reinserted an uncritical reference to Nikolai Bukharin. They even included a photograph of Mayakovsky with a dedicatory inscription to Boris Pasternak, the latest in the long list of Soviet writers to run afoul of authorities. At the end of March, the Central Committee rebuked Mikhail Khrapchenko, the former chairman of the Committee on Artistic Affairs and the highest ranking party member on the almanac's editorial board, for his "irresponsible attitude." After a forthcoming volume on Chekhov was delayed, however, and after an investigation in October revealed persisting problems at the almanac, the Central Committee ordered the Academy of Sciences to transfer control from the Literature and Language Section to the Institute of World Literature, citing its abundance of "specialists."[27]

At the same time that the institute was entrusted with *Literaturnoe nasledstvo*, it was embroiled in its own controversy over Mayakovsky's legacy. In June 1959, the institute submitted the penultimate volume of a planned thirteen-volume anthology of Mayakovsky's writings to the State Literature Press. It included several works that were plainly controversial: "The Manifesto of the Ephemeral Federation of Futurists," which reflected Mayakovsky's early association with an art movement that sought to destroy inherited culture; the poet's speech at the First All-Union Conference of Proletarian Writers, which included positive references to opposition figures like Bukharin, Leon Trotsky, Aleksei Rykov, and Karl Radek; as well as forty-seven letters to Lili Brik that were first published in *Literaturnoe nasledstvo*. One of the institute's deputy directors, Vladimir Shcherbina, asked the press to abstain from "violating the author's wishes" by excising controversial passages; instead, editors provided a lengthy commentary to "help the reader relate properly" to the text. The Central Committee responded by ordering the State Literature Press to delete two references to Trotsky and Bukharin, and to exclude

27. L. Pushkareva, ed., "Vokrug tvorcheskogo naslediia Maiakovskogo," *Voprosy literatury* 2 (March–April 1994): 199, 205, 208–9, 213–14; *Ideologicheskie komissii TsK KPSS*, 141–49; and TsAODM, f. 2472, o. 1, d. 20, l. 30. Much of the correspondence between Mayakovsky and Brik was republished in 1991. See Vladimir Mayakovsky, *Liubov eto serdtse vsego: V. V. Maiakovskii i L. Iu. Brik, perepiska, 1915–1930* (Moscow, 1991).

altogether "The Manifesto of the Ephemeral Federation of Futurists" and nineteen of the most "intimate" letters to Brik.[28]

Full disclosure of Mayakovsky's writings was complicated by his post-mortem promotion to "poet of the revolution." Despite his centrality in Soviet literature, there was a side of Mayakovsky's life that was unknown to most Soviet citizens. IMLI scholars wrongly assumed that the thaw allowed for a more evenhanded depiction of Mayakovsky. They thought the same about Maxim Gorky, whose permanent return to the Soviet Union in 1933 after more than a decade in the West was widely trumpeted as a Soviet public-relations coup. After Gorky's death in 1936, the institute became the primary repository for his manuscripts and correspondence. Its scholars were the chief defenders of Gorky's legacy, both at home and abroad. They published dozens of monographs and articles about Gorky's fiction and edited anthologies of his papers and correspondence. But not everything in Gorky's archive enhanced his official image. In June 1960, Anisimov—conscious of the previous controversy involving Mayakovsky—sought instruction from the Central Committee about correspondence between Gorky and the French writer Romain Rolland, which was then being prepared for publication. The friendship between Gorky and Rolland was itself uncontroversial. Prior to his death in 1944, Rolland was one of the most vocal Soviet allies in the West, and many of the letters between the two writers had already been published within the Soviet Union. Much of the remaining correspondence, however, was clearly scandalous, since it dated from the period immediately following the revolution when Gorky was in opposition to the Bolsheviks. Anisimov noted that it was not the practice of Soviet literary scholars to "cover up temporary mistakes," but he worried that it would be "inappropriate and even tactless" to publish letters in which Gorky was critical of Soviet power. Moreover, the institute's usual practice of abridged publication was complicated by the fact that the original copies of the letters were in the possession of Rolland's widow in France. Concealing the truth could have an "undesirable resonance abroad."[29]

Anisimov's concern about the foreign reaction to domestic editorial decisions reflected the institute's growing engagement with the Western academic world, another issue that was the cause of a great deal of controversy. As early as 1954, IMLI scholars began to challenge stereotypes of Soviet culture then circulating in Western academic circles, especially the

28. Pushkareva, "Vokrug tvorcheskogo naslediia Maiakovskogo," 215–18.
29. E. Orekhova, ed., "V obstanovke fal'sifikatsii i total'noi lzhi," *Voprosy literatury* 6 (November–December 1995): 281–96.

view that Soviet writers were "artists in uniform."[30] In 1957, the academy's Literature and Language Section began preparations for the Fourth International Congress of Slavists, which Moscow was hosting the following year. It also started to facilitate long-term research trips abroad for scholars in the Slavic and German fields, where there were friendly socialist countries available to host.[31] After the invasion of Budapest, the Literature and Language Section trained its sights on the Hungarian philosopher György Lukács, who served as a minister in Imre Nagy's government. It later attacked the French critic Henri Lefebvre for trying to "overthrow" socialist realism, and the Italian writer Alberto Moravia for his "idealistic and revisionist theories." In 1959, IMLI scholars targeted the work of Berkeley's Gleb Struve, the son of the émigré Marxist apostate Petr Struve, and Columbia's Ernest Simmons.[32] The institute also followed foreign evaluations of its own work in journals like *Books Abroad*. In 1964, Struve unknowingly caused a stir when he praised an IMLI essay collection as "the first in the history of Soviet literary criticism that more or less serves its name, and is comprised of many informative materials." One scholar worried that American Sovietologists were trying to show Soviet attempts to "repudiate socialist realism"; books they positively reviewed were thus deficient for use at home. Another referred to one of the institute's recent books on Gorky, which Western scholars were using "to prove that Gorky was not simply mistaken in his evaluation of Stalin, but was a militant defender of mass repressions."[33]

While IMLI scholars embraced engagement with the foreign world, they were also aware that it produced new pretexts for interference from

---

30. TsAODM, f. 2472, o. 1, d. 13, l. 130. This is a reference to Max Eastman's book, *Artists in Uniform: A Study of Literature and Bureaucratization* (London, 1934).
31. TsAODM f. 2472, o. 1, d. 17, ll. 77, 87; T. Ia. Mikhel'son, "Godichnoe sobranie Otdeleniia literatury i iazyka Akademii nauk SSSR," *IAN SSSR. OLIa* XV, vyp. 2 (March–April 1956): 185; and D. E. Mikhal'chi, "Godichnoe sobranie Otdeleniia literatury i iazyka Akademii nauk SSSR," *IAN SSSR. OLIa* XVI, vyp. 3 (May–June 1957): 276.
32. V. Etov, "Sovetskaia literatura i ee amerikanskie istolkovateli," *Voprosy literatury* 11 (November 1966): 87–88; S. I. Kozlov, "Obshchee sobranie Otdeleniia literatury i iazyka AN SSSR," *IAN SSSR. OLIa* XVII, vyp. 5 (September–October 1958): 473–74; V. Sereda and A. Stykalin, eds., *Besedy na Lubianke: sledstvennoe delo Dierdia Lukacha. Materialy k biografii* (Moscow, 1999), 220–25; and "Otchet Otdeleniia literatury i iazyka," 4–5.
33. TsAODM, f. 2472, o. 1, d. 24, ll. 36, 39, 45; and Lazar Fleishman, "Iz arkhiva Guverovskogo instituta. Pis'ma Iu. G. Oksmana k G. P. Struve," in *Stanford Slavic Studies,* ed. Lazar Fleishman, Gregory Freidin, Richard D. Schupbach, and William Mills Todd, III (Stanford, Calif., 1987), 1:45. Eleonory Gilburd has uncovered a similar concern about the Western reaction to Soviet editorial and translation policies. See *Foreign Literature, 1955–1964: The Strategies of Mediation and Manipulation of Cultural Exchange in Khrushchev's Russia*" (unpublished manuscript, single-spaced version, 1998), 27–93.

above. Scholars who failed to display the requisite tendentiousness or tact while interacting with foreigners, or who mistakenly thought the new-found openness was itself a virtue, quickly ran afoul of authorities. In 1962, the party organization rebuked Il'ia Fradkin, a specialist in German literature, for arguing in a speech in East Germany that the key event of the Twenty-second Party Congress (1961) was Khrushchev's denunciation of Stalin. The American Deming Brown, an exchange scholar at the institute during the early 1960s, was also the cause of considerable anxiety. One party member cited Brown as proof that "our workers . . . consider it humiliating to engage in polemics with ideological opponents." Another worried that Western scholars like Brown were promoting the "peaceful coexistence of ideas" in order to disarm their Soviet counterparts.[34]

A bigger storm occurred in 1964 when the institute fired Iulian Oksman, a prolific specialist in nineteenth-century Russian literature. A KGB investigation revealed that Oksman corresponded with Gleb Struve through Martin Malia and Kathryn and Lewis Feuer, then American exchange scholars in Moscow, and that he published articles under pseudonyms in émigré newspapers.[35] Few IMLI scholars had more accomplished résumés. Despite studying in Heidelberg and Bonn before 1917, and then associating himself with the Left Communists who opposed the Treaty of Brest-Litovsk that ended Russia's participation in the First World War, Oksman advanced steadily through the Soviet aca-demic and political worlds during the 1920s and '30s. He eventually became the deputy director of the Institute of Russian Literature in Leningrad (Pushkin House) and a member of the presidium of the city's soviet. Oksman's career was interrupted in 1936 when he was arrested and sent to a camp in Kolyma, a timber region in far eastern Siberia. He was probably targeted because of his friendship with the former opposi-tion figures Nikolai Bukharin and Lev Kamenev, and because of his offer to adopt Kamenev's daughter after the latter's arrest in 1934. Upon his release in 1947, Oksman found a position at Saratov University, and then moved to the Institute of World Literature a decade later.[36] To the mortification of IMLI administrators, however, Oksman's experience in

34. TsAODM, f. 2472, o 1, d. 22, l. 104; d. 23, l. 42; and d. 24, l. 6. Brown later got into additional trouble when he endorsed the supposed liberal pedigree of *Novyi mir* in an advertisement that University Microfilms sent to several Soviet libraries. See Goriaeva, "Glavlit i literatura," 292–93.
35. GARF, f. 8131, o. 31, d. 95946, ll. 1–20.
36. Fleishman, "Pis'ma Iu. G. Oksmana k G. P. Struve," 15–21; Dmitrii Zubarev, ed., "Iz zhizni literaturovedov," *Novoe literaturoe obozrenie* 20 (1996): 145–46; and Elena Korobova, "Iu. G. Oksman v Saratove, 1947–1957 gg.," in *Korni travy: sbornik statei molodykh istorikov,* ed. L. S. Eremina and E. B. Zhemkova (Moscow, 1996), 145–54.

prison did not make him any more diplomatic. He frequently used the institute's gatherings to complain about the restrictions placed on interaction with foreign scholars and travel abroad. At a general assembly of IMLI employees in 1962, he challenged official, uncomplimentary evaluations of the work of Western scholars like F. D. Reeve, Malia, Vladimir Markov, Roman Jakobson, Waclaw Lednicki, Struve, and others. On another occasion, he railed against the "hangmen of Ezhov and Beria," the leaders of the secret police under Stalin, who were still at the institute. One of the articles he sent Struve concerned the activities of his colleagues Roman Samarin, Iakov El'sberg, and Vladimir Ermilov, whose denunciations in the 1930s and '40s resulted in the arrest of innocent friends and colleagues.[37] Oksman also smuggled to the West Anna Akhmatova's cycle of poems about Stalinist repression, *Requiem,* and Osip Mandelstam's contemptuous poem about Stalin. The latter work—never before seen outside the Soviet Union—was one of the reasons why Mandelstam perished in the gulag in 1938.[38]

Two years before Sinyavsky's arrest, Oksman offered a preview of the debate that dissidence would provoke. The party bureau determined that Oksman's transgressions were facilitated by a climate of excessive permissiveness. He repeatedly flaunted the rules for contact with foreigners by inviting Malia into his apartment. And he crossed the bounds governing discussions of the Stalinist past by brazenly denouncing colleagues complicit in repression. The institute had served as an incubator for Oksman's dissidence, but his colleagues "were silent" during his gestation. Close observers, nonetheless, knew that there were fissures in the supposedly monolithic "collective" when it came to Oksman. Bureau members criticized scholars who acted as if Oksman were an unexpected "bomb blast." They wondered about the loyalties of his colleagues in the Russian literature section. And they criticized scholars who continued to fraternize naively with their Western counterparts, as if unaware of their hostility.[39] After Sinyavsky's arrest, these fissures grew into a far-reaching debate over the implications of de-Stalinization.

---

37. On Samarin and El'sberg, see Ianevich [Evnina], "Institut mirovoi literatury," 118–32; and Nadezhda Mandelstam, *Hope against Hope,* trans. Max Hayward (New York, 1999), 37.

38. On Oksman's contacts with Western scholars, see "Pis'ma Iu. G. Oksmana," 22–26, 36, 42, 56, 61; N. N., "Donoshchiki i predateli sredi sovetskikh pisatelei i uchenykh," in *Sotsialisticheskii vestnik* 5/6, no. 777/778 (May–June 1963): 74–76; and TsAODM, f. 2472, o. 1, d. 24, ll. 137–38. I am indebted to David Engerman for sharing with me material from the Lewis Feuer Collection at Brandeis University (Special Collections, box 38, folder 28, 1–7) that detail Kathryn and Lewis Feuer's contacts with Oksman.

39. Zubarev, "Iz zhizni literaturovedov," 146–47.

On one side were persons who were convinced that dissidence was a product of excessive scholarly autonomy, dangerous inquiries into Stalinism, and careless contact with foreigners. On the other side were persons who were determined to preserve the reforms of the previous decade, however flawed they were.

Scholarly Autonomy Imperiled

On the morning of September 8, 1965, the KGB arrested Andrei Sinyavsky while he sat at a bus stop near Nikitskie Gates, not far from his apartment on Khlebnyi Lane, just off Arbat Square. Later that day, Iulii Daniel was detained at Moscow's Vnukovo Airport. For two months, party leaders refused to comment on the arrests, despite anxious inquiries from family and friends, and from foreign dignitaries like William Styron, Alberto Moravia, and Lillian Hellman.[40] During a trip to Paris in November, Aleksei Surkov, chief of the Union of Writers, admitted that Sinyavsky and Daniel were in custody for crimes against the Soviet people. Yet Soviet citizens were told of the arrests only on January 13, 1966, when *Izvestiia* published a caustic article by Dmitrii Eremin, the secretary of the Moscow Section of the Union of Writers, in which he accused Sinyavsky and Daniel of "duplicity" for publishing anti-Soviet works abroad under pseudonyms and maintaining the image of loyal Soviet citizens at home. A week later *Literaturnaia gazeta* (Literary Gazette) provided more details with "The Heirs of Smerdiakov," a reference to the villain in Dostoevsky's *The Brothers Karamazov*, by the IMLI scholar Zoia Kedrina. Kedrina admitted that she did not know the "extent" to which Sinyavsky and Daniel "were culpable in legal terms"; nonetheless, she claimed that their works were inspired by "hatred for the socialist system."[41]

As early as 1959, after the publication of Abram Tertz's first work in the West, his provocative essay "What Is Socialist Realism?" the KGB suspected that Tertz was an IMLI scholar. According to Galina Belaia, then a

40. On the foreign reaction to the trials, see Aleksandr Ginzburg, *Belaia kniga po delu A. Siniavskogo i Iu. Danielia* (samizdat, 1966; Frankfurt, 1967), 9–19, 26–30, 38–57, 117, 346–54, 417–27.
41. For translations of the articles, see Hayward, *On Trial*, 212–32. For analysis, see Hayward, *On Trial*, 24–35; Rothberg, *The Heirs of Stalin*, 145–67; Catherine Theimer Nepomnyashchy, *Abram Tertz and the Poetics of Crime* (New Haven, Conn., 1995), 5–11; and Harriet Murav, *Russia's Legal Fictions* (Ann Arbor, Mich., 1998), 202–8.

graduate student at the institute, Anisimov told the Soviet literature section, where Sinyavsky worked, that Tertz was "someone among us," and ordered scholars to find him. In the early 1960s, Sinyavsky drunkenly confided his alter-ego to Belaia and another graduate student. After his arrest, administrators alleged that Andrei Men'shutin, a researcher in the Soviet literature section, and an "underground" of Sinyavsky's friends also knew of Tertz's identity.[42] Men'shutin was later fired from the institute; the art critic Igor Golomshtok, supposedly a member of the "underground," was sentenced to six months "corrective labor" for refusing to disclose where he had obtained copies of Tertz's writings.[43] Yet the majority of IMLI scholars did not find out about Tertz's identity until September 9, a day after he was seized by the KGB. While Moscow was abuzz with rumors that two writers had been arrested for "hard-currency contraband," IMLI scholars began to take sides in the most serious controversy to engulf the institute since the anti-cosmopolitan campaign two decades earlier.[44]

Open discussions about Sinyavsky's arrest were delayed by the official reticence surrounding his case and uncertainty about what Tertz had written. At the beginning of October, Vladimir Semichastnyi, the head of the KGB, and Roman Rudenko, chief of the Procuracy, asked the Central Committee to inform the institute's administrators about the reasons for Sinyavsky's arrest.[45] Several days later, the institute's party bureau scheduled the first substantive discussion about Sinyavsky for the end of November, by which time it hoped the full scale of his crimes would be known. In the middle of November, the Central Committee's Ideological Commission summoned Arfo Petrosian to discuss "the disorder and vacillation" at the institute. According to Petrosian's subsequent report to the institute's party organization, party leaders cast the writings of Sinyavsky as one component in a broader campaign to discredit the party and manipulate the cult of personality to slander Soviet life. The Ideological Commission demanded that IMLI scholars "decline from

42. Galina Belaia, "'Ia rodom iz shestidesiatykh . . .' Memuarnoe vystuplenie na prazdnovanii 70-letiia G. A. Beloi na istoriko-filologicheskom fakul'tete RGGU," www.yavlinsky.ru/culture/index.phtml?id=2200; and Dmitrii Zubarev, "Iz zhizni literaturovedov," 155–56. Men'shutin also penned a rebuttal to Kedrina's article. See Hayward, *On Trial*, 246–48. On efforts to identify Tertz, see "Po sledu Tertsa v TsK KPSS iz Soiuza pisatelei," *Nezavisimaia gazeta*, February 6, 1998, 12.
43. GARF, f. 8131, o. 36, ll. 7–8, 14.
44. Evgrafov and Karpov, "Po statei 70-oi," 21; and Alliluyeva, *Only One Year*, 178.
45. L. Lazarev, T. Domracheva, and L. Charskaia, eds., "Smotreli na kazhdym. 'Palata no. 7,'" *Voprosy literatury* 2 (March–April 1996): 296.

using the phrase 'the period of the cult,' because behind it all the achievements of the Soviet government are forgotten."[46]

On November 30, 1965, the institute's party bureau met to discuss a speech that Vladimir Borshchukov, a specialist in Soviet literature, was scheduled to deliver to party members on December 7–8, the first sizeable gathering devoted to Sinyavsky's arrest. Despite the intercession of high officials, there was still a great deal of uncertainty about Sinyavsky's specific crimes, a phenomenon that paralleled a debate in the Procuracy about whether it was the act of publishing abroad that was illegal, or the content of what was published, and whether Sinyavsky was mentally fit to stand trial.[47] In lieu of these specifics, Vladimir Shcherbina, the institute's deputy director, drew a parallel that literary scholars unfamiliar with Sinyavsky's work might understand, namely, that Sinyavsky was a "mixture of the Zamiatin affair" of the 1920s, when the writer Evegenii Zamiatin was hounded into emigration after the publication of his dystopian novel *We,* and the "nauseating Fronde of 1954–56," a reference to the unconventional prose and criticism of the early thaw. Similar to the aristocratic uprisings against growing autocratic power in seventeenth-century France, the Soviet literary Fronde challenged the supremacy of socialist realism. Another administrator claimed that Sinyavsky's writings were a "rehash of Orwell and Zamiatin." Shcherbina also raised the question of culpability for the first time. He asked why Sinyavsky was promoted to senior research assistant over the objections of administrators. Another bureau member wondered about "the responsibility of colleagues who meet with foreigners." Sinyavsky, after all, had smuggled his writings abroad through a visiting Frenchwoman.[48]

When the bureau met with party members the following week, administrators steered the discussion away from Sinyavsky's still indeterminate crimes to questions of individual and collective culpability. Borshchukov targeted Sergei Bocharov, a member of the editorial board at *Voprosy literatury* (Literary Issues), a journal of liberal repute that the institute had published since 1957. Bocharev was a "politically uneducated" person prone to the same mistakes as Sinyavsky. Several speakers attacked Iurii Burtin, a graduate student who had recently finished his dissertation on Aleksandr Tvardovskii. During his defense, Burtin thanked Andrei

46. TsAODM, f. 2472, o. 1, d. 25, ll. 164–65.
47. GARF, f. 8131, o. 31, d. 99561, ll. l, 26; and "Ambulatornyi akt no. 15a: sudebno-psikhiatricheskoi ekspertizy na ispytuemogo Siniavskogo, Andreia Donatovicha," *Nezavisimaia gazeta*, February 6, 1998, 13.
48. TsAODM, f. 2472, o 1, d. 26, l. 256; and Zubarev, "Iz zhizni literaturovedov," 150–51.

Sinyavsky, then in pretrial detention, for his assistance. But the chief targets for criticism were Sinyavsky's colleagues in the Soviet literature section, who gave positive evaluations to Sinyavsky's scholarly work and were slow to respond to his arrest. Aleksandr Ushakov, the institute's scholarly secretary and reputed KGB informant, accused the Soviet literature section of shielding Sinyavsky from criticism. Ushakov claimed that the section was silent when Sinyavsky argued in the presence of visiting German scholars that the repressed writer Isaac Babel represented the "central line" of Soviet literature and the officially acclaimed Dmitrii Furmanov a peripheral line. After Sinyavsky mumbled an obligatory denunciation of his friend Pasternak during the Nobel Prize controversy in 1958, when Pasternak was forced to decline the award, only Vladimir Shcherbina, an outsider to the section, took him to task. Petrosian likewise objected to party members who were "sighing as if we were hit by a bolt from the blue." The implication was that Sinyavsky's colleagues should have anticipated his crimes.[49]

Administrators deemed two persons in the Soviet literature section especially culpable for Sinyavsky's crimes. The first was Aleksandr Dement'ev, the section's deputy director and chief editor of the three-volume *History of Soviet Literature,* to which Sinyavsky had contributed several chapters. Dement'ev was also a deputy editor at *Novyi mir* (New World), where he had asked Sinyavsky to write book reviews "on account of his talent," suddenly a very dubious measure. Dement'ev augmented his culpability by admitting (in the words of another) that he "knew Sinyavsky was capable of thinking like Abram Tertz," and that he did not denounce Sinyavsky's errors, because he wanted to foster a free exchange of ideas. Under pressure, Dement'ev supported efforts "to draw the broadest conclusions" from Sinyavsky's arrest, but later undermined his contrition by refusing to serve as the public accuser in Sinyavsky's trial.[50]

Administrators also thought that Mikhail Kuznetsov, the secretary of the party cell in the Soviet literature section, shared responsibility for Sinyavsky. On February 17, less than a week after the conclusion of the trial, the party bureau met to review a report on the "moral-political composition" of the Soviet literature section, which would be presented the following week to the section's party cell. Administrators hoped to do two things at the coming meeting. First, the Central Committee

49. "*Voprosy literatury—40 let,*" *Voprosy literatury* 2 (March–April 1997): 9; Ianevich [Evnina], "Institut mirovoi literatury," 173; TsAODM, f. 2472, o 1, d. 25, ll. 165–66, 186–87; Belaia, "Ia rodom iz shestidesiatykh"; and Zubarev, "Iz zhizni literaturovedov," 152–55.
50. TsAODM, f. 2472, o 1, d. 25, l. 167; and Belaia, "Ia rodom iz shestidesiatykh."

ordered the institute to draft a "collective letter" denouncing Sinyavsky, similar to one that eighteen of Sinyavsky's acquaintances at Moscow State University, including the prominent Pushkin scholar Sergei Bondi, recently published. According to Evnina, Anisimov "was horrified by such a course of action," but knowing he could not refuse, ordered the Soviet literature section to draft the letter.[51] Second, Ushakov pushed for extraordinary elections in the section in order that Kuznetsov could be replaced. Ushakov's contention that the previous election had been flawed was not without basis. Two months earlier, district party officials had alleged that the section's autumn elections were evidence of the "political immaturity" of Sinyavsky's colleagues. Several party members had abstained from voting; some had even circulated pamphlets defending Sinyavsky. During the intervening period, Kuznetsov's position had worsened. Not only had he failed to "unmask" Sinyavsky and discourage an "atmosphere of excessive praise," he had also compared Sinyavsky's fate to Aleksandr Herzen's, the founding father of Russian socialism forced into exile more than a century earlier by Nicholas I.[52] Nonetheless, according to party protocol, personnel changes had to be approved by party members in the Soviet literature section, so the bureau postponed further discussion until February 24 when the bureau was scheduled to meet with the section's party cell.

From the standpoint of administrators, the February 24 meeting was a debacle. After the head of the bureau warned that municipal party officials had criticized Kuznetsov's stewardship, the section's party members reacted not with the contrition that administrators sought, but disgruntlement. Kuznetsov argued that the section had responded properly to Sinyavsky's arrest and that he could not be held responsible for duplicity that even the KGB had difficulty unmasking. He claimed that the section's slow response to Sinyavsky's arrest was necessitated by the secrecy surrounding the trial and that a full appraisal of Sinyavsky was possible only in retrospect. Dement'ev also criticized the meddling of outside officials and claimed that the section had tried to set Sinyavsky on the proper ideological bearing prior to his arrest.[53] Svetlana Alliluyeva, who was Stalin's daughter, Sinyavsky's colleague, and, up to that point,

---

51. Ianevich [Evnina], "Institut mirovoi literatury," 141; and Zubarev, "Iz zhizni literaturovedov," 156. The letter from Moscow State University faculty was published as "Net nravstvennogo opravdaniia," *Literaturnaia gazeta*, February 15, 1966, 4.

52. TsAODM, f. 2472, o 1, d. 25, l. 194; d. 27, ll. 69, 74–75; and Zubarev, "Iz zhizni literaturovedov," 154, 156.

53. TsAODM, f. 2472, o 1, d. 27, ll. 79–80.

an infrequent participant in party meetings, wondered why the administration was "throwing dirt" at the section.

> I strongly protest. I don't understand what's going on today. Everyone knows that the events with Sinyavsky are tragic. . . . And now it seems as if the Soviet section produced him. . . . Sinyavsky was criticized in the section, but to unmask him is undercover work, for the investigative organs. I protest the slandering of the collective in the Soviet section. Sinyavsky did not spring from the section's party work, nor its scholarly work. But here they want to prove that he did.[54]

When the meeting resumed on February 28, the protests grew wider. Vsevolod Keldysh, a young Gorky specialist and the nephew of the academy president, admitted that many in the section knew that Sinyavsky was not entirely clean, "but from here to Tertz the distance is huge." Elena Evnina criticized administrators for caving in to outside pressure to levy blame. Several speakers insisted that Sinyavsky was a gifted and perceptive critic in spite of his crimes, an assessment that matched Aleksandr Tvardovskii's pre-arrest assessment.[55] Administrators' efforts to force the Soviet literature section to draft a collective letter denouncing Sinyavsky were also proving futile. After the bureau meeting on February 7, Kuznetsov dutifully convened the party cell to write a letter on behalf of the entire section. One woman locked herself in a bathroom during the meeting so that she would not have to participate. After Dement'ev read the completed letter aloud, two persons, at considerable risk to themselves, declined to add their signatures. Belaia, still only a graduate student, refused because she thought Sinyavsky had received enough punishment from the court; Evgenii Tager, a future activist in the Soviet human-rights movement, refused because he thought the letter was too "late" to achieve its intended purpose.[56]

The institute's administrators did not look kindly upon the resistance. One complained that the February 24 and 28 meetings had degenerated

54. Alliluyeva's block quote comes from the stenographic report of the meeting (TsAODM, f. 2472, o. 1, d. 27, ll. 85–86); "throwing dirt" from Evnina's memoir (Ianevich [Evnina], "Institut mirovoi literatury," 142). Evnina remembered a more combative speech than the stenographer recorded. This may reflect a retrospective bias born out of Alliluyeva's 1967 emigration to the West, or the fact that Alliluyeva "corrected" the stenographic report after the meeting, a common Soviet practice.
55. TsAODM, f. 2472, o 1, d. 27, ll. 92, 94; and Aleksandr Tvardovskii, "Po sluchaiu ubileia," *Novyi Mir* 1 (January 1965): 4.
56. Belaia, "Ia rodom iz shestidesiatykh"; Zubarev, "Iz zhizni literaturovedov," 158; and Ianevich [Evnina], "Institut mirovoi literatury," 143.

into an elaborate defense of the Soviet literature section, led by those who were most culpable for its deficiencies. Another criticized scholars who thought "that no one in our midst bears personal responsibility for Sinyavsky." Nonetheless, administrators were determined to see the affair through to an appropriate conclusion. Anisimov insisted that two days of discussion had shown that "the issue of the section's consolidation remains acute" and warned that the full party organization would decide the fate of an unrepentant section. He responded tepidly to suggestions that the entire institute draft a letter about Sinyavsky for the press, claiming that such an initiative would have to come from the academic council, a mostly impotent organization that was elected annually by the institute's scholars. In the meantime, it was the "duty" of the Soviet literature section to publish a letter, even one without all the necessary signatures. Yet when Anisimov asked whether the section's communists would "recognize their guilt," Kuznetsov interjected, "But why us? You . . . write it." According to Evnina, Anisimov left the room grasping his chest. He died in a hospital a short time later. The letter he sought was never published.[57]

By March 15, the mood at the institute was rebellious enough that Lev Smirnov, the chairman of the RSFSR Supreme Court, a participant in the Nuremberg Trials, and the presiding judge in Sinyavsky and Daniel's trial, met with scholars to stress the gravity of Sinyavsky's crimes.[58] During the following week, the party organization convened to decide the fate of the Soviet literature section. The head of the bureau warned that the chief of the Moscow Party Committee, Nikolai Egorychev, not a person to be taken lightly, wondered whether IMLI scholars remembered the lessons of the Oksman affair. Yet even in the face of pressure from above, Irina Neupokoeva, a specialist in European literature whose father, a former Minister of Finance, had been shot in the late 1930s, condemned the bureau's attempts to levy blame on the entire section. Many of the institute's party members had come to see the attacks on the Soviet literature section as a violation of the "democratic system of work" established after the Twentieth Party Congress. Just as the party bureau had previously denounced the meddling of administrators, so too did scholars now challenge the bureau's "ideological unscrupulousness in scholarship."[59] During the summer and fall of 1966, even a handful of bureau members began to question the bureau's penchant for intervening in the affairs of the

---

57. TsAODM, f. 2472, o. 1, d. 27, ll. 96, 98–99. The stenographer did not record Kuznetsov's interjection, which comes from Evnina's memoir (Ianevich [Evnina], "Institut mirovoi literatury," 142–43).
58. TsAODM, f. 2472, o 1, d. 27, l. 6.
59. TsAODM, f. 2472, o 1, d. 25, l. 170; and d. 27, ll. 18, 21.

Soviet literature section. In September, several rejected a plan to establish stricter oversight for graduate students, a development spawned by the perception that the "rogue shock worker" Sinyavsky and the Beatles had far too much authority among young people. In October, Boris Bialik, a Gorky specialist who was nearly fired during Stalin's anti-cosmopolitan campaign, criticized the bureau's continuing obsession with Kuznetsov after reviewing a draft of the bureau's annual report. When the report was released in final form prior to bureau elections in February 1967, it mentioned only that the bureau had reviewed the "ideological-educational work" of the Soviet literature section. Evnina thought that even this was insufficient. She argued that it was "necessary to remember . . . what was bad in the work of the bureau"; there were "improper attempts to settle old scores" by lumping blame for Sinyavsky on innocent persons. Irina Neupokoeva, Elena Evnina, and Vsevolod Keldysh were among the fourteen party members elected to the bureau in February 1967. They had all been outspoken in support of the Soviet literature section.[60]

Kuznetsov and Dement'ev managed to avoid penalties by arguing that their supervision of Sinyavsky was consonant with the institute's accepted norms. Along with their supporters, they pitted their alleged culpability against the widely popular notion that sections were autonomous, self-regulating organizations, protected for the sake of scholarly objectivity from outside pressure. They forced the party bureau to choose between political expediency and the reforms it once advocated. Once the uproar over Sinyavsky subsided in the latter half of 1966, the bureau opted for the latter. Nonetheless, there were some types of culpability that were more difficult to dismiss. In 1966, Gennadii Gritsai, a former graduate student at the institute, ran afoul of the KGB for serving as a conduit between the literary critic Ivan Svetlichnyi, who had been arrested for smuggling "anti-Soviet works" abroad, and a Ukrainian-American woman visiting Moscow. Under interrogation, Gritsai admitted that he had lived for two and a half weeks in Iulii Daniel's apartment and offered money to Daniel's wife after his arrest. Gritsai tried to justify his actions to the institute's party organization by arguing that he saw nothing criminal in Sinyavsky and Daniel's writings, a defense Shcherbina called "bourgeois solidarity." By a vote of fifty nine to one, with eight abstentions, the IMLI party organization revoked Gritsai's membership.[61]

60. TsAODM, f. 2472, o 1, d. 25, l. 191; d. 27, ll. 157, 169; and d. 28, ll. 8, 14.
61. TsAODM, f. 2472, o 1, d. 27, ll. 37–46; and Zubarev, "Iz zhizni literaturovedov," 163–67.

Gritsai was excluded from the party because he failed to distance himself from Daniel, and because he maintained under questioning that Sinyavsky and Daniel were innocent. In the ritualistic interaction of criticism/self-criticism, Gritsai refused to play the role that the party demanded of him. Yet a similar case indicates that many of the institute's party members were hesitant to punish their colleagues even in these circumstances. At the beginning of 1968, a young literary critic at *Voprosy literatury*, V. S. Nepomniashchii, signed a letter that was broadcast on Voice of America in support of Aleksandr Ginzburg, Iurii Galanskov, Aleksei Dobrovol'skii, and Vera Lashkova, the authors of the *White Book* anthology on Sinyavsky and Daniel. From the outset, the majority of the party bureau was reluctant to expel Nepomniashchii, knowing it would end his scholarly career. "But how could he be saved," Evnina asked in her memoir, "when that evil machine—the campaign to prosecute 'dissidents'—was in full gear?" Nepomniashchii admitted that he signed the letter rashly, but steadfastly refused to reveal the name of the person who gave it to him. To the delight of many, he challenged accusations that his signature provided fodder to foreign enemies by arguing that Soviet courts had brought attention on themselves by acting illegally, as they did in 1937. He was eventually expelled from the party when his case was forwarded to the district committee, where he again refused to disclose the name of the person who had given him the letter. But the district committee first had to overturn the verdicts of the institute's party bureau and organization, which had voted only for a reprimand.[62]

The institute's defiance of the campaign against dissidence was also evident in the search for Anisimov's replacement as director, which coincided with new elections to the Academy of Sciences in 1966. The institute put forth two candidates for the corresponding member slot reserved for a literary scholar: Roman Samarin, a specialist on Gorky and Friedrich Schiller, and Vladimir Shcherbina, the institute's deputy director and the author of several impenetrable books on socialist-realist theory. The Institute of Russian Literature in Leningrad forwarded the candidacy of Aleksandr Ovcharenko, a young specialist in Soviet literature rumored to be the frontrunner, since he had the support of Viktor Vinogradov, chair of the academy's Literature and Language Section. IMLI scholars understood that the new corresponding academician would likely become the director of the institute. According to Evnina, "nothing could

62. Ianevich [Evnina], "Institut mirovoi literatury," 149–51; and TsAODM, f. 2472, o.1, d. 29, ll. 49–59.

be worse" than Ovcharenko, a man infamous for abusing scholars who did not toe the official line. (Several years later, Ovcharenko helped smear the poet Aleksandr Tvardovskii before he was fired from the editor's post at *Novyi mir*.) IMLI scholars drafted a letter to the academy challenging Ovcharenko's ethical and scholarly qualifications, yet almost no one was willing to sign it for fear that Ovcharenko would use his "secret connections" with the KGB to retaliate. The secretary of the institute's party bureau even refused to schedule a discussion of the letter. In the end, twelve people put their heads "in the noose" and added their signatures. Viktor Zhirmunskii read the letter aloud at an academy meeting and announced his intention to vote against Ovcharenko. After recessing to allow the far-flung writers Mikhail Sholokhov (in the Don region) and Oleksandr Korniichuk (in Ukraine) to cast their votes, the academy unexpectedly elected a little known specialist in Bulgarian literature from the Institute of Slavic Studies. Ovcharenko failed to garner even a third of the votes. To the relief of many, Boris Suchkov, a former gulag prisoner and deputy editor of the journal *Znamia* (Banner), became the institute's new director. Unbeknownst to his new subordinates, Suchkov had written an internal review of Tertz's work for the KGB, an act that had put him in good stead with authorities.[63]

In the months following Sinyavsky's arrest, only a small number of IMLI scholars openly challenged official attempts to "draw the broadest conclusions" from his crimes and create a more rigid scholarly climate. Most kept their silence, or begrudgingly acquiesced to the demands of administrators, party bureau members, and outside authorities. Yet the vocal minority prevailed on almost every front. Outspoken scholars prevented retribution against Sinyavsky's superiors in the Soviet literature section. They delayed drafting the collective letter that the Central Committee demanded until it was a moot point. And they nixed the candidacy of Ovcharenko to the Academy of Sciences to prevent him from becoming the institute's new director. There were other victories as well. After Sinyavsky's arrest, administrators at the Institute of World Literature attacked so-called "young geniuses" who were "in the business of international contacts," but they took few steps to curtail these contacts. In 1967, more than forty of the institute's scholars traveled abroad for professional reasons. Destinations included reliable Soviet allies in Eastern Europe, but

63. Ianevich [Evnina], "Institut mirovoi literatury, 145–48; and "Slovo pisatelei. Vnutrennie retsenzii na knigi Abrama Tertsa, napisannye chlenami SP SSSR po zakazu KGB," *Nezavisimaia gazeta*, February 6, 1998, 13.

also the United States and a Czechoslovakia in the throes of reform communism. The institute's party organization continued to defend the value of foreign research topics, as well as familiarity with the work of Western specialists for those scholars working on Russian and Soviet literature. In the fall of 1967, the institute streamlined its guidelines for reviewing foreign works in order to provide researchers with greater access to materials published abroad, including the works of Michel Foucault.[64]

The institute's scholars did not save Sinyavsky, of course, but that was never their intention. Instead, they tried to limit the repercussions of his arrest and preserve the imperfect reforms of the previous decade. In this, they were remarkably successful, perhaps because their protests were not altogether unique.

OUTSIDE THE INSTITUTE

No single event belies the perceived dichotomy between the Khrushchev and Brezhnev eras like the popular upheaval that the trial of Sinyavsky and Daniel unleashed. Between 1965 and 1968, hundreds of Soviet cultural figures sent letters to the Procuracy, to prominent political figures, and to journals like *Novyi mir* voicing their disgruntlement with the dissident trials.[65] Their letter-writing campaign overwhelmed official attempts to rally Soviet citizens against the dissidents and destroyed for good the image of the monolithic public that the party hoped to preserve.[66] Like IMLI scholars, letter-writers feared that the trials jeopardized the fundamental achievements of the previous decade, particularly the rule of law. Many drew parallels between the fate of Sinyavsky and Daniel and the violence of 1937, the height of Stalin's purges. In a country where it had once "rained blood," they were horrified that Sinyavsky and Daniel were held criminally responsible for the content of their prose, and that the authors of the *White Book* were punished for speaking their consciences. Some argued that a "ban on thinking incorrectly" was the same as a "ban on thinking in general." Both were contrary to the

64. TsAODM, f. 2472, o 1, d. 28, ll. 7, 52, 60, 75, 121–22, 153, 163–65; and d. 29, ll. 35, 90, 136.
65. V. V. Zhuravlev, ed., *Vlast' i oppozitsiia. Rossiiskii politicheskii protsess XX stoletiia* (Moscow, 1995), 238; Hayward, *On Trial*, 233–51, 284–301; and I. Iu. Kuberskii, ed., *Mif o zastoe* (Leningrad, 1991), 59–61.
66. For a selection of letters and other reactions from Soviet citizens that were critical of Sinyavsky and Daniel, see Ginzburg, *Belaia kniga*, 57–60, 101–4, 354–84.

spirit of the thaw.[67] Letter-writers claimed they were motivated to protest by a growing sense of civic-mindedness. They expressed frustration with, and, in some instances, anger over the lack of glasnost in the trials. And most important, they agonized about a return to Stalinism. Their letters, however, indicate that the principal outcome of the inquisition that party leaders launched against Sinyavsky and Daniel was the very sort of heresy that is typically associated with the thaw.[68]

Many letter-writers based their right to protest on their identities as citizens. Both Boris Vakhtin, a member of the Leningrad branch of the Union of Writers who attended part of the trial and helped compile the transcript that became the basis for the *White Book,* and his son Iurii, a researcher at the Institute of Cytology, felt that this right was guaranteed by the Soviet constitution and socialism's recognition of individual human worth. Nina Levidova, a member of the Union of Journalists, premised her protest on her identity as "citizen, voter, writer, and scholar." Others regretted not exercising their right to protest earlier. Many of these citizen letters are marked by a stridency that bordered on recklessness, since citizens tended to "insist" and "demand" rather than "ask." In a letter to Roman Rudenko, the head of the Procuracy, 116 persons, including the dissidents Pavel Litvinov and Petr Grigorenko, insisted on their right to attend Ginzburg's trial regardless of the amount of space in the courtroom. Four Leningrad writers warned Rudenko that a day of reckoning would come if he failed to rectify illegalities in Sinyavsky and Daniel's prosecution. Nina Lisovskaia, a Moscow scholar, insisted that Brezhnev and Rudenko bring criminal charges against officials who authorized closed judicial proceedings. Thirty persons, including Daniel's wife, Larissa Bogoraz-Bukhman, demanded the immediate release of Ginzburg and an investigation into the actions of the KGB. Several Moscow workers, a group poorly represented in extant letters, demanded that Kremlin leaders curtail KGB surveillance of Ginzburg's friends and supporters and respect the freedoms of speech, press, and assembly guaranteed by the constitution.[69]

67. GARF, f. 8131, o. 31, d. 89189a, l. 127. These are also the themes of Lidiia Chukovskaia's famous rebuttal to Mikhail Sholokhov's speech at the Twenty-third Party Conference. See Hayward, *On Trial,* 286–91; and Ginzburg, *Belaia kniga,* 390–94.

68. On deviance as a characteristic of the thaw, see Nancy Condee, "Cultural Codes of the Thaw," in *Nikita Khrushchev,* ed. William Taubman, Sergei Khrushchev, and Abbott Gleason (New Haven, Conn., 2000), 164–66.

69. GARF, f. 8131, o. 31, d. 89189a, ll. 99 (116 signees), 127 (Leningrad writers), 128–280b (Lisovskaia), 133 (Levidova), 134 (30 signees), 150 (Vakhtin), 161–610b (workers).

It is not surprising that "citizen" was the most common self-identification among letter-writers. Even though Stalinist traditionalism had retarded the transition from supplicant to citizen, members of the intelligentsia were more inclined than other segments of Soviet society to identify themselves as citizens.[70] Yet the dissident trials brought something new to the citizenship discourse: the characterization of protest letters as a "civic duty." During the 1930s, allusions to duty and loyalty were common in letters of denunciation, since they helped establish the altruistic motives of denouncers.[71] Thirty years later, letter-writers referenced civic duty to justify actions and beliefs that were contrary to the policies of the Soviet state.

In March 1968, the French weekly *Le nouvel observateur* printed an essay by Ginzburg's attorney, Boris Zolotukhin, who asked how Ginzburg might have responded differently to a verdict he deemed unjust.

> As a citizen, how should he have acted, what should he have thought? He could have been fully indifferent to the affair, but instead it evoked in him a civic response. . . . I do not know which of these reactions the court prefers. But I do know that indifference is inconsonant with the calling of a citizen.

Zolotukhin's assessment was not unique. In the days immediately following Ginzburg's arrest, his mother argued much the same in a letter to Brezhnev, Rudenko, Aleksei Kosygin, and six others. She claimed that her son acted in the only manner open to an "honest and principled person" confronted by injustice. Letter-writers frequently duplicated Ginzburg's defense strategy by characterizing their own protests as acts of duty. A scholar at Latvian State University was moved by a desire to preserve "the honor of my country and the principles of Soviet democracy." Forty-six persons told Brezhnev, Kosygin, and Nikolai Podgornyi, the chair of the Supreme Soviet, that a sense of "civic responsibility" obligated them to demand that Ginzburg's sentence be overturned. Another letter-writer told "citizen" Brezhnev that patriotism demanded he emulate the novelist Konstantin Paustovskii, who had been outspoken in his support of Sinyavsky and Daniel.[72]

70. On letter-writing in the Stalin period, see Sheila Fitzpatrick, "Supplicants and Citizens: Public Letter-Writing in Soviet Russia in the 1930s," *Slavic Review* 55, no. 1 (Spring 1996): 78–105.

71. Sheila Fitzpatrick, "Signals from Below: Soviet Letters of Denunciation in the 1930s," in Sheila Fitzpatrick and Robert Gellately, eds., *Accusatory Practices: Denunciation in Modern European History, 1789–1989* (Chicago, 1997), 91–95.

72. GARF, f. 8131, o. 31, d. 89189a, ll. 70 (mother), 111–12 (Latvian), 195 (46 signers); d. 89189b, l. 72 (Zolotukhin); and d. 99561, l. 120 (Paustovskii).

Letters premised on civic duty are significant because they represent an alternative to the rights-based rhetoric found in many citizen letters. It may be the case that letter-writers thought expressions of duty were safer than assertions of rights, since they were easier to conflate with patriotism. Nonetheless, the divide was not absolute, and writers often referenced both their right and duty to protest. These discursive strategies were sometimes linked by an emphasis on conscience. As Zolotukhin argued in defense of Ginzburg, citizens were duty-bound to act according to conscience, even if it contradicted the party line. Some thought the same standard applied to party leaders as well. One anonymous letter-writer asked Rudenko to sequester himself with his conscience, and consider the meaning of "freedom, democracy, open court, inquisition, comedy, tyranny, parody." Another letter-writer appealed to Kosygin's reputedly liberal conscience and rumors of a split with Brezhnev. Some letter-writers attacked the party for demanding the subordination of conscience to politics. V. I. Bukasov, a scholar in Fergana, Uzbekistan, asked the editors of *Novyi mir* why his fellow Soviet citizens, who from the distant reaches of Central Asia seemed quiescent, failed to speak their consciences. "The answer, I am sure, is the *diktat* of the monopolistic, fanatical, censorious party." Others pointed out that their own consciences had not been tainted by BBC and Voice of America.[73]

Letter-writers also complained about the lack of glasnost in the dissident trials, which they saw as an important restraint on the capriciousness of government. They were inspired by Aleksandr Esenin-Vol'pin's legalist strand of dissidence, which challenged the Soviet government to honor its own laws, and the protesters on Pushkin Square. They argued that judicial authorities were violating basic constitutional protections of due process by staging a closed trial.[74] A man from Ivanovo told Rudenko that the "absence of any information" in the press on Aleksandr Ginzburg forced him to doubt the "correctness of the court's decision." A man from Kaluzhskaia oblast argued that "complete glasnost" was the only guarantee against injustice. Larissa Bogoraz-Bukhman told Brezhnev, Rudenko, and the editors at *Pravda* that excessive secrecy fueled rumors of a return to Stalinism. Nina Levidova feared that *neglasnost'* hurt the international prestige of the Soviet Union. Dozens of other writers

73. GARF, f. 8131, o. 31, d. 89189a, l. 141 (anonymous); d. 99563, l. 122 (Kosygin); and RGALI, f. 1702, o. 9, d. 220, ll. 5 (Bukasov), 14 (BBC/VOA).
74. Robert Horvath, "The Dissident Roots of *Glasnost*," in *Challenging Traditional Views of Russian History*, ed. Stephen G. Wheatcroft (New York, 2002), 176–77; and Daniel, *Piatoe dekabria*, 4.

demanded access to the trials so they could safeguard the rights of the accused. A smaller number asked that the trials be publicized so that they could evaluate for themselves the legitimacy of the charges. Four Leningrad writers, feigning nostalgia for the well-publicized show trials of the 1930s, argued that open trials might serve a valuable didactic function: "Television, radio, and newspapers can show in great detail the face of our enemy." Forty-two signers of a more litigious letter argued that there was no legal basis for closing the dissident trials; the charges, after all, did not concern the dissemination of state secrets.[75]

In January 1968, a senior aide to Rudenko unsuccessfully petitioned the Moscow municipal court to open the doors to the trial of Ginzburg, Galanskov, Dobrovol'skii, and Lashkova.[76] He cited the degree of "public interest" in the case, undoubtedly a reference to the flood of mail the Procuracy had received. Rudenko likely understood that much of the public outrage over the trials—especially outside the literary world—stemmed from excessive secrecy rather than the terms of the indictment. The fact that his petition was denied interestingly suggests that the court, contrary to the suspicions of many, was not in lockstep with the Procuracy. Fifty-two persons argued that the absence of glasnost empowered the KGB, which was using dissident trials to "settle scores with good-for-nothings . . . who spoke in defense of the constitution and demanded the observance of legality." One Muscovite thought the KGB was trying to poison public opinion by circulating rumors that Sinyavsky was "a swine, scum (*podonok*) who was motivated by American dollars." Numerous letter-writers complained about the KGB's harassment of Ginzburg's family and friends, who had gathered outside the court during the trial. Another letter-writer claimed that judicial secrecy was a deliberate attempt to cover violations of civil rights.[77] Letter-writers were also critical of the scant information about the trials that had been published. More than one-hundred persons took issue

---

75. GARF, f. 8131, o. 31, d. 89189a, ll. 125 (Ivanovo), 128 (Leningrad writers), 133 (Levidova), 136 (42 signers), 204 (Kaluzhskaia oblast); and d. 99561, l. 37 (Bogoraz). Complaints about the lack of glasnost were also expressed in the Moscow Section of the Union of Writers. See RGALI, f. 2464, o. 3, d. 211, ll. 43, 45.

76. GARF, f. 8131, o. 31, d. 89189a, l. 109.

77. GARF, f. 8131, o. 31, d. 89189a, l. 143 (judicial secrecy); d. 89189b, l. 87 (52 signers); and d. 99563, l. 1 (Muscovite). KGB harassment of the families and friends of the accused was also the subject of letters that Bogoraz-Bukhman, Daniel's wife, and Rozanova-Kruglikova, Sinyavsky's wife, sent to authorities. See Ginzburg, *Belaia kniga*, 80–83.

with official claims that Sinyavsky and Daniel had ties with the National Labor Union (NTS), an anti-Soviet émigré organization in Frankfurt. The Leningrader, Ernst Orlovskii, wrote a lengthy refutation of several of the more absurd charges in Dmitrii Eremin's article in *Izvestiia*, including his allegation that Sinyavsky was trying to fan anti-Semitism by writing under an ostensibly Jewish pseudonym. Igor Golomshtok, who later spent six months in a work camp for refusing to reveal how he obtained copies of Sinyavsky's writings, sent a similar rebuttal of newspaper coverage to the Supreme Court. Twenty-five artists and writers, including the future émigrés Vassily Aksyonov, Naum Korzhavin, and Vladimir Voinovich, told Brezhnev and Kosygin that coverage of Ginzburg and Galanskov's trial in *Komsomol'skaia pravda* (Komsomol Pravda) and *Izvestiia* only "deepened disbelief" among the public. Fourteen of Ginzburg's friends argued much the same in another letter.[78]

The tendentious press coverage encouraged many people to look elsewhere for news, particularly to Voice of America and BBC. Despite occasional attempts to jam shortwave broadcasts, large numbers of Soviet citizens had been listening to foreign newscasts for more than a decade. The repercussions were potentially significant. Party members could be reprimanded or expelled for tuning in to "anti-Soviet propaganda." Nonetheless, the dissident trials provoked an unprecedented frankness about the listening habits of Soviet citizens. One letter-writer claimed that he was "forced" to listen to Western radio after finding little about the trials in the Soviet press. There he was surprised to discover that pro-Soviet luminaries like Louis Aragon opposed the trials. Another letter-writer admitted that he heard about Ginzburg and Galanskov's trial on a London radio station, and then read about it in *L'Humanité*, the newspaper of the French communist party. Others admitted that they listened to Bogoraz-Bukhman and Litvinov's letter "To the World Public" on Voice of America, which (contrary to its title) called on Soviet citizens to recall judges who perpetuated judicial secrecy. More than 180 persons asked Brezhnev, Kosygin, and other political leaders to respond to Bogoraz-Bukhman and Litvinov's charges. A resident of Riga asked Rudenko to

78. GARF, f. 8131, o. 31, d. 89189a, ll. 181–86 (14 friends), 190 (25 signers); d. 89189b, l. 100 (NTS); RGALI, f. 1702, o. 9, d. 220, l. 8 (Orlovskii); and f. 2887, o. 1, d. 572, ll. 23–30 (Golomshtok). A copy of Golomshtok's letter can also be found at RGALI (f. 2887, o. 1, d. 572, ll. 23–32) and in Ginzburg (*Belaia kniga*, 157–62). For a penitent account of the *Izvestiia* reporter at the trial, see Yuri Feofanov and Donald D. Barry, *Politics and Justice in Russia: Major Trials of the Post-Stalin Era* (Armonk, N.Y., 1996), 38–49.

prevent criminal charges from being filed against Bogoraz-Bukhman and Litvinov for smuggling their appeal to the West.[79]

It is not clear whether letter-writers were routinely punished for signing protest letters, like the *Voprosy literatury* critic Nepomniashchii. In general, party leaders were more concerned about the circulation of protest letters abroad than their content at home. Persons whose letters fell into the hands of Western journalists could be reprimanded, fired from their jobs, expelled from the party, or imprisoned for spreading anti-Soviet propaganda.[80] Eduard Gureev, a Moscow engineer, was sentenced to five years hard labor and three years internal exile for distributing 700 pamphlets that called on Muscovites to vote against their local soviet deputies to protest the arrests of Sinyavsky and Daniel. Five of Gureev's co-conspirators received lesser sentences. The gravity of Gureev's crimes was augmented by his alleged ties with Western journalists and NTS.[81] Nonetheless, the high percentage of letters that were signed suggests that the repercussions were usually minimal for letters sent to domestic institutions. The Moscow Section of the Union of Writers refused to condemn the writer Konstantin Paustovskii for signing a protest letter because he was not a party member. The Union was more critical of the future dissident Lev Kopelev, a party member, but still sanctioned no punishment.[82] The dissident Boris Kagarlitsky later argued that authorities went "too far" in their harassment of Sinyavsky and Daniel, and were forced to retreat after the intelligentsia became "agitated."[83] If Kagarlitsky is correct, the sheer volume of letters may have been the best guarantee against retribution.

Letter-writers were less successful realizing their demands than their counterparts at the Institute of World Literature, largely because their demands were more extensive. The Soviet government did not release Sinyavsky and Daniel from prison; it did not file criminal charges against the KGB agents and prosecutors in charge of the investigation; and it did not show any greater respect for the supposedly inviolable freedoms of speech and press guaranteed by the Soviet constitution. Yet there may be some truth in Kagarlitsky's contention that letter-writers

79. GARF, f. 8131, o. 30, d. 89189a, ll. 112 (Aragon), 140 (Riga resident), 171 (180 signers), 177–78 (Bogoraz/Litvinov).
80. Josephson, *New Atlantis Revisited*, 296–302; and Alexeyeva and Goldberg, *The Thaw Generation*, 167–69.
81. GARF, f. 8131, o. 31, d. 99976, ll. 1–7, 12, 20.
82. RGALI, f. 2464, o. 3, d. 211, l. 54.
83. Boris Kagarlitsky, *The Thinking Reed: Intellectuals and the Soviet State from 1917 to the Present*, trans. Brian Pearce (London, 1988), 189.

prevented a more extensive crackdown. At Moscow State University, for instance, letter-writers managed to lessen the punishment of a colleague who got into trouble over Sinyavsky and Daniel. In March 1966, administrators at the university tried to fire Viktor Duvakin, a Mayakovsky specialist who was the lone witness to testify on behalf of Sinyavsky and Daniel. Duvakin had known Sinyavsky since the mid-1940s, when both Sinyavsky and Hélène Peltier-Zamoskaia, the daughter of the French naval attaché assigned to Moscow and Sinyavsky's future conduit to the West, enrolled in his seminar on Mayakovsky. Official efforts to fire Duvakin failed when several of his colleagues argued in a petition to the Twenty-third Party Congress that retribution against witnesses discredited the entire Soviet justice system. Duvakin was instead reassigned to library work.[84]

In addition, some evidence suggests that prosecutors were more reluctant to prosecute aberrant behavior after the uproar over Sinyavsky and Daniel. In 1965 the KGB discovered that Sinyavsky helped Andrei Remizov, an employee at the State Foreign Language Library, smuggle anti-Soviet writings to the West under the pseudonym I. Ivanov. One of Remizov's works appeared in *Encounter,* the journal of the anti-communist Congress for Cultural Freedom. Despite the similarity to Sinyavsky and Daniel's crimes, Remizov managed to avoid charges by disavowing his writings and serving as a witness for the prosecution in Sinyavsky and Daniel's trial. He claimed that he was "disoriented by Khrushchev's political initiatives," and that he consequently mistook "Khrushchev's fallacious remarks as the official line of the Central Committee."[85] For prosecutors still shocked by the uproar over Sinyavsky and Daniel, Remizov's politically astute and timely self-criticism and cooperation were punishment enough.

Notwithstanding their modest results, most letter-writers wrote with the expectation that their protests would have some impact.[86] "The time before the trial [of Sinyavsky and Daniel] had been a time of hope for justice," Galina Belaia wrote in the late 1980s,

---

84. Hayward, *On Trial*, 39, 300–301; Galina Belaia, "Yea So Shall It Be Known to All . . . ," trans. Catherine T. Nepomnyashchy, *Russian Studies in Literature* 28, no. 1 (Winter 1991–1992): 20–21; and "Protokol doprosa svidetelia Duvakina, Viktora Dmitrievicha," *Nezavisimaia gazeta,* February 6, 1998, 14.

85. GARF, f. 8131, o. 36, d. 111, ll. 4, 18–19; and Mar'ia Rozanova, "Teatr absurda, ili profil'fas," *Nezavisimaia gazeta,* February 6, 1998, 9.

86. For an exception to this optimism, see GARF, f. 8131, o. 31, d. 89189a, l. 127.

for the power of legal protest, the weight of public opinion. It was the highest point in the development of civic consciousness, the pinnacle of trust in authority, desire to get through to those "on top," to find a common language with them. The wives of arrested men wrote, their friends wrote, people unacquainted with them wrote. They did not hide their names.[87]

Belaia's comments suggest that the act of writing was as important as the results. Like Trotsky's metaphor for the disappearance of the state under socialism—the candle that flames up before it goes out—the heresy associated with the thaw intensified at the very moment the thaw was supposedly in full collapse. Letter-writers agonized about Stalin's return to the Kremlin, but they were acting in a way that was wholly inconsonant with Stalinism. Similarly, scholars at the Institute of World Literature refused to scapegoat friends and colleagues whom they knew to be innocent, often at considerable risk to their own careers. They rallied to defend the scholarly autonomy they fought for in the previous decade, however imperfect it was. And to the chagrin of administrators, they elected persons sympathetic to Sinyavsky to the institute's party bureau. As Elena Evnina noted in her samizdat history of the Institute of World Literature, the late 1960s was a "politically ambiguous" era that was "still the 'thaw,' but already its end."[88]

Few of these persons, it seems, were aware that their actions belied their fears, probably because the trial of Sinyavsky and Daniel, though hardly the catastrophe that many envisioned, marked real changes in Soviet cultural policy. Transgressions that warranted only a sharp rebuke under Khrushchev, earned a lengthy prison sentence under Brezhnev. Borrowing from Sinyavsky's trial testimony and his later writings on Soviet culture, the literary scholar Harriet Murav characterized these developments as the suspension of a metaphor's "referential status." Just as the Moscow court mistook a first-person fictional narrator for Sinyavsky, so too did it confuse what was metaphorical in Sinyavsky's writings with what was real. It was this "literal-mindedness" that led the court to deny that fiction could be purely imaginary. Literature, in its view, was fundamentally a vehicle for politics.[89] As the young bard Vladimir Vysotskii sang in an impromptu ode to Sinyavsky: "They say

87. Belaia, "Yea So Shall It Be Known to All . . . ," 21.
88. Ianevich [Evnina], "Institut mirovoi literatury," 149.
89. Murav, *Russia's Legal Fictions,* 197, 208–9.

that the best guy was arrested for three words."[90] In 1968, when Ginzburg, Galanskov, Dobrovol'skii, and Lashkova were tried for compiling and distributing the *White Book,* the court further tightened the reins by rejecting assertions that individual conscience was a basis of authority in Soviet politics. Patriotism demanded the subordination of conscience to the state.

In their autobiographical accounts of the late 1960s, both Galina Belaia and Aleksandr Solzhenitsyn criticized the "apostasy" of intellectuals who collaborated with authorities in the prosecution of dissidents, like the eminent Pushkin scholar Sergei Bondi, who signed a letter denouncing his former student, Sinyavsky. Belaia and Solzhenitsyn juxtaposed the alleged cowardice of apostates in their midst with the courage of dissidents who refused to recant, a practice that the poet Joseph Brodsky initiated in his trial for "parasitism" (having no job) in Leningrad in 1964. Similarly, Mar'ia Rozanova-Kruglikova, Sinyavsky's wife, never forgave Aleksandr Tvardovskii, the editor of *Novyi mir.* Tvardovskii sat in the front row at her husband's trial, but refused to make eye contact with the man he had once extolled as a great talent.[91] In truth, however, the apostasy of the intelligentsia was wider and more multifaceted. While some cultural figures renounced their beliefs or refused to speak in defense of the accused because it was politically or professionally expedient, many others began to look anew at the thaw, a type of apostasy that went largely unnoticed. According to Solzhenitsyn, who had earlier admitted his "relief" when Khrushchev was ousted from power, Sinyavsky and Daniel's trial produced a "change of hearts" regarding the past, since it underscored how "fragile and precarious were the freedoms—to talk, to possess manuscripts—that had been bestowed under Khrushchev and had expired with him."[92] The dissident trials cemented the sense that the thaw was, above all, a "magical era" of cultural autonomy and political tolerance.[93] Beginning in September 1965, many Soviet citizens feared that the new Kremlin leadership had terminated the thaw, and in death they grew quite fond of it.

There were many things remarkable and surprising about the end of the thaw. Sinyavsky's friends and coworkers fought hard to preserve

90. Rozanova, "Teatr absurda," 9.
91. Ibid.
92. Belaia, "Yea So Shall It Be Known to All," 24; and Solzhenitsyn, *The Oak and the Calf,* 90, 108.
93. Masha Gessen, *Dead Again: The Russian Intelligentsia after Communism* (London, 1997), 12.

reforms that they had deemed flawed only a few years earlier. Their success suggests that the impact of the thaw on Soviet society was in many ways permanent, even at the moment when they feared the thaw was in full eclipse. And most important, an era whose contradictory reforms and disorienting ideological climate bred so much nostalgia for the pre-Stalin period, quickly became an object of nostalgia itself. In this sense, the trial of Sinyavsky and Daniel was truly a turning point.

The Arbat and the Thaw

The Arbat emerged from the thaw a very different place from what it had been fifteen years earlier. Its transformation was most evident in the Novyi Arbat project, which split the neighborhood in half, and whose skyscrapers cast long shadows over the low-rise, pre-revolutionary buildings that lined the narrow alleys north of the thoroughfare. But there were other changes—evident in the trajectory of the Arbat's experienced thaw—that were more subtle and important. During the early and mid-1950s, teachers and administrators at the Gnesin Institute wondered whether the thaw was anything more than a temporary reprieve from Stalinism. Their concerns were reinforced by the uneven pace and ad hoc nature of Khrushchev's reforms, and, especially, by the political and cultural retrenchment of late 1956, when the Central Committee warned that enemies were manipulating the Twentieth Party Congress to discredit the Soviet Union. Consequently, without clear guidance from above, few teachers were willing to extrapolate from the congress to the realm of curricular reform. Their reluctance was part of the survival instinct that Stalinism had honed. Ten years later and a few blocks to the west, Andrei Sinyavsky's friends and coworkers at the Institute of World Literature fought hard to preserve the reforms of the Khrushchev era. In the wake of Sinyavsky's arrest, they openly flaunted demands to punish his superiors in the Soviet literature section. They criticized colleagues who sanctioned a broader crackdown. They thwarted the appointment of a widely despised scholar from Leningrad as director of the institute.

And, of course, they were joined in protest by thousands of artists, writers, and scholars from outside the institute, who were outraged by the imprisonment of two writers for the content of their prose. Unquestionably, a great deal had changed.

In the introduction, I indicated that the trajectory of the Arbat's experienced thaw—from uncertainty to enthusiasm, and then to anger and disappointment—had much to do with the way different generations responded to reform. During the initial years of the thaw, the "fathers"—people who had come of age in the 1920s and '30s—were understandably worried about stepping beyond the parameters of reform. Conversely, the "sons"—teenagers and young adults at the time of Stalin's death—pressed their superiors to follow the logic of de-Stalinization to its end; they enthusiastically embraced the Soviet Union's opening to the outside world. Finally, Andrei Amalrik's "generation of 1966" felt betrayed by the renewed authoritarianism of the early-Brezhnev years. It is dangerous to be overly reductionist about all of this, for what was valid on the aggregate did not always hold true for the individual. It is also true that generational divides were never concrete, and that many persons whose age put them in one generation shared political and cultural sensibilities with those in others.

Nonetheless, it is clear that age and experience were important factors in structuring the way individuals responded to reform, and that generational issues, consequently, were ubiquitous in the culture and politics of the thaw. Teachers at the Gnesin Institute feared that students held them responsible for the sins of the past. Ruben Simonov tried to resurrect the egalitarian spirit and youthful creativity he remembered from his younger days in Evgenii Vakhtangov's studio. And members of the Moscow Section of the Union of Architects wondered whether contemporary Soviet architecture was as significant as what their constructivist "fathers" had achieved in the 1920s. The prominence of generational issues, however, is not necessarily evidence of the sort of schism that Ivan Turgenev had described a century earlier, where the young rejected the conventions and values of the old. In the Arbat, in fact, the opposite was often the rule. Young and old people alike embraced the cultural achievements of the pre-Stalin period. In *Princess Turandot* and early-Soviet constructivism, they saw what Soviet culture might have been had it not been regimented by Stalinism. In the historical preservation movement, special esteem was reserved for persons like Igor Grabar' and Petr Baranovskii, old-timers ("grandfathers," really, since they had come of age before 1917) who had been central figures in early-Soviet preservationist circles. Old people, in short, were not hopelessly out-dated. They were victims of Stalinism and surviving vessels of an uncor-rupted pre-Stalinist past. As Iulian Oksman, the IMLI literary scholar who was fired for outing former NKVD informers in the émigré press, knew all too well, there were villains among them but also much more. It is perhaps telling that the only instance where guilt for the past was pinned on a generation—at the Gnesin Institute—it appears to have been largely self-ascribed by the "fathers," and then was easily assuaged by continuing reform.

The absence of a conventional generational schism amid so much generational rhetoric is important for two reasons. First, it suggests, paradoxically, that there might have been something to Khrushchev's 1963 denial of a "father and son problem." In the aftermath of the trial of Sinyavsky and Daniel, any young person who was convinced that elders were unrepentant needed to look closely at the "generation of 1966." It included young jazz aficionados who were convinced, as one Gnesin teacher put it, that the older generation had not yet "discovered America," but also older people like Lev Kopelev, a former "true believer" who had helped seize grain from starving Ukrainian peasants in the early 1930s.[1] (Granted, this is probably not what Khrushchev had in mind when he touted the generational unity of the Soviet people.) Second, the tendency to identify older people as victims of Stalinism glossed over relationships between the intelligentsia and the state that were considerably more complex. This was especially evident in archi-tects' uncritical embrace of constructivism. They saw in Kaganovich's 1931 denunciation of constructivism and in the Soviet government's subsequent endorsement of neoclassicism proof that constructivism was the antipode of Stalinism. The truth, of course, was not so clear-cut.

It seems unlikely that MOSA architects purposefully obfuscated the past. Rather, in the context of the thaw, where so many things associated with the Stalin period had been discredited, and Soviet citizens of all stripes were licking their wounds, it struck many as entirely logical that constructivist architects had always been the implacable foes of Stalin-ism. Moreover, in the context of heightened Cold War tensions and the aesthetic crisis that had plagued Soviet architecture since 1954, con-structivism had definite political utility. As James Wertsch argues, col-lective memories, because they are constantly shifting in response to the political and cultural texts that mediate them, typically offer narratives

---

1. Lev Kopelev, *Education of a True Believer* (New York, 1980).

of the past that are politically useful and intuitively valid.[2] Consequently, collective memories have little to do with historical accuracy. Wertsch's rule of thumb is valid for much of the Arbat's retrospective gaze. For the *vakhtangovtsy*, the idealized view of Evgenii Vakhtangov's studio was consonant with the broader search for alternate cultural and political models in the 1920s that was characteristic of the thaw. Insofar as it informed the revival of *Princess Turandot* in 1963, it also offered a useable past that promised to rectify the Vakhtangov Theater's diminished stature, and establish Simonov as Vakhtangov's principal heir. Similarly, the image of the thaw as an idyllic period of political tolerance and cultural experimentation seemed entirely logical in a context where writers were suddenly being prosecuted for the content of their prose. It was also politically useful because it could be used to rally the Soviet intelligentsia against what seemed to be an increasingly authoritarian regime.

The collective remembering that went on in the Arbat was only the tip of the neighborhood's engagement with the past. Interest in Russian and Soviet history was widespread during the thaw. It was evident in efforts to rewrite music history textbooks, in the growing historical preservation movement, and in the re-publication of forgotten and disgraced writers from the Silver Age and the NEP period. It reflected a natural desire to tally as accurately as possible the victims of Stalinism, and was encouraged by the fact that so many political and cultural standards were in flux. In the latter sense, the Arbat's engagement with the past was part of the devolution of political power that is often associated with the Khrushchev years. The historical preservation movement, for example, openly challenged official appraisals of past culture by calling for a greater degree of public input in decisions regarding demolition and restoration. Similarly, IMLI scholars struggled to cast aside the "inertia" of their old ways by showing greater initiative and independence when choosing research topics.

These activities amounted to more than political opportunism. Cultural figures in the Arbat looked for meaning in the past, given that the present was so disorienting. In Simonov's successful efforts to restore the reputation of his teacher, Evgenii Vakhtangov, and in the insurrection that historical preservationists mounted in the spring of 1965, it is easy to see the outlines of the "magical era" that the intelligentsia remembered in the wake of the dissident trials. But the thaw also triggered emotions that

2. James V. Wertsch, *Voices of Collective Remembering* (Cambridge, 2002), 7, 9.

were less memorable: confusion, doubt, even disappointment and fear. At the Gnesin Institute, teachers who had suffered personally during the Stalin period began to question their own complicity for repression and obscurantism. The Vakhtangov Theater was scandalized by the performance of a bitterly anti-Stalinist play, which, ironically, was taken as proof that little had changed since Stalin's death. At MOSA, Khrushchev's denunciation of the neoclassical and gothic structures of Stalinism ushered in what can only be described as the dark age of Soviet architecture. Moreover, the tools that the intelligentsia used to make sense of reform were changing alongside the rest of Soviet society. Actors at the Vakhtangov Theater discovered that some types of political patronage had become unacceptable, even though patronage was a practice that was deeply embedded in the history of the theater. Historical preservationists found that their usual method of thwarting the reconstruction plans of local officials—appeals to higher authorities—were less effective than demands that local officials respect the opinion of the public. And Gnesin teachers resorted to the most tried and true method for obtaining clarification from above: they patiently waited for someone to explain to them how the Central Committee's 1948 decree on Vano Muradeli's opera *Great Friendship* was consonant with the spirit of the Twentieth Party Congress. They might have tried something different had they known their wait would last more than two years!

Herein lies the chief moral of the Arbat's experienced thaw: de-Stalinization ushered in such rapid and sweeping ideological change that it was hard for the intelligentsia (and even political leaders) to make sense of it all, much less foresee the problems it would cause. In the introduction, I argued that there are good reasons to privilege ideological change in analyses of the thaw. First, it allows for a better accounting of the myriad responses it provoked from Soviet citizens than traditional analyses that define the period in terms of political liberalization. In this regard, it is worth noting how seldom cultural and political debates in the Arbat broke down along the conventional liberal/conservative, Stalinist/reformist axes. Both the architects who designed Novyi Arbat and the historical preservationists who opposed it, for example, claimed the mantel of reform. Their debate was not about whether de-Stalinization was good or bad, but which reforms had priority, those that rehabilitated the innocent victims of Stalinism, or those that sought to create enthusiastic citizen-activists out of a population browbeaten by Stalinism. Even at the Institute of World Literature, where Sinyavsky's defenders were more prone than others in the Arbat to frame their struggle as a fight against inveterate Stalinists, it is striking how many of the accomplishments of the thaw went unchallenged by all sides, like the idea that good scholarship was best served by some degree of scholarly freedom. After all, this is what Arfo Petrosian, one of Sinyavsky's most vocal antagonists, had fought for a decade earlier. Growing scholarly freedom and institutional autonomy also made it possible for Sinyavsky's allies to advance their agenda through existing frameworks, like elections within the Soviet literature section and the institute's party organization. Moreover, privileging ideological change in narratives of the thaw may make it easier to avoid false dichotomies between the Khrushchev period, on the one hand, and the Stalin and Brezhnev periods, on the other. These dichotomies are invariably based on the presumption that the Khrushchev period was less repressive and more liberal than what came before and after. They contain much that is true, but they also obscure how many of the seeds of de-Stalinization were sown before 1953, like efforts to reform the Gnesin Institute's curriculum, and how the image of the idyllic thaw was constructed retrospectively, despite a great deal of continuity across the divide marked by the dissident trials.

Yet perhaps the best reason to emphasize ideological change in narratives of the thaw is that it better reflects the sense of indeterminacy that was embedded in Ilya Ehrenburg's original metaphor. In the spring of 1953, amid the grief and hope that followed Stalin's death, who could have known what lay ahead? Who could have predicted the many problems that would arise as the Soviet Union changed in ways subtle and obvious? This uncertain thaw was both exhilarating and treacherous.

Of course, the end of the thaw was not the end of the Arbat. For Bulat Okudzhava, that came later, in the mid-1980s, when urban planners began work on the Arbat pedestrian mall. Okudzhava complained that municipal officials were unresponsive to calls that the pedestrian mall be halted, even though they pledged to respect residents' concerns. In a show of goodwill, Mossovet invited Vladimir Nikolaev, a satirical poet who had written a great deal about the reconstruction of Moscow, to do a reading for delegates. When Nikolaev finished, municipal officials "clapped him on the shoulder, took him to the buffet, and went on building as before." "I imagine there is some kind of administrative-economic or construction section," Okudzhava told participants at a roundtable on the pedestrian mall in 1986, "where sits some illiterate boss, who is charged with 'coping' with us. And he copes. And no one among us can influence him in any way."[3] The pedestrian mall was especially bitter because urban planners couched it as a preservation and restoration project; they ignored Okudzhava's argument that the antecedent they were recreating—the tourist district and bazaar of yore—had never existed.

The historian Sigurd Shmidt was only slightly more equivocal about the fate of the neighborhood during the 1980s. The political changes of the Gorbachev years provided opportunities to look anew at *arbattsy* like Marina Tsvetaeva, Andrei Belyi, and Mikhail Osorgin, writers whose legacies were clouded by repression or emigration. Shmidt was one of the chief organizers of celebrations in 1993 to mark the Arbat's pentacentennial. But he was also angered by the daily discomfort caused by the pedestrian mall. The Arbat had become a "gaslight" district, a recreation zone, and a tourist attraction that was lacking in conveniences like bakeries and mailboxes. Architects claimed they were recreating a lost Arbat idyll, but its central component, the pedestrian mall and the "free cultural zone" that quickly developed, made normal life impossible.[4]

Like the pre-revolutionary populists who were saddened to discover that Russian peasants were not only uninterested in toppling the autocracy, but hostile to the thought, Okudzhava and Shmidt acknowledged their alienation from what urban planners called (with no irony) the "new, old Arbat." Okudzhava claimed to have nothing in common with persons who settled in the neighborhood in the 1960s and '70s, mostly party and managerial elites who occupied new, yellow-brick apartment buildings in the southern and western parts of the neighborhood, and pre-revolutionary structures that had been consolidated into single-family apartments. (Okudzhava was apparently unworried about being accused of snobbishness.) On Plotnikov Lane, there even opened a hotel that catered to Central Committee members. One of the newcomers was Nikita Khrushchev's widow, who moved to Starokoniushennyi Lane to live with her daughter after Khrushchev died in 1971. She was unable to bring with her Khrushchev's best friend and "sole companion" during his retirement years: a German shepherd her daughter had named Arbat. Arbat died shortly before his master. According to Okudzhava, these persons were "not a part of the Arbat, and [were] totally indifferent to it."

3. "Arbat. 16 rakursov odnoi ulitsy," *Arkhitektura SSSR* 4 (April 1986): 34.
4. Ibid., 36–37; Sigurd Ottovich Shmidt, *Put' istorika: izbrannye trudy po istochnikovedeniiu i istoriografii* (Moscow, 1997), 331–38; and Esfir' Semenova, "Marinin dom," interview by Mariia Semenova, *Arbatskie vesti* 1 (January 2002): 3.

They "passively and without curiosity" related to the neighborhood's past. "Over the last quarter century, my own personal, biased opinions about the Arbat have changed irreversibly," Okudzhava admitted in 1981, "which makes it impossible for me to think about the Arbat now as the native land of my childhood friends and me."[5]

The anger that surfaced in the Arbat in the 1980s was ostensibly linked with the pedestrian mall, but it had deep roots. By the mid-1960s, the Arbat myth—the notion that present-day Arbat was only a shadow of its former self and that the neighborhood had been targeted for destruction precisely because it was home to what Immanuil Levin called the "flowers of the Moscow intelligentsia"—was firmly entrenched in the writings of Okudzhava and Anatolii Rybakov.[6] By then, Rybakov was nearing completion of *Children of the Arbat*, which treated the neighborhood as a symbol of the crushed innocence and idealism of the first Soviet generation, and Okudzhava's poetry had shifted from the optimistic, celebratory tones of "A Little Song about the Arbat" (1959) to more somber verses that explored a past that was "impossible to bring back" (1964). The myth that Okudzhava and Rybakov honed comprised elements that would have been familiar to many persons in the neighborhood, even those who had never stumbled across their work. Like actors at the Vakhtangov Theater and architects at MOSA, Okudzhava and Rybakov romanticized the pre-Stalin period. Their celebration of the old Arbat's lively streetscape and intimate courtyards was easy to juxtapose against the unpopular, modernist nightmare that was under construction a few blocks to the north. Their view of the old intelligentsia as a moral and cultural compass would have had great appeal at the Gnesin Institute, where teachers worried about their own authority in the minds of students. And, undoubtedly, their contention that the Arbat was targeted for repression, because of its longstanding ties to the intelligentsia, would have elicited rueful nods from Sinyavsky's friends and coworkers. In many ways, the Arbat myth encapsulated the Arbat's experienced thaw.

5. "Arbat. 16 rakursov odnoi ulitsy," 34, 36–37; and Bulat Okudzhava, "Net zadvorok u Arbata," in *Arbatskii arkhiv,* vyp. 1, ed. S. O. Shmidt (Moscow, 1997), 139, 141. On the Khrushchev family and dog, see Sergei Khrushchev, *Khrushchev on Khrushchev: An Inside Account of the Man and His Era,* ed. and trans. William Taubman (Boston, 1990), 160–61, 229; and idem, "The History of the Creation and Publication of the Khrushchev Memoirs, 1967–1999," in *Memoirs of Nikita Khrushchev: Volume I, Commissar, 1918–1945,* ed. Sergei N. Khrushchev (Providence, R.I., and University Park, Penn., 2004), 800.
6. Im. Levin, *Arbat: odin kilometr Rossii* (Moscow, 1993), 5.

Finally, it is important to ask why the Arbat myth has proven so durable and why it continues to resonate in tourist guidebooks, in the *kraevedenie* (local studies) literature, and in the stories that lifelong residents tell. The answer may lie within the changing role and prestige of the intelligentsia during the late-Soviet and post-Soviet periods. Beginning in the Brezhnev years, subscriptions to "thick journals," once de rigueur reading for educated persons, began to decline. Soviet youth turned their attention from the classics of Russian literature to a subculture of apathy, rock-and-roll, and Western fashion. The perceived value of a higher education was eclipsed by an economy that privileged hucksters and entrepreneurs. And after 1991, self-identified *intelligenty* were two to three times more likely than other social groups and classes to live in poverty.[7] When Soviet dissidents emigrated to the West in the 1970s and '80s, they were often disappointed to discover that their skills were not highly valued in their new societies. Soviet cultural figures who remained at home may have come to similar conclusions. If so, it would not be surprising that a myth that posited an intellectual and cultural utopia in old Arbat, and that explained the neighborhood's demise in a way that affirmed the supposedly adversarial relationship between the intelligentsia and the state, would prove so durable. The Arbat myth may resonate because it offers an analgesic to an intelligentsia suffering with its own obsolescence.

7. L. Gudkov and B. Dubin, *Intelligentsiia: zametki o literaturno-politicheskikh illiuziiakh* (Moscow and Kharkov, Ukr., 1995), 67–68. On the plight of the post-Soviet intelligentsia, see Masha Gessen, *Dead Again: The Russian Intelligentsia after Communism* (London, 1997).

Selected Bibliography

1. ARCHIVAL SOURCES

Central Moscow Archive of Literature and Art (TsALIM)
fond 306   Gnesin Children's Music School

Central Moscow Archive of Scientific-Technical Documentation (TsANTDM)
fond 655   Institute of the Master Plan (Technical Materials)

Central Moscow Archive of Social Movements (TsAODM)
fond 4   Moscow City Party Committee
fond 88   Frunzenskii District Party Committee
fond 1249   Party Organization of the Main Architectural-Planning Administration
fond 2472   Party Organization of the Gorky Institute of World Literature
fond 2890   Party Organization of the Administration for the Design of Public Buildings and Structures (Mosproekt-2)
fond 3954   Party Organization of the Vakhtangov Theater
fond 4081   Party Organization of the Gnesin Music-Pedagogy Institute

Central Moscow Municipal Archive (TsMAM)
fond 150   Moscow City Soviet (Mossovet)
fond 496   Main Administration for Tall Buildings and Hotels
fond 534   Main Architectural-Planning Administration
fond 655   Institute of the Master Plan
fond 773   Administration for the Design of Public Buildings and Structures (Mosproekt-2)

Russian State Archive of Literature and Art (RGALI)
fond 674   Union of Architects
fond 1702   Journal *Novyi mir*
fond 2329   USSR Ministry of Culture
fond 2464   Moscow Section of the Union of Writers
fond 2466   Moscow Section of the Union of Architects

fond 2887	Evgenii Borisovich Tager
fond 2927	Gnesin Music-Pedagogy Institute
fond 2931	Journal *Moskva*

Russian State Archive for Recent History (RGANI)

fond 5	Central Committee of the Communist Party of the Soviet Union
	o. 30 General Affairs Department
	o. 36 Culture Department
	o. 55 Ideological Department
fond 89	Collection of Declassified Documents

Russian State Economic Archive (RGAE)

| fond 5 | USSR State Construction Committee |

State Archive of the Russian Federation (GARF)

| fond A-259 | RSFSR Council of Ministers |
| fond 8131 | USSR Procuracy |

2. RUSSIAN AND SOVIET PERIODICALS

Arbatskie vesti
Arkhitektura SSSR
Biulleten' ispolkoma Moskovskogo gorodskogo Soveta (BIM)
Gorodskoe khoziaistvo Moskvy
Izvestiia
Izvestiia Akademii nauk SSSR. Otdeleniia literatury i iazyka (IAN SSSR. OLIa)
Komsomol'skaia pravda
Kuranty
Literatura i zhizn'
Literaturnaia gazeta
Moskovskaia pravda
Moskva
Na dne
Neva
Nezavisimaia gazeta
Novoe literaturnoe obozrenie
Novyi mir
Ogonek
Partiinaia zhizn'
Pravda
Sotsialisticheskii vestnik
Sovetskaia muzyka
Sovremennaia arkhitektura
Stroitel'stvo i arkhitektura Moskvy (Arkhitektura i stroitel'stvo Moskvy after 1986*)*
Trud
Vecherniaia Moskva
Vestnik vyshei shkoly
Voprosy literatury

Index

Brik, Lili, 184–86
British Broadcasting Corporation (BBC), 63, 203, 205
Brodsky, Joseph, 10, 209
Brown, Deming, 188, 188n
Bruk, Mirra, 59–61, 59n, 65
Budapest uprising, 1, 63, 187
Bukasov, V. I., 203
Bukharin, Nikolai, 4, 9, 139, 185, 188
Bulgakov, Mikhail, 22, 25
Bunin, Ivan, 19–20, 26
Burtin, Iurii, 192–93
Bushmelev, Boris, 172
Butovskii proving ground, 25–26

Candilis, Georges (Gheorghios), 132–34
Cathedral of Christ the Savior, 112, 146
Chaadaev, Petr, 141
Chechulin, Dmitrii, 117, 151, 169
Chekhov, Anton, 22, 185
Chernyshev, Sergei, 114–17
Chetunova, Nataliia, 154–56
Chopin, Frédéric, 47
Chukovskaia, Lidiia, 201n
Chukovskii, Kornei, 3–4
Church of Boris and Gleb, 20
Church of Simeon Stolpnik, 170
Church of the Holy Mother of Rzhev, 24
Church of the Holy Trinity, 24
Church of the Revelation of St. Nicholas the Miracle Worker, 23–24
Clark, Katerina, 8, 11n
Cohen, Stephen, 8n
Cold War, 107, 124–26, 173, 213
Colton, Timothy, 157, 170
Comédie Français, 79
commedia dell'arte, 80–81, 90
Committee for State Security (KGB):
Ginzburg, arrest of, 201, 204
Gritsai, arrest of, 194
informants, 193, 199
Oksman, arrest of, 188
Remizov, arrest of, 207
Sinyavsky and Daniel, arrest of, 175, 190–91, 194, 206
surveillance of the intelligentsia, 177, 201, 204
Communist Party of the Soviet Union, Central Committee:
Agitprop Department, 62, 185
Aleksandrov, denunciation of, 62

architectural and historical preservation, involvement in, 154, 160–62, 165
architecture, decree on, 117
Culture Department, 88, 185
Great Friendship, decrees on, 46–48, 59, 62, 64–66, 69, 70–73, 215
higher education, decree on, 72–73
housing for members and staffers, 24, 217
Ideological Commission, 99, 191
Ideological Department, 97, 162
Khrushchev, dismissal of, 162–63, 167, 207
literary affairs, involvement in, 180–82, 184–86
Manège affair, in wake of, 125
plenums, 125, 127, 145
Rainstorm, response to, 95n, 96–97
Science and Culture Department, 181
Sinyavsky and Daniel affair, involvement in, 191, 193–94, 199
Soviet youth, concern with, 44, 64
theater repertoire, decree on, 94
Twentieth Party Congress, response to, 63–65, 69, 211
Vakhtangov Theater, dispute at, 88
Communist Party of the Soviet Union, Politburo, 169
Communist Party of the Soviet Union, Presidium, 6, 55, 92, 95, 112, 123
Communist Party of the Soviet Union, trial of, 64
Communist Party of the Soviet Union, Twentieth Party Congress:
constructivism, efforts to rehabilitate, 136
musicology, impact on, 59–61, 65, 71, 73–74, 215
Gnesin Music-Pedagogy Institute, impact on, 56–65
Gorky Institute of World Literature, impact on, 181–83, 186
popular perceptions of, 6
Stalin, criticism of, 1, 4, 43–44, 55–56
"thaw generation," impact on, 14, 56–57
Communist Party of the Soviet Union, Twenty-second Party Congress, 17, 107, 126, 160, 188
Communist Party of the Soviet Union, Twenty-third Party Congress, 175–177, 201n, 207
Congress for Cultural Freedom, 7, 207

Malenkov, Georgii, 4, 44, 114, 150
Malevich, Kasimir, 143
Malia, Martin, 188–89
Malyi Kakovinskii Lane, 20
Malyi Kislovskii Lane, 20
Malyi Levshinskii Lane, 25
Malyi Theater, 78, 99
Mandelstam, Osip and Nadezhda,
  25, 189
Manège Exhibit Hall, 4, 7, 21, 44, 125, 128
Manège Square, 146
Mansurovskaia Studio, 76
Mansurovskii Lane, 76
Marx Avenue (Mokhovaia Street), 21, 33,
  106
Marx, Karl, 144
Marxism-Leninism, 4, 10, 43, 52–54, 58, 63.
Mayakovsky, Vladimir, 37, 45, 133–34, 142,
  184–86, 207
McDonald's restaurant, 28
Melnikov, Konstantin, 107–8, 166
Mel'nikova, E. V., 53, 58, 70
memory:
  Arbat myth, 37–39
  collective, 2n, 15, 107, 139, 146, 173,
    213–15
  in Okudzhava's work, 30, 34
  "sites of memory," 2, 2n, 106
  of victims of Stalinism, 26n, 111
Men'shutin, Andrei, 191, 191n
Mertvyi Lane, 22
Meyerhold, Vsevolod, 77, 86
Mezentsov, Boris, 127
Mikhailov, Boris, 153–54, 161–62
Mikhailov, Nikolai, 88, 150.
Mikoian, Anastas, 88
Ministry of Culture:
  architectural and historical
    preservation, impact on, 152–53, 161
  Gnesin Institute, impact on, 52, 72
  Vakhtangov Theater, impact on, 92–93,
    96, 98–100, 103
MKhAT. See Moscow Art Theater
Mndoiants, Ashot, 112, 129–31
Molotov, Viacheslav, 44
Molotov-Ribbentrop pact, 55
Moravia, Alberto, 187, 190
Mordvinov, Arkadii, 115
MOSA. See Moscow Section of the Union
  of Architects
Moscow Art Theater (MKhAT), 40, 76–79,
  84–85

Moscow Conservatory, 40–41, 48–49,
  70–71, 73
Moscow Institute of Transportation
  Engineers, 35
Moscow Party Committee, 114, 128,
  157–58, 160
Moscow Section of the Union of Architects
  (MOSA):
  architectural and historical
    preservation, role in, 150–54,
    162–73
  architectural-theory section, 133–36
  collective memories of, 213, 215
  constructivism, rehabilitation of, 106–7,
    109–11, 132–37, 212
  Eighth Conference of Moscow
    Architects, 120, 125
  as a forum for discussion, 145
  Moskva roundtable, 159–60
  Ninth Conference of Moscow
    Architects, 126, 137, 162, 171
  Novyi Arbat, discussions about, 130–32,
    137–38, 160
  preservation section, 160, 163
  Stalinist architecture, denunciation of ,
    114–15
  Tenth Conference of Moscow
    Architects, 136–37, 168
  tipovoe proektirovanie, criticism of, 119
  urban-planning and construction
    section, 150
  Western architecture, discussions about,
    124–26, 138
Moscow Section of the Union of Artists,
  154, 163, 168
Moscow Section of the Union of Writers,
  97, 154–55, 190, 204, 206
Moscow State University, 21, 64, 175, 194,
  194n, 207
Moscow, city government:
  Finance Administration, 148
  Housing Administration, 149
  Main Administration for Residential
    and Civil Construction, 117–18,
    121
  Mosproekt, 118, 121, 125
  See also Architectural-Planning
    Administration (Moscow); Mossovet
    (Moscow City Council)
Moses, Robert, 110
Moskva (Moscow), journal, 154–60, 162,
  164–66

Mossovet (Moscow City Council):
architectural and historical
preservation, role in, 147–48, 153, 156,
160–61, 163–65, 216
Noyvi Arbat, role in, 121–22
urban planning, 114–15, 118–19
Muradeli, Vano, 46–48, 59, 62, 70–71, 215
Murav, Harriet, 208
Muromtsev, Iu. V., 49–50, 53–54, 58, 63,
67, 69, 73.
music:
folk, 46–48, 66
jazz, 46, 62, 66–67, 73–74, 82, 213
polyphony, 48
polytonality, 69–70
rock-and-roll, 44, 66, 219
thaw on, impact of, 13, 16, 56, 65–66,
70–71
variety (*estrada*), 46, 53
Western, 16, 43, 51, 54, 62, 67, 72
zhdanovshchina, impact of, on, 46–48, 71
Mussorgsky, Modest, 64

Napoleon I, Emperor of France, 19, 146
National Labor Union (NTS), 205–6
Neglinnaia River, 20
Neigaus, Genrikh, 41
Nemirovich-Danchenko, Vladimir, 77, 79
Nepomniashchii, V. S., 198, 206
Neupokoeva, Irina, 196–97
New Economic Policy (NEP), 75–76,
139–40, 183, 214
New York, 110, 124, 131, 165, 172
Nicholas I, Tsar, 141, 194
Nikolaev, Viktor, 180
Nikolaev, Vladimir, 216
NKVD. *See* Soviet Union, government:
People's Commissariat of Internal
Affairs
Nordlander, David, 7
nostalgia:
for the pre-Stalin period, 38, 74–76,
103–4, 106, 138–39, 203–4, 214
for thaw, 6, 18, 178, 204, 210
Novokirovskii Avenue, 138
Novyi Arbat:
architectural crisis, as solution to, 120,
128–29, 137–38
casualties of, 141–42, 150
construction, 17, 26, 105–6, 120–24,
129–31, 138, 211
description of, 19, 26, 105, 123, 131, 170

housing on, 130–31, 137–38
initial plans for, 111
new party program on, impact of,
129–32
opposition to, 106, 137–38, 142–46, 156,
159–63, 165–66, 168–73
as "site of memory," 104, 106, 110–11,
131–32, 140, 215
tunnel, plans for, 28
Novyi mir (New World), journal, 69, 107,
188n, 193, 199–200, 203, 221

Oksman, Iulian, 188–89, 196, 213
Okudzhava, Bulat:
Arbat myth, 16, 32–34, 36–38, 218
background, 29, 43, 75
daughter, 32n
"Little Song about the Arbat," 20, 34, 218
Novyi Arbat and pedestrian mall,
opposition to, 106, 172–73, 216–18
on Pushkin, 21
statue of, 29–32
writings of, 20, 30, 34, 45
Old Moscow, 144, 154
Oltarzhevskii, Viacheslav, 131–32
oprichnina, 20
Orlov, Mikhail, 141
Orlovskii, Ernst, 205
Orochko, Anna, 87, 89, 102
Osorgin, Mikhail, 217
Osterman, Natan, 137–38
Ovcharenko, Aleksandr, 198–99

Palace of Congresses, 110, 145
Palace of Soviets, 112, 146
Palace of the English Court, 151
Palekh, 28
Paris, 2, 41, 82, 124–25, 134, 157, 190
Partiinaia zhizn' (Party Life), journal,
57–58
Pashkova, Galina and Larisa, 100–101
Pasternak, Boris, 6, 22, 41, 73, 175, 185, 193
patronage, 11, 91–93, 97, 102, 121, 159, 215
Paustovskii, Konstantin, 202, 206
Pekelis, Mikhail, 60–61, 71–72, 74
Peltier-Zamoskaia, Hélène, 207
perestroika, 12
Perfil'ev, V. P., 141–42
Peter the Great, 12, 20
Petrosian, Arfo, 179–82, 191, 193, 216
Plekhanov, Georgii, 183
Plotnikov Lane, 30–31, 41, 217